Pre-Primary Education
Philosophy and Practice

By the Same Author

Know Your Child

About the Author

Professor G. Pankajam (M.Sc., M.A., M.Ed., Ph.D.) has the experience of teach ing Child Development, Exceptional Children and Pre-school Education sinc 1965. Starting her career as a lecturer in Lakshmi College of Education, she ro upto the Principal of the College for 16 years and then the Vice-Chancellor c Gandhigram Rural Institute (Deemed University), Gandhigram.

Prof. Pankajam received Alumni Achievement Award from M.S. University, Baroda and the Best Principal Award from Government of Tamil Nadu. She has ten books to her credit on pre-primary education, child development, higher education, and women and child welfare.

Pre-Primary Education Philosophy and Practice

PROF. G. PANKAJAM
Former Vice-Chancellor
Gandhigram Rural Institute
Deemed University
Gandhigram

CONCEPT PUBLISHING COMPANY, NEW DELHI-110059

Cataloging in Publication Data—DK
Courtesy: D.K. Agencies (P) Ltd. <docinfo@dkagencies.com>

Pankajam, G. (Gnanasundaram), 1939-
Pre-primary education : philosophy and practice/ G. Pankajam.
p. cm.
Includes bibliographical references (p.)
Includes index.
ISBN 8180692337

1. Education, Preschool—Philosophy. 2. Education, Preschool. 3. Education, Preschool—India. I. Title.

DDC 372.210 1 21

ISBN: 81-8069-234-5 (PB)

First Published 2005

Published and Printed by
Ashok Kumar Mittal
Concept Publishing Company
A/15-16, Commercial Block, Mohan Garden
New Delhi-110059 (INDIA)

Phones : 25351460, 25351794
Fax : 091-11-25357103
Email : publishing@conceptpub.com

Preface

This book *Pre-Primary Education — Philosophy and Practice* deals with the philosophies of Pre-primary education, trends and practices in India as well as at the global level. The aim of the book is to throw light on the origin, growth and existing patterns of Pre-primary education in India and in other countries. It also aims at making the parents, educationists especially who are interested in the welfare and education of young children understand and plan for the kind of education which will be more conducive for pre-schoolers.

One of the primary aims of writing this book has been to plan curriculum and strategies of teaching and learning for children between 3 and 5 in the Indian context. The author's experience in the field for about 4 decades made her convinced that education of young children takes place best in a stimulating and in an enriched environment.

The Tamil version of this book first published by Lakshmi Seva Sangam of Gandhigram Trust in 1980 had a very encouraging reception from the educationists, teachers, students, parents and all those who are interested in young children. The same book has come out now as 5th edition in 2001. Nearly fifteen thousand copies of the book have been sold out.

The author felt that writing this book in English will help the non-Tamils to have an idea of different practices in Pre-primary education we have in india and how it has been modified to suit our soil, over a period of time.

The author is thankful to her students, the Balasevikas and the Pre-schoolers who were of inspiration for writing this book. In fact they were instrumental in her experiments with some of her ideas in this book.

The author is deeply grateful to Ms. K.P. Kala, Ms. R. Vijayarani,

Ms. M. Vanmathi, Ms. P. Senthamarai, Ms. KH. Ringsuachang Aimol, Ms. Kavitha and Ms. P. Gomathi for their untiring help in my experiments and while preparing the manuscript, and to my nephew Mr. G. Nadimuthu and my niece Mrs. N. Devaki for their assistance.

I am thankful to the Concept Publishing Company, New Delhi for bringing out this book in record time.

G. PANKAJAM

Contents

Part I

Philosophical and Historical Foundations

1

Pre-Primary Education
A Historical Perspective

Children constitute the supreme form of wealth of any nation. They are the sacred trust of the family, community and nation. Children are the valuable human resources on whose development depends the future of the nation. Hence a special responsibility lies on us—the elders, to ensure that every child in the world grows into a responsible adult possessing a strong character and unique calibre and a profound knowledge of our culture.

The early years are the most impressionable and crucial period in a child's life. Great changes in the destiny of mankind can be effected only through training the minds of little children. So education provided to him/her should be received by him/her as a pleasure rather than as pain. Pre-primary education should be a new paddle given to the child to take him/her to the right destination in his/her life.

If we want the humanity to have a future of a wonderful kind, it is very much essential that the foundation of the pre-primary education is structured properly.

Importance of Pre-Prmnimary Education

Known by different nomenclatures like Pre-Primary Education, Pre-School Education, Early Childhood Care Education, Balwadi, Anganwadi, Nursery, Kindergarten, Montessori School etc. It is this significant period of education for the children in the age group of 2½ years to 6 years, that lays the foundation for the optimum development of their personality.

Kothari Commission recognizing the merits of Pre-Primary Education, hailed the Pre-primary education as "an essential adjunct" of the national system of education.

Every child in this country has the right to receive the very best the country can give him/her especially with regard to education. But most of the home environment in our country is appallingly poor. Lack of space, shortage of toys and play material, absence of proper psychological methods of dealing with children are the grave limitations in most of our homes. In such circumstances how will these parents be able to channelize the spontaneous flowing of the creative abilities of their children in the right direction. Researchers proved that children brought up in good socio-economic and cultural environment where they get the needed inspiration, display the better talents than those who are deprived of such congenial atmosphere.

When parents create a world of toys for their children, the children develop curiosity to learn about them, label them, understand how they work and play with them. The educated parents try to provide some apt answers to the curious "Whys" of their children. But, the economically poor and educationally backward parents are at a disadvantage and cannot provide such facilities to their children. Children, whether they are from villages or towns, literate or illiterate families, have the same requirements for the development of their potentials. This impressionable, plastic and educationally potent period of a child's life has to be fully utilized and enjoyed by him. What his home and parents have failed to give him or have been unable to give him should be given in his pre-primary school, which is an extension of home.

Parents should find time to play with the children, interact with them and provide experiential content that is required for the wholesome development of their children.

Though mother is the first educator to the child, the idea of pre-primary education through an organized institution outside the home of the child is not just a new one. This idea was put forth by Plato even 2000 years before. In our country the movement took its first roots in the minds of few educationists who lost faith in the educational system introduced by foreign rulers. At a later stage as a result of industrial revolution, breaking down of joint family system, women's emancipation and realization of importance of early years in learning, it has become a necessity to start pre-primary schools in India.

An attempt is being made in this chapter to trace the history of pre-primary education system in the world as well as in India.

2

Comenius

INTRODUCTION

Comenius was born at Nivnitz, a Moravian Village, in 1592. Both parents died when Comenius was a child and so he received only a meagre education in reading, writing, hymn singing and arithmetic during his early years. After the age of sixteen he spent some years in the college of Horborn and Amsterdam and later became a great educator.

The Pansophic Plan of Education

Comenius, plan of pansophic education comprehended the art of teaching everyone everything. 'Pansophia' means 'Universal Wisdom'. Comenius had an exaggerated conception of the intellectual capacity of the masses of people.

He believed that the forces making for goodness are stronger than those leading toward evil. He affirmed that "seeds of knowledge, virtue and piety" are found in all normal individuals, and are susceptible to unlimited cultivation. No educator has had a stronger faith in the power of education to save mankind and thus to bring it back to its original divinity.

Democracy of Education

Another fundamental quality of Comenius was his profound sympathy for the common man. No great champion of the education of the masses had yet risen into prominence in educational history. This emphatic declaration of Comenius must have been shocking in an age moving rapidly forward political absolutionism.

"The education that I propose includes all that is proper for a man, and is one in which all men who are born into this world should share. All, therefore, as far as possible, should be educated together, that they may stimulate and urge on one another."

Children are not born human, according to Comenius, but all are born with the capacity to become human; and they can became human only by proper training in the society.

Aim of Education

The purpose of "education was universal wisdom" may be taken as Comenius' aim for all education. Three words summarize his aim: Knowledge, virtue, and piety. Comenius made piety the supreme purpose of education. Comenius had a sublime confidence in the power of education to regenerate human life; he was convinced that "there is no more certain way under the sun for raising sunken humanity than the proper education of the young".

Function of the School

To attain his educational objective, Comenius asserted that three things were essential: good text books, good teachers and good methods. The school is an institution where children work and live together under conditions which resemble the activities of the play ground. The school must provide opportunity for movement, spontaneity, social relations, rivalry, good order and pleasurable exercises in learning.

Comenius believed that education is the indispensable process by which the young are made human. This process must begin at birth and not merely when the children enter school. Comenius pleaded for independent thinking: to see with one's own eyes, and to became wide by using one's own mind.

Organisation of the School System

Comenius' generous concepts regarding the functions of education were to be realized in a clear-cut system schools. His school system is divided into four levels of six years each:

(*i*) For infancy —The mother's knee
(*ii*) For childhood —The vernacular school

(*iii*) For boyhood —The Latin School
(*iv*) For youth —The university and travel.

A mother-school should exist in every house, a vernacular school in every hamlet and village, a gymnasium in every city, and a university in every kingdom. All schools shall begin at a uniform date, and children shall be admitted at no other time. A daily and yearly schedule of work shall be followed. The subjects of instruction are to be so divided that each year, each month, each week, each day, and even each hour may have a definite task appointed for it. A separate room with a special teacher shall be appointed for each class.

Comenius objected to the rigorous practice of forcing young children to study six or eight hours a day. For younger children, he specified four hours of school work a day; for older ones, six. No home work shall be required. The morning hours shall be devoted to work which taxes the intellect and memory; the afternoon, to handwork, music and practical activities.

SCHOOL OF INFANCY

Education begins at birth; the home is therefore the first school. He anticipated the thinkers of later centuries, and gave the world a sketch of pre-school training astonishing in its completeness. His "The school of infancy" is filled with information and suggestions that testify to extraordinary insight into the nature and needs of young children.

Comenius taught each child at this stage the fundamental parts of all the sciences. The school of infancy has its special functions the exercise of the external senses, early social training, and instruction, in religion. But he did not propose any activity beyond the scope of the real, spontaneous interests of normal children. Moreover, he was an enthusiastic advocate of fairy tales, Mother Goose rhymes stories, play, manual constructivity, music and even of humour.

VERNACULAR SCHOOL

Comenius demanded a well-rounded elementary education for every child, poor or rich, high-born or low, boy or girl. It was obligatory that every child attends the vernacular school, for it was to furnish the elementary training necessary for life and, at the same time to give preparatory training to those who were to enter the Latin School and prepare for the learned professions.

According to the programme of Comenius, the vernacular school should train "the internal senses, the imagination and memory in combination with their congate organs". The course of study includes reading, writing, practical arithmetic, singing, religion, morals, economics and politics, general history, cosmography and the mechanical arts.

LATIN SCHOOL OR GYMNASIUM

According to Comenius, the Latin School was not a special educational route which only the learned on higher classes may travel. This was designed as the institution for development in the adolescent age.

Psychologically, the purpose of the Latin School is to train the pupil "to understand and pass judgement on the information collected by the senses" in the former period. The means to this end are logic, grammar, rhetoric, and the science and arts "that are based on principles of causation". Four languages are to be learned the vernacular, Latin, Greek and Hebrew. For the introduction to Latin, Comenius prescribed his own texts.

The Latin School is divided into six classes, or years, called after the subjects, grammar, natural philosophy, mathematics, ethics, dialectic and rhetoric.

UNIVERSITY AND TRAVEL

The University course travel from the highest level of education. A university is to be established in every kingdom or province. Comenius expected only brightest students, who were also of high moral character, to attend the universities. The solution was to be made by a public examination of the students who completed the Latin School.

He believed that "the curriculum should be really universal, provision being made for the study of every branch of human knowledge". He fully recognized that research is also a function of the universities. Comenius believed in the advantages of travel in furnishing direct information concerning human nature and institutions. He felt that such experience should follow the university earlier, after moral habits were fully formed.

Teaching the Young Children

Comenius' principles and methods of instruction were based upon a fairly well-formed theory of the mental ability and the growth of children. He possessed a remarkably active capacity for observation of phenomena in many fields. He observed carefully the development of plants and animals, the operation of the manual arts and crafts, and the spontaneous activities and interests of children.

Another strong trait, but one which frequently led him into vagaries of imagination, was his life-long tendency to reason and analogy. Because of this he sought the basis for his principles of method in the analogies of external nature and of the mechanical arts. He understood clearly the idea that the true basis of educational science must be the natural growth of the child. He was firmly convinced that "the exact order of instruction must be borrowed from nature."

The greatest weakness of Comenius' ideas arose from the want of a deep and accurate knowledge of the mental life.

Knowledge Through the Senses

The five senses are "the gateways to man's soul". This doctrine formed the basis of the principles of method which he applied in the school of infancy and in the vernacular school.

Imagination

This faculty is the inner sense, just as seeing and hearing are the outer senses. It develops from sensibility and is indispensable for the further development of the child's knowledge and spiritual being.

Individual Differences

Educational theorists from the time immemorial, recognizing that all children are not alike, had insisted that they should not be treated in precisely the same manner. Comenius pointed out some of the chief differences and discussed how to deal with them wisely.

Adaptation to Stages of Develoment

Comenius possessed extraordinary insight as to what children at each stage of development could comprehend, and what would interest them.

Comenius proposed a text covering each year of school life; in each of these texts he set down, in graded order, everything suitable to the comprehension and interest of the child.

Learning by Doing

Comenius' theory of learning is expressed very clearly in 'The Great Didactic'. He believed that the increase of power comes through the exercise of particular and not of general functions.

Memory and Formal Discipline

Memory is important in the education of the young; but teachers had realised upon it too much and, as a result, instruction had become a mere examining process. He believed that memory could be developed and strengthened through practice writing, pictures, and repetition fix impressions more permanently in memory and are constantly to be employed. For this purpose he advised the greater use of blackboards, diagrams, and other similar means.

Reason or Understanding

This faculty, according to the psychological views of Comenius, "measures and determines, what, where and how far anything should be sought after or avoided. The faculty of judgement has its function to utilize the materials brought to the mind through the senses and the imagination. Judgement emerges especially during the adolescent years of life when reflection and reasoning are the nascent developments.

Emotions and Will

Comenius was greatly in advance of his time in recognizing the prime importance of the emotions of children and in diagnosing their relation to the process of education. The insistence upon interest, attention and sense of need in connection with everything to be learned and anticipated to present day theories. He would foster the native curiosity, or "desire to see, hear or handle everything new". He recognized that in these emotional tendencies nature provides the inner striving after knowledge. Thus Comenius assigned the foremost place in human experience to the will and moral nature, which form the capstone in the process of development.

THE CURRICULUM

Pansophic Curriculum

The Curriculum proposed by Comenius is encyclopaedic scope. Everyone is "to know all things, to do all things, and to say all things".

Comenius did not intend that the details of each subject should be fully mastered, but merely that the outlines, or principal ideas, should be learned.

So far as languages are concerned; he urged less attention to Latin, Greek, and Hebrew than was the custom, but exalted vernacular, and what is particularly worthy of note, he advocated the study of modern foreign languages.

The Latin language as well as the vernacular was to be employed in learning the trivial and quadrivial subjects: grammar, rhetoric, dialectic, arithmetic, geometry, astronomy and mustic. In addition, Comenius included physics, geography, chronology, history, novels and religion. For history he had extraordinary regard.

"An acquaintance with history is the most important element in a man's education, and is, as it were, the eye of his whole life".

Comenius insisted upon the manual arts and industry in connection with the vernacular school. In the interests of happiness and healthy Comenius advocated plenty of physical activity and play.

Comenius revealed his most unique insight when he urged the development of the sense of humour or wit as a means of education. No other educator was gone wild so far in his declaration that children "ought to be taught, and that thoroughly, to understand what is said in a joke". Moreover humour is not to be indulged merely for idle fun, but it should be employed for the purpose of sharpening their intellects".

METHODS OF TEACHING

Professor Laurie says, "Comenius is to be regarded as the true founder of modern method".

In his observation of nature, Comenius saw many operations that by analogy suggested principles of instructions. A few examples may be given.

(*a*) *Nature observes a suitable time*: The birds hatch their eggs in the spring, and the gardener plants his seeds at that season. From this, Comenius drew the principle that "the education of men should be commenced in the spring time of life."

(*b*) *Nature prepares the material before she begins to give it a form*: In the schools, the study of form should precede the learning of subject matter. For illustration, languages are taught before the sciences, which is to teach expression before the child has knowledge to express.

(*c*) *In all the operations of nature, development is from within*: A subject should be thoroughly understood by the child before he is called upon to memorize any definitions. Grammar is the most striking example of the application of this new method.

(*d*) *Nature, in its formative process, begins with the universal and ends with the particular*: In instruction, the large, simple, general elements come first, details follow.

(*e*) *Nature makes no leaps, but proceeds step by step*: A chicken develops slowly and without sudden changes. So all studies should be carefully graded by minute steps.

"Nothing should be taught to the young, unless it is not only permitted but actually demanded by their age and mental strength".

Basic Principles Involved in Methods of Teaching: Everything Through the Senses

This is one of the fundamental principles which Comenius frequently repeated. He was the first sense-Realist. Everything should as far as possible, be placed before the senses. If the thing is not available, representation may be used. The walls of the room should be hung with pictures, and books should be full of them. Charts, maps, drawings, diagrams, models, engravings and other apparatus should be freely employed.

Grading of Subject Matter

So far as subject matter is concerned, Comenius was the first to apply a system of grading on the basis of psychological ability. All studies should be graduated in such a way that those coming first may prepare the way for and throw light upon those that follow.

Everything Without Compulsion

The common use of the rod to force children to learn is clear evidence of the unfortunate lack of true educational insight of that day. Comenius would not require anything by force. The school should be a pleasant and happy place. The intellect should be forced to nothing for which it does not have a natural bent. Learning should always be made attractive.

Socialization

Comenius advocated the advantage of encouraging pupils to tell others what they have learned. He said, "Whatever has been learned should be communicated by one pupil to the other that no knowledge may remain unused". Comenius recognized knowledge and expression as co-ordinates which must always proceed together, for knowledge is a social commodity, and is most readily acquired when a need is felt to communicate it to others. He approved the plan of forming classes and the school as a whole into "a republic, its senate and proctor, which will hold sessions occasionally, and pronounce judgement on conduct". In this manner he would train the individual for self-government and social life.

Integration or Correlation

Another fundamental principle which Comenius recognized is that of properly combining, or integrating the materials that are learned.

The senses should be daily exercised in conjunction. Words, and things, style and thought should be correlated.

From the Known to the Unknown

Children at that time learned by rote without any understanding of the meaning of what they memorized. The little fellows were made to learn words and long passages which were just so many nonsense syllables to them. Comenius declared that "to teach the unknown through the medium of that which is equally unknown".

Avoiding Confusion in the Child's Mind

Comenius was afraid that the methods pursued were producing confusion in the child's mental growth. To avoid this danger, he recommended a number of principles. One, and only one, text is to be used in a subject. Many texts for young children lead to distraction of mind. One, and only one, teacher is to be in-charge of a class. The whole class is to have the same exercises. All languages are to be taught by the same method.

Conclusion

Comenius' contributions to the field of education of young children make others to call him, the prophet of modern education system. Actually he was a restless and resourceful observer and a creative thinker himself. He took a profound interest in nature in all its varied operations. Most important of all, he caught the genetic point of view. All of his principles find analogy in the processes of nature, such as growth of trees, plants, and the human body.

Comenius' text books, which embodied his principles of method attained extra-ordinary popularity. His curriculum recommendation for young children, were neverthless in harmony with the new trend in subject matter. Thus in all sense he could said to be a prophet of modern education for young children as we have borrowed heavily from his principles curriculum and methodology.

3

Plato

Life

Plato, the first Western Educational Philosopher, was born in Athens in 428 B.C. He was an aristocrat and so he did not mix up with ordinary people. He was a good wrestler and warrior. At the same time he had a taste for literature and politics. At the age of 20, he became a disciple of Socrates who was then sixty years of age. He worshipped Socrates as the God or Deity of knowledge.

Plato's Academy

After the death of Socrates, he left his country and wandered for about 10 years. Then he returned to Greece at the age of forty. By that time he had grown quite mature and wanted to put his ideas into actual practice. So he opened his school in 386 B.C. which was known as 'Academy'. He propounded the view that before imparting education the virtue of the educand must be well understood. This was what Rousseau and Dewey had suggested later on. He was a great philosopher not only of his time but for all times. His views are important not only for education but for all branches of knowledge, society, politics etc. In his Academy he tried to give practical shape to his ideas. These very ideas have been collected in 'Republic'. He aimed at making an individual an ideal citizen. So in his Academy he taught psychology, philosophy, music, politics, mathematics etc.

Plato's Concept of Knowledge and Soul

Socrates said that the true knowledge is not acquired through sense organs but it is acquired through mind or reasoning power. Plato hold that true knowledge is innate. He thinks that knowledge does not come to the soul at or after birth. In fact, it is a part of the soul itself and it is always with the soul. The three elements of soul are appetite, will and reason.

(*a*) *Appetite*: It is the point that inspires desire, wishes and other activities of the body. Self control and discipline is the quality of this element.
(*b*) *Will*: This is the second element of the soul. It resides in the human heart. It controls the spiritual qualities and will power of man. It is this element that gives courage, activity, tolerance and other such qualities in man.
(*c*) *Reason*: Mind is the residence of this particular element of the soul. All good and praise worthy acts of man are guided by it. Knowledge is the quality of man.

When all these three elements are well organised and work together, man's life is praise worthy, high and full of lust acts. First of all, it is the appetite that grows in the child. Then comes will and lastly reason which is invariably accompanied by knowledge. Plato has said that body is unreal and transitory but the soul is eternal and immortal.

Three Sources of Knowledge

1. *Knowledge acquired through sense organs*: According to Plato, the knowledge acquired through sense organs is not permanent. He calls it unreal. He even says, the sense organs are unreal and so the knowledge acquired through them is unreal. The realisation of heat, cold, colour, smoothness etc., is the knowledge acquired through sense organs.

2. *Knowledge acquired through instruction*: In the view of Plato the knowledge acquired through counsel or instruction is neither real nor permanent. He says that a particular counsel given under certain circumstances may be correct for the time being, but this may not be universal and eternal.

3. *Knowledge acquired through reason*: Acçording to Plato the knowledge acquired through reason is true, permanent and eternal. 'Truth', 'Beauty' and 'Goodness' are the products of this very sort of knowledge. Such a knowledge does not change. It remains universal and unchangeable.

Works of Plato on Education

Plato was the foremost Greek Philosopher and Educationist. He wrote about 400 books but only the following are available to us:

(*a*) *Republic*: This book contains Plato's conception of an 'Ideal State' and speaks on justice.
(*b*) *Protagoras*: This is a book in which the virtues, principles and ideas of Socrates have been dealt with.
(*c*) *Laws*: It seems that this book was written to clarify certain national portions of 'Republic'.
(*d*) *Symposium*: This book contains his views on the ideals of 'the Truth', 'the Beauty' and 'the Good'.

The Stages of Education

1. *Nursery Education*: (3–6 years): Education begins at birth. The child is taught the fundamental habits by the mother, when the child is three years old, his nursery education begins. As the child grows, he begins to jump and shout. These activities should be trained gradually by the use of rhythm, tune and a sense of time. Education at this stage should be given through the stories of Gods and Goddesses. The environment should be happy and congenial for the development of the personality of the children.

2. *Primary Education*: (6–10 years): The education at this stage, should include all such subjects which lead to the growth of virtues in the child. Play, physical exercises, riding and use of simple arms should also be taught to both boys and girls. This creates better soldiers and good citizens for the state.

3. *Secondary Education*: (10–16 years): At this stage, 3 Rs are taught to the children. They learn mathematics, geometry, astronomy and music. This will help the growth of their personality. Ugly and uninterested things should not be allowed to reach these children. Education, at this stage, should have a good deal of material for amusement and recreation; it should lead to the balanced development of the body as well as soul.

4. *Education for Youth*: (16–30 years): Plato has suggested higher education for those who have completed secondary education successfully. Those who are interested in the military education should be given the training of horse riding, use of arms and the way to lead a

military life. This would lead to their proper physical development. The bright young men are taught scientific subjects like Mathematics, Geometry, Astronomy etc. Those who do not prove to be very good at secondary education, should be given some vocational or occupational education.

5. *Education for the Matured Persons*: (above 30 years): The education, at this stage, includes the learning of Philosophy and Oratory. The men study Ethics and Psychology also. These subjects develop their knowledge and they become wise men. They shall grow up as administrators; they shall occupy various offices of importance and responsibility and serve the state. They prove to be good guardians.

Aim of Education

According to Plato, 'Education consists of giving to the body and the soul all the perfection of which they are susceptible'. At the time of Plato, the state was indifferent towards Education. He believed that state was responsible to make the life of the individuals perfect and ideal. So he gave out his views in regard to education in this context. The citizens of the state belonged to three classes:

(*a*) Soldiers, (*b*) Administrators, and (*c*) Businessmen. Plato thinks that businessmen and their children need not be educated. But he does feel that the children of the other two classes of people must be educated. He emphasised that compulsory education should be given to the boys and girls. The children belong to the state rather than to their parents. Plato believed, 'education provides perfection not only to the body but to the soul as well. Education should aim at the achievement of the absolutes of 'Truth', 'Beauty' and Goodness.

1. *Inculcating the idea of good citizenship and virtues*: Plato has suggested that the children should be given virtues and the qualities of citizenship should be developed in them. This will maintain unity and integrity of the state.
2. *Development of body as well as soul*: Education should aim at the harmonious development of the body as well as soul. In the absence of a sound body, a man can not have a sound mind which is essential for good education. So Plato's famous saying, 'A sound mind lives in a sound body'.

3. *Vision of Truth*: Plato believed that God is truth. The 'truth', 'beauty' and 'goodness' are the internal qualities of God. The education should aim at the achievement of these aims.
4. *Appreciation of beauty*: Beauty is one of the eternal aim of life. Education should train the child to appreciate beauty when it comes before him.

Plato and Curriculum

Music and Physical Training: During infancy or early years of childhood, Plato has suggested that music and physical training must be taught. He was of the view that education should begin with music and then physical training. This will lead to harmonious development of the body as well as soul.

Mathematics and Geometry: Plato believes that mathematics and geometry lead to exactness in the children. The subjects lead to the formation of the background of Philosophy. He has also suggested timely examinations in order to test the knowledge acquired by the children.

Curriculum for Higher Education: Plato has prescribed higher mathematics, geometry, mathematical music, Astronomy, Philosophy, etc. He has praised mathematics. These subjects are useful in practical life. Philosophy brings to the mind the truth in all its forms.

Plato and Methods of Teaching: Plato has suggested only one method of teaching and that is presentation of the subject material through lecture in the most interesting manner. While teaching the children, their interest should be taken into consideration. If not effective education can not take place.

Play is given much importance in Plato's system of education. The pleasure that is created by play has great importance in education. If education could be imparted through the pleasure, its effect is sure to be lasting and useful.

Women Education

Plato was the supporter of women education. He believed that educated mothers can build up good citizens. So he has suggested that women should also be educated like men. There needs not be any difference in the education of men and women. Women also should be given physical training, taught music and given the training of the battle fields. In fact, the real aim of Plato's education is to bring out the proper development of the body as well as soul of young men and women. What Plato said about 2000 years back was that there should be no distinction between the education of men and women is accepted and practiced today. His views hold good in many respects.

Famous French Philosopher and Educationist, Rousseau remarked, "If you wish to know what is meant by public education, read Plato's Republic...it is the finest treatise on education ever written".

Limitations of Plato's System of Education

1. Plato's education is not based on variety and individual differences. He suggested one type of education to all. It is a fact that there are individual differences and the education should vary according to the differences. Psychologically speaking, education devoid of variety and not based on variation of interests and faculties, is not very scientific.

2. He has prescribed for 'State' controlled education which in fact, does not fit in with his concept of democracy. Education should have a free atmosphere. But in the educational pattern suggested by Plato, there shall be no freedom. Human personality can grow only in a free atmosphere.

3. Plato has completely ignored family in his pattern of education. This goes against nature. It is a recognised fact that the development and growth of a child, in his early years, takes place only in the family. Nurseries, however well equipped they may be can not provide to the child that is available in the family. Love and affection can find their outlet only in the family and so early education can be properly attended to only in the family.

4. Plato's scheme of education has no provision for the education of the heart. If the faculties of heart do not grow, the man cannot have real and balanced personality. It has also been recognised that a person is very much guided by feelings and emotions. Therefore, a sound education must provide for the education of the heart as well and here Plato lags behind.

Plato's Contribution to Pre-school Education

Stages of education as suggested by Plato could be considered as one of his major contribution to Pre-school education. He talks about nursery education to 3 to 6 years old children and emphasises the importance of activities and play during this period. He also talks about the importance of a conducive and happy atmosphere for learning young children. Even today the stress is on play in the pre-school level though many parents are to anxious to have their children to be taught Reading, Writing and Arithmetic – the 3 Rs. Plato's concept of nursery education is based on the psychological principles of child development and gives importance to the child, than to the curriculum, teacher and the method.

4

Rousseau

Jean Jacques Rousseau was an educational philosopher who believed in Naturalism. The experiences which he had during his early years made him love children by letting them free. He was a vagabond without family bonds or social status with no literary training and with little knowledge, has influenced education in its organization. Rousseau was born on 28th June, 1712, in Jeneva. The next day after his birth his mother passed away. During his early days itself, he developed bad habits like telling lies, carelessness and lack of discipline. At the age of 10 he was admitted in a village school since he had no liking for schooling, he left the school. He developed liking for gardening, love for nature, drawing and painting. Then he worked in a Registrar office, that also he didn't like and left the job. But he was fond of music. Till his sixteenth year of age, he suffered a let in this world. This gave him an opportunity to observe different phases of nature and men from closer contact. During this phase he came across a beautiful woman called *Madam Dewarrance*. Her contact inspired him to learn many occupations. But he succeeded in more of them.

In short, it can be said that from the age of twelve to twenty nine, he went about aimlessly from one place to other, meeting different types of people and different types of situations. This life had an educative influence on him. He learnt to symphathise with poor, worship nature and revolt against conservatism and convention of society.

'Emile'

'Emile' is Rousseau's famous educational treatise. Emile has justified and been called "the Gosepel' of childhood". If it had no other claims to consideration, it would deserve the homage of parents and teachers by reasons of that sacredness with which it invites the personality of every child. In the 'Emile' Rousseau aims to replace the conventional and formal education of the day with a training, that should be natural and spontaneous. In it he divides man's life into four stages, namely 'Infancy' (1-5), Childhood (5-12), Boyhood (12-15) and youth or Adolescence (15-20).

He deals separately with all these stages. He prescribes the type of education appropriate for each period.

Infancy : 1-5

Rousseau condemns all the checks on freedom during this period. He recommends country life, freedom, sports and outdoor games. The child has a desire for physical activities. The child should play with natural objects like, branches of a tree, fruits and flowers etc.

Plain and simple language should be used with young children. The child should not be made to talk prematurely. He should not be made to learn 3 Rs, he can speak or understand by touching things and lifting them by comparing them with each other. His ways of seeking, thinking and feelings differ from those of adults. Nature wants children should be children before they are men. Education of child at this stage lies in its natural experience. No artificial education is needed at this stage.

Childhood: 5-12

Rousseau says that this is the largest period of child's life. The main aim of education of this stage is the development of sense organs. Proper development of these sense organs depends upon their natural activities. The child should be allowed to learn by his experience, trials and errors. During this stage, child should be given negative education allowing the child, what he likes to do and not compelling him to learn which he doesn't want to learn.

Boyhood: 12-15

This is a period of transition in the child's life. He has reached a stage to be understand things and so he should be taught things which are useful for the development of his personality. This is the apt period to begin formal education. The only book that Rousseau recommended during this period is *Robinson Crusoe*. He emphasised that education should be based on the psychology of the child and in accordance with his nature.

Adolescence: 15-20

This period is predominently of moral education. Hither to the child has been educated in duties, concerning to himself only. Now the growth must be brought up so as to understand social relationships. He should be taught to respect and love others.

Rousseau suggested that his 'Emile' is to be taken to social places like infirmaries, hospitals and prisons to observe concrete examples of miseries in all stages of human being so that he will understand the realities of the world.

Rousseau's Aims of Education

The aim of education in infancy is to develop well regulated freedom. In childhood education is to provide the child with the strength which he needs for the attainment of well regulated freedom. In boyhood the aim is to acquire such knowledge which may satisfy the wants of the child and must be functionally useful. In adolescent period the aim of education should be religious, moral and social. The sex instinct which is sufficiently developed by this time is to be supplemented by re-directing it to the love of some noble ideas and keeping the young person occupied in work and activity.

Rousseau aimed at developing the individual to enter whole-heartedly into all the basic relationships of humanity. He had in view the education of the upper classes. He stated that, the lower classes do not need an education. The circumstances of life produce in them the sense of equality, simplicity, spontaneity and all the other virtues of which they shared in need. But it is the children of the rich and high-born, who are brought up in luxury and artificiality, who stand most in need of natural education.

The child is to be educated, not for some, uncertain future, but only to act in the present. No one rejected so firmly and boldly the appeal to the child's future good. He is to be best prepared to meet any situation when it shall arise.

Curriculum

Rousseau has not suggested any fixed curriculum. He says that every child is given the right to determine its own curriculum. He is expected to learn directly from nature through personal experience. He says that subjects like, nature study, Agriculture, Art, Craft, Botany, Geology, Zoology, Geography, Astronomy etc. can be learnt directly from nature. Because they are in keeping with the nature of the child. They include those subjects in the curriculum which contribute directly to the enrichment of the health, vocational life, family life and social life of the child. Languages are included because they are considered for understanding the science subject. Negative education is recommended for children, which gives freedom for child in his movements and activities.

Methods of Teaching

Rousseau advocated simple and direct method of instructions and urged experience before expression and objects before words. The emphasis was on 'learning by doing'. Rousseau says, "Give your child no verbal lesson, but he should be taught experience alone". Two factors are involved in any methods, namely the subjects to be taught and age of the child. Heuristic method and play-way method are emphasised. Because they create spirit of joyful and creative activity. Co-education is also emphasised. Because it will develop the family and community life in school.

Role of Teacher

Rousseau says that, teacher is an observer of the child's development, rather than a giver of information, ideals, ideas and will power. Teacher should not interfere with the activities of the child. He should not dictate them what they have to do. The children know better what, when and how they should learn. According to this concept, teacher is only a setter of the stage, a supplier of material and opportunities, a provider of an ideal environment and creates conditions which will be conducive to the natural development of the child.

Discipline

The child is given freedom to do and to learn what he likes. According to Rousseau child should not be punished. He says that "whenever a child goes wrong, natural reaction is a proper punishment for them".

There is always a possibility that a child will suffer in almost all cases than he actually deserves. For regulating the conduct of the children Rousseau evolved a concept of 'Self Government' which is quite intune with the demand of democratic society.

Conclusion

Rousseau keeps the child in the fare-front in the entire process of education. Teacher, school, curriculum method of teaching and evaluation are not important to the child who is to be educated. But he emphasised that the school should provide a conducive environment for the free development of the growing child. The whole school is to be organised as free, natural society in which the child contributes his well beings. Education should be based on the psychology of the child which is the basic concept of the Pre-school. Thus, whatever, Rousseau has advocated that could be applied even today.

5

Friedrich Froebel

"Come, let us live for our children!"

—this was the call of the great German Educationist Friedrich Froebel (1782-1852)—the founder of the Kindergarten system of education.

"Kindergarten" is a German word which means 'the children's garden' *i.e.* a place in which young human plants are cultivated. Froebel regarded the school as a garden and the teacher as a gardener who carefully tends the little human plants under his care, and helps them to beauty and perfection.

It could be said that Germany was the pioneer in pre-primary education and perhaps it would be right to look deeper into the system of Kindergarden Education when India is trying to evolve her own educational system suited to the needs and requirements of Indian children.

The Philosophical Principles Underlying Froebel's Kindergarten Method

The Law of Unity or Interconnectness

Froebel says that in all things there lives and reigns and eternal law—the law of unity. This eternal unity is God and all the phenomenon around is interconnected. Just as different branches of a tree come from one organ—a seed-all things in the world, though they seem to be different, have one origin which is God. The whole universe is simply a unity and this unity is three-fold in nature.

(*a*) *Unity of substance*: Man and nature are made of one substance *i.e.* the spirit which animates them both.

(*b*) *Unity of origin*: All things come from one source which is God.
(*c*) *Unity of purpose*: All things strive towards a divinely ordained perfection *i.e.* God.

The Principle of Development

The life is continuous evolution of development, as we march towards unity. All parts of the universe are growing and they are growing from within through the force of the inner law of their own beings.

The Principle of Self-activity

Real growth and development is possible only through self-activity. Our minds are self-active, we bring with us when we are born, the tendencies which prompt us to action. Children, when left to themselves, reveal spontaneous activity in their thoughts and movements.

Development of Individuality Through Social Institutions

Self-activity, self-expression, self-realisation and the development of individuality, must come through a process of socialisation. Froebel stresses that the individual child can only be properly educated in the company of other children. The life of the individual is bound up with the social institutions, the home, the school, the church, the state—is a place for the activity of the individual, and through these the child attains the development of individuality.

'KINDERGARTEN'—The Second Home of a Child

The small child, at the age of three, tries to make his own steps into the world. The child lets the hands of his mother and learns to accept other persons. Hence, the kindergarten should be called as the second home of the child.

The child should be fit in its physical and psychological development. It should not go to school too early. The small child should be brought up all-around in his own world and this happens in the family and often also by the help of Kindergarten Education.

The Kindergarten Education aims at the following objectives:

1. To provide a centre for the free growth of the child's personality along sound lines of physical and psychological development.
2. To train little children in hygienic and social habits and to guide them into modifying their behaviour as members of group.
3. To meet generally the social, emotional, intellectual and physical needs of the child by providing opportunities and the necessary equipment.
4. To enable the child to handle situations according to his age and learn to feel ease in a group situation.
5. To give the child training in the use of language (correct pronunciation, enlargement of vocabulary and clear expression of thoughts).
6. To provide the child with rich experiences to enable him to understand the world.
7. To help the child to develop his own creative ability and to give scope to his fantasy, by all sorts of free and guided play.
8. To enable the parents to study child life and its needs in co-operation with trained workers of the Kindergarten and to get help for themselves by educational discussion in the modern way to bring up their children from the view-point of psychology in the best possible way.

Play Activities at Kindergarten

1. Play with dolls. The children play mother and child and various occupations of life.
2. Threading beads.
3. Puzzles and manipulating toys.
4. Constructive materials. (Providing bars, screws, screwdrivers, wheels etc., so that the child could make car, boat or any other toy which he likes.)
5. Building with blocks.
6. Art activities like drawing, painting, clay work.
7. Handwork like making toys from paper.
8. Story-telling.

9. Role play.
10. Rhythmic exercises, songs, instrumental music, dance.
11. Domestic activities—brooming, washing plates, cleaning chairs and tables, polishing shoes etc.

These play materials are simple and they give scope for stimulation. The child starts interpreting and understanding the things around him in his own way. A child's social attitude and behaviour can be traced through his play activities. His inner desires come out through his play activities.

Outdoor Activities

The outdoor equipments like swings, sea-saw, jungle gym, climbing apparatus, etc., keeps children of different age groups live together in a big community and share their rights.

Group activities are provided to children, like making them sing a song together, dance or play a fairy tale. The children are taken to small excursions to a nearby garden, zoo, park, post-office etc.

The Songs of Kindergarten

The nursery songs in this system of education intend to exercise the child's sense, limbs and muscles to make him familiar with the common objects around him.

The teacher determines the selection of the song in accordance with the development of the child. There are three parts in each song:

1. A motion for the guidance of mother or teacher.
2. A verse with the accompanying music.
3. A picture illustrating the song.

She is to give the idea of the concept presented to the students as she demonstrates the thing. For example,

Cube Song

When she presents a cube, she sings a cube song:
Eight corners, and twelve edges see;

And faces six, belong to me;
One face behind, and one before,
One top, one bottom, that makes four.
One at the right, at left side one,
And that counts six, if rightly done.

Sphere Song

While presenting a sphere, she sings the songs of the sphere:

1. The ball is such a pretty thing,
   About it I do over to sing.
   So round it is, and light and soft
   I hold in my hands full of.
2. This made of wool, and do you know
   That on a sheep the wool did grow?
   Until some men the fluce did take
   Warm clothes and Pretty ball to make.

Music Activities

For music activities the children are provided with instruments like metallophones, xylophones, simple rhythmical instruments like rattles, triangles, sticks, drums etc.

Froebel's Gifts

For the complete education and training of child Froebel devised a series of gifts. The gifts comprise carefully graduated series of material, which possess all the novelty of play things, yet they form the basis of his educational method. They are to train the senses of sight and touch, to give the child an idea of size and surface, and to present him a correct idea of number. The activities suggested by these gifts are called occupations. The gifts are to be given in a certain order. The gradation and order of gifts is determined by the principle of development.

Gift I

Gift I consists of six coloured woolen balls, three in primary colours red, yellow and blue and three secondary colours, orange, green and purple. The occupation consists in rolling them about in play. Thus they develop in the children the idea of colour and material, form, motion, direction and muscular sensibility.

Gift II

Gift II consists of a sphere, cube and cylinder made of hardwood. In playing with these the child notices the difference between the stability of the cubes, and the mobility of the sphere. He observes that the cylinder is both stable and movable and that it harmonises both the qualities in one.

Gift III

Gift III is a large cube divided into eight smaller equal cubes. From these the child can build up a number of useful artistic forms such as benches, doors, bridges etc; and for this reason, the third gift is often called 'the first building box'. The child can also gain elementary ideas of addition and substration through these.

Gift IV

Gift IV consists of large cubes divided into eight oblong prisms. In each of these, the length is twice the breadth and the breadth is twice the thickness. This helps the child to construct different kinds of buildings and patterns when combined with the third gift.

Gift V

Gift V is very much like the third gift. It consists of a large cube divided into twenty seven small cubes, three of which are again divided diagonally into halves and three into quarters. The child can construct many beautiful forms and patterns by combining the third, fourth, and fifth gifts, and it gives him great pleasure to do so. Form and number can very well be taught by the use of this gift.

Gift VI

Gift VI is again similar to gift IV. In it a large cube is divided into 18 whole and 9 small oblong blocks. Still further designs in forms and constructions may be made by the child and it will also be useful in teaching numbers.

Gift VII

Gift VII is a set of square and triangular tablets made of very fine wood in two colours. It provides materials for many exercise in geometrical forms and mosaic work.

The duty of the teacher while the gifts are being presented to the children is not to remain passive. She gives an idea of the occupation to them by demonstrating them.

Though the gifts are altogether 20 in number, only the first seven are given here.

Boyhood and Education

Froebel does not ignore the second stage of development. At this stage, play is not the most important thing. Just as play is the characteristic activity of childhood, the most striking characteristic of boyhood is work. Manual work helps in the development of skill, creative power and exercises of muscles. For this, gardening, carpentary, wood work and other subjects are included in the curriculum.

Froebel attached very great importance to 'nature-study' at this stage. He believed that nature-study would result in moral development, religious uplift and spiritual insight.

The Kindergarten Teacher

The Kindergarten teacher or 'The Kindergartcn' has to be devoted to her profession because she has to fulfill responsible task in our socialisation. She surpervises, guides and takes care of the children in a general way. She has to observe the children while giving them full chance for free play and occupations. She gives advice to the mothers about the physical and emotional needs of the children. This will be done during 'mother's evenings'. She should have love and affection for the children. She must have abilities in music and play as music activities play a very important role in Kindergarten.

The Youth Leader

The youth leader or the 'Jugendleiterin' is the one who conducts a Kindergarten, teach and train the Kindergarten teacher, guide the Kindergarten teacher in her duties and practical work.

The youth leader should be qualified to work as a co-ordinating agent between the various people who all work for child welfare. She can be an adviser or specialist in welfare boards and associations.

The Kindergarten Inside

The inside of a Kindergarten will be pleasant and colourful. The first room will have a peg with many symbols. Each child will know their individual symbols and hang their coats and bags in it.

There will be wash room with low pegs and low basins with the same symbols outside. There will be a towel and comb hanging on the respective peg. This will be used by the children for cleaning themselves.

There are low toilets, surrounded by wall which are 1-1½ meter trigs so that the teacher is to give proper toilet training to the child.

Next is the play room with different lay activities. The play room will also have low and attractive furniture.

The walls will be painted with beautiful colours and pictures.

One corner will be the doll's corner with variety of dolls. Even the window of the room will be very low so that the children could enjoy looking the courtyard outside.

The time-table will be flexible. Children start coming to school from 8 and 9 in the morning and will be there till 12 noon.

The Influence of Froebel's Kindergarten on Modern Educational Practice

1. Froebel was the first educator to give us the idea of the Kindergarten and to name the children's school 'the child's garden'. This has stressed the need of making the child's school have an atmosphere of beauty and delight for the children to learn.
2. His method raised the need for the school to function as a miniature society where the responsibility is shared by all, individual rights are respected by all and brotherly sympathy is developed and voluntary co-operation being practised by all.
3. His method has made people think and realise the need for care given to children during early childhood education and

the necessity for giving them the best impression and atmosphere in a school.

4. Kindergarten education said good-bye to the old dogmatic methods of education. Children were made to understand the concepts easily through play-way methods.
5. Froebel's method of introducing the graded concepts to students through gifts has pictured the importance of teaching abstract ideas and phenomenon to students systematically.
6. The Kindergarten education was the first to introduce the concept of learning by doing for better understanding.

Criticisms and Limitations of the Froebel's Method

1. Froebel expects too much of the child when he thinks that he will be able to understand abstract ideas while playing with the gifts.
2. Some songs and pictures given by Froebel are outdated. They have to be modified according to the environment of the school and needs of the children.
3. The gifts of Froebel are of a formal nature and their order of presentation is some what arbitrary. Many schools have discarded the use of gifts because they feel that sense training could also be given through other means.
4. There is no correlation of subjects in Froebel's Kindergarten.
5. There is too much emphasis on social unity and little emphasis on the development of individual child.

The Kindergarten experience makes the passage of the child from home to elementary school smooth and easy. It makes high ripe and receptive to formal and uniform type of instruction of the elementary school.

Froebel also wanted the child to learn everything only when it is fit psychologically and physically to understand it so that we could see the best in him.

6

Madam Montessori

Madam Montessori was one of the great pioneers in the education of young children. In fact it would be no exaggeration to say that there have been few discoveries in education and the principles and philosophy on which it is based could have been so epoch making. She completely changed the approach to children's education and opened a new world to parents and educators.

Montessori Method of Education

Dr. Montessori called her method not as a 'system' because—a system is something that 'stand'. But a 'method' is a 'way', a 'path'. A 'path' invites us to 'follow'. As Madam Montessori always suggested, those who wish to follow her, should not focus their attention on her person but on what she had been indicating; the moving developing child revealing himself, his needs and the extent to which we try to help him, and follow him.

The Four Phases of Education

The teacher must observe the child, not with the idea of educating him, but to be taught how to educate him. So, the child becomes an important person in front of us and we can talk of the child's prerogatives and rights.

First Phase (Birth to Six years of age)

In this stage, we observe that the child "valorises" has personality. The child realises that he can be independent and achieve things through his own efforts. In order to reach these results it is necessary to place the child in a free environment where he can make social contacts on his own.

Second Phase (Seven to Twelve years)

At this phase, the child changes completely. He becomes less attractive. He is no longer so beautiful, he develops his full teeth with which he clings to life. He moves from concrete to abstract. He asks what is good? What is bad? He needs a different and a greater effort. He requires to go out into the world to make wider contacts.

Third Phase (Adolescence)

A totally different psychology develops in this individual who passes from feeling for himself to feeling for others, whom he has never seen. They identify themselves with society and feel that they themselves are valued by the society.

Fourth Phase (Adulthood)

This man should be as a live spark, aware of the open gate of life, its possibilities and responsibilities. He should decide for himself how far he can proceed in a culture that belongs to the whole of humanity.

MONTESSORI'S APPROACH TO PRE-SCHOOL EDUCATION

Aims of Pre-school Education

1. Montessori was concerned about what she called direct preparation for academic learning.
2. The principal feeling that is clearly recognised in Montessori schools and for which satisfaction is deliberately sought is the joy of achievement.
3. Teacher recognises that emotions play a part in learning. Teachers should neither reward nor praise the child. It is the inward satisfaction of a child which is his strongest motive to learn.

View of the Child

1. Education is based on the great responsiveness of children's senses and also on their desire to master real skills.
2. Montessori sensed the unique nature of early intelligence, employed it in her method and understood that by only using methods appropriate to the age level, maximum acceleration of cognitive development can be achieved.
3. She talked about *"sensitive periods"*. Children between 3 to 6 years are sensitive to sensory. Motoric activities are the foundations for the following intellectual development.

How Children Learn

1. As an expert physician Dr. Montessori knew that young children learn through movement.
2. She believed that all learning was cumulative and the beginnings of reading and writing were clearly to be found in child's first years.
3. Montessori believed that through the materials children master complex skills from the trial and success points of view. 'Never let a child risk failure until he has a reasonable chance of success.'
4. Montessori believed that children learn first by seeing teacher demonstrating, second the child imitating the demonstration and third the child repeating the imitation.

Curriculum and Classroom Environment

1. Montessori's notion of the environment not as a classroom but a 'room to learn' is very important.
2. Emphasis is on a planned sequence of activities and here child sets his own pace.
3. According to Montessori environment is excellent in helping children, to internalize certain behaviour limits.
4. She allowed children to work independently and in small groups rather than to group them arbitrarily for instruction. According to her, children tend to combine with and break apart awarding to their developmental status.
5. For most part children are expected to work alone.

6. According to Montessori, her method has for its base, "The liberty of the child and liberty of activity". There is order and control but the control comes through organisation or environment rather than direct control of the child's behaviour by the teacher. This provides a valuable island of autonomy to each child.
7. Learning of domestic skills is divided into systematic sequences of steps and when a child has mastered the whole sequence he keeps on repeating it.
8. In Montessori school field trips are systematic and structured in their presentation. The aim is to bring to the child, awareness of the inherent order and structure in nature.

Ideas of Play, Play Material and Use of this Material

1. Montessori has a 'reality orientation' and does not believe in fantasy.
2. Montessori preferred the word 'work to' 'play', she did not arbitrarily divide work from play.
3. Planned pieces of equipment to be used in ways intended by Montessori.
4. All materials are self corrective. This stimulates repeated use of material and results in self education. The child perfects himself through his own efforts.

Teacher's Role

1. Teacher is a programmer, who prepares in advance of the child's coming, information and motives of activity (Things to do). In this prepared environment, child is free to learn in his own way.
2. Montessori counsels exemplary teacher behaviours because much of child's social behaviour is acquired through imitation.
3. Montessori exposes an awareness of the individual and group rhythms of children's lives in a learning environment.
4. Montessori's idea of readiness is that the child is always ready. It is the task of the teacher to find out for what the child is ready at a given moment.
5. Observation is a form of pedagogy. The teacher should observe before intervening.

6. Montessori allowed the children space upon which to impose their own style of growth and development. In order to do this she conceived of a teacher who was less directive in the verbal interaction sense, she felt that gesture was a foundation of learning.

Activities and Montessori Methods

The first contact of the child with the world is sensorial and he observes everything that is being done on him, for him and around him by means of this sensory organs. With regard to this, the activities conducted in Montessori method is classified under the following four heads:

1. Activities related to elementary movements, such as holding, putting down, picking up, rolling, unrolling etc., of all that forms part of the child's daily environment and actions such as walking, sitting down, getting up etc.
2. Then there are activities related to looking after the environment, both animate and inanimate, such as dusting, cleaning, polishing, washing and sweeping and also taking care of the plants and animals in one's environment.
3. Activities such as dressing, undressing, buttoning etc., help the child to look after himself and others.
4. Lastly, those activities which help him to maintain social relations with grace and courtesy—such as greeting, offering, accepting etc.

In case of a young child, these activities have a much more important and personal function. They are truly constructive, not with regard to the child himself.

These activities directly help the child become more dependent of adult help with regard to performance of elementary movements, looking after himself and his environment and maintain social relations properly.

Sensorial Activities and Montessori Method

The sensorial activities are presented to child at about 3 years of age in a Montessori house of children. Whatever object we wish to use for the education of the senses, it is of necessity to present many diverse qualities like weight, roughness, colour, form, size, etc.

The sensorial material helps him to know all basic properties of things and to recognise them and their relevance in every day life. Later he also discovers that they exist in various degrees of intensity and combinations.

Simultaneously, everything appertaining to the child's higher energies become a stimulus, setting his creative powers to work and extending the interests of his exploring mind. The sensorial material provides a kind of guide to observation because it classifies the impressions that each sense receives the colours, notes, noises, forms and sizes, touch, sensations, odours, and tastes. The child who has worked with these sensorial approaches has not only acquired greater skill in the use of his hands, but has also achieved a higher degree of perceptiveness towards those stimuli which come to him from the external world.

Cultural Activities and Montessori Method

"When you find a great treasure, place it at the feet of the child so that he may preserve it"— Dr. Maria Montessori.

The treasure she spoke of refers to the treasure from the treasure-house of human culture.

Language represents one of the greatest treasures of human culture. To start with, when the child is 2 ½ years, this help is offered by means of spoken language, story telling, recitation, planned conversations are some of the means used. The Montessori method considers it as a duty and privilege to provide the child with all possible opportunities to come into contact with the best of all fields; music, dancing, drawings and paintings. It takes all efforts to remove cultural illiteracy. It helps the child in his present needs so that the future would be safe in his hands.

Atmosphere in a Children's House

A Montessori school is 'a children's house' where the atmosphere is congenial for the development of the individuality of the child. Generally, it is a house with many rooms and a garden attached. Children look after the garden. The garden is so planned that children may play as well as rest over there. If they so desire, they may bring out the tables and the chairs and eat in the neighbourhood of the nature. This house provides them with an opportunity to live in the open air and also protection against sun and rain. The main room of the house is the place where children study. Attached to this big room are certain small rooms that are used as a laboratory, a lunch room, a common room and a place for manual work, a gymnasium and a rest room. Children are taught, in this house, to lead a natural and decent life.

Special Equipments

The special feature of this house is that it is equipped for the use of the children only and the furniture is so designed. There is that 'Didactic Apparatus' which brings about the intellectual development of the children. Children have to look after the arrangement and cleanliness of this house. There are various types of chairs, sofas and tables in the house. Every child is provided with a drawer in which he is supposed to keep his own things. There are low cup-boards in which children keep their didactic material and take them out when they need it. On the walls of the rooms, pictures and paintings are hung. There are small pieces of carpets of different colours to enable the children to sit on them and work with their didactic material. The sitting room is called the club room. In this room, are various types of equipments and materials for the amusement and recreation of the children. Flowers, toys and indoor games are also there.

The lunch room has low tables, chairs and drawers. In the drawers trays, spoons, knives, tables cloth, napkins etc. are kept. Children have to lay their own table and sometimes it gives pleasure to see these small children handle the brittle China plates and other things.

Dressing room has a little shelf for every child, where he keeps his soap and towel for washing, whenever he needs. There are low sinks and water taps for the use of the children.

Self-Help in Practice

In the Children's House, children themselves do every thing. They dust the room and the furniture, wash clothes and do all the things that are done in a family. They learn to wash themselves, to dress and undress. They are also taught to take care of their clothes.

Equipment of the house, to keep a record of physical development of the children

In every Children's House, there is a "Peadometer" for measuring of the heights of the children. This instrument has a little stool, from the centre of which rise two wooden posts, at top of which there is another flat piece of metal. Attached to this piece, there is an indicator which moves up and down the rod. The child has to stand on the instrument and measure himself. Two children can measure themselves at a time. They learn the use of the 'Pedometer' and keep a 'physiological record of their own'. This not only gives them an opportunity to handle an instrument and keep a record of their own, but also gives them an opportunity to learn, to work with their fellowmen.

Methods Applied for the Achievement of the Aims of Education

Three methods are applied to achieve the aims of education in the Montessori system. They are given below:

(a) Motor Education: The opportunity to manage the Children's House in which children live and educate themselves, provides them 'Motor Education'. A physically developed personality has a balanced and healthy mind. Only Motor Education can bring about such a development. Various sense organs have not only to be kept clean but also put to proper use. Such a use develops the co-ordination to the head, heart and body.

Without the guidance, the movements of the children are simply disorderly. The teacher has to guide them to walk properly, to handle things properly and take care of their own body and manage the house and garden. Dressing and undressing are also taught. As already stated, they have to perform small domestic duties than form a routine of a household. Along with it, they are also taught gardening, clay modelling etc. Certain Arithmetic exercises are also given to children. They are also taught to walk properly and undertake exercise in accompaniment with music. All these things provide for the Motor Education.

(b) Sensory Education: This education is completed with the help of the 'Didactic Apparatus' which consists of the following:

1. Three sets of solid insets.
2. Three sets of solids. They are graduated in sizes and contain the following:
   (*i*) Pink cubes.
   (*ii*) Brown prisms.
   (*iii*) Rods. These rods are green coloured and alternately coloured as red and blue.

3. Various Geometric solids like prism, pyramid, sphere, cone, cylinder, etc.
4. Tables of rectangular shape and size with surfaces rough and smooth.
5. Collection of various 'tuffs'.
6. Small wooden tables of various weights.
7. Two boxes. Each of them contains 64 coloured tablets.
8. A chest of drawers which has plane insets.
9. Three series of cards. On these Geometrical form of papers are pasted.
10. A collection of closed boxes cylindrical in shape. They are called sounds.
11. Lastly, there is a double series of music bells. Wooden boards with lines painted on them are used in music. Then, there are small wooden dishes for the notes.

(c) Language Teaching: In this process, there are letters made of wood. Children are made to learn those letters and move their hands over them. When they get acquainted with them, the teacher asks them to recognise a particular letter and take it out. While doing so, the teacher also asks them to pronounce that particular letter. There are also tables and boards on which the letters have been engraved. Children are asked to move their fingers or the pencil on those letters. While the children are doing so, the teacher pronounces those letters. By doing so, the children get acquainted with those letters in a natural and spontaneous manner and also learn reading and writing. Teaching of language consists of a desk, small balls and cards with letters pasted on them and also coloured boards of certain measurement with letters engraved on them. With the help of all these things, the aim of Montessori Education is achieved.

Montessori has thus given us a cosmic plan for the education of young children which could never be forgotten and it is up to us to try and follow it and further it for the benefit of human society.

7

John Dewey

"All education proceeds by the participation of the individual in the social consciousness of the race." This is the deliberate view of John Dewey, the veteran pragmatist, American philosopher, psychologist and a practical teacher. He was born in Vermont in new England in 1859. He was the son of a shopkeeper and was brought up in rural environment. The experience of early years brought to him two convictions: (1) that traditional methods of schooling were useless, and (2) that human contacts of everyday life provide unlimited, natural dynamic learning situations.

Dewey's Writings: Dewey was not only a great teacher but was also a great thinker. He had written various books on Philosophy, Psychology, Ethics, Political Science, Education and of course literature as well. His versatile contribution has helped him to make his mark in the various fields of life. Most well known on education are: (1) Relation of theory to practical in the education of teachers, (2) The School and the Child, (3) Moral Principles in Education, (4) How we think, (5) Schools of Tomorrow, (6) Democracy and Education. (7) Education Today.

Philosophy of John Dewey: Dewey's philosophy is a combination of the theory of evolution of Darwin and pragmatic concept of James. It has resulted in the blending of naturalism and pragmatism. He tested ideas in every form including their consequences. So, experience has become the core of his philosophy. Since experience is the central idea of his philosophy, it points towards the practical side of life and state of affairs which are the concern of pragmatic philosophy.

Dewey's Concept of Education: Pragmatism has gone around and influenced all facts of life, but it has special importance in the field of education. According to Dewey, "Education aims at the development of all those capacities in the individual which will enable him to control his environment and fulfil his faculties". He pointed out the defects in the prevalent system of education. There is more emphasis on the bookish knowledge than the practical working. This kills the initiative in the child.

According to Dewey, there are two elements of education—Psychological and Social. (1) *Psychological factor*: The interest and the tendencies of the child should be first studied and then education should be framed accordingly. (2) *Social factor*: All education proceeds by the participation of the individual in the social consciousness of the race and, therefore the aim of education should be to create an atmosphere by active participation in which the child may take part in the social consciousness of the race."

Education has to be in accordance with needs of the society. Dewey remarked, "What nutrition and reproduction are to the psychological life, education is to social life." He suggested that school should be a miniature society by living in which the child may learn the requirements of the social life. Dewey believed that the development of the child's mind takes place by his collective participation in activities that lead to social good. Living in co-operation brings about the development of the human personality and mind.

Experiences bring about the development of mind. Experience is the basis of education. Education is a process involving continuous reconstruction and reorganization of experiences.

Society and Democracy: We are living in an age which believes that democracy is the best form of life. It is the government of the people, for the people and by the people. Therefore, education should be such that it may be in accordance with the democrate set-up or capable of establishing co-ordination between the individual interest and the social interest. So the aim of education should be to inculcate the spirit of democracy in young children so that when they go out in life they may prove to be ideal and good citizens. This can happen only when a school is a democratic society in miniature.

Dewey's Educational Theory: *Aims of Education:* According to Dewey, "The function of education is to help growing of helpless young animal into a happy, moral and efficient human being." Education should aim at the 'stimulation of the child's powers through the social medium'. Since the interest and the capabilities of the children differ from child to child the education cannot grow according to set aims. This will hamper the proper growth of their personality. It should only aim at the growth of the innate nature of the immature child as to help him to be able to live upto the social standards and the demands that are made upon him. It should aim at 'social efficiency'.

The Aim of Education Can be Divided Under Two Heads

(1) *Individual and* (2) *Social.*

1. *Individual Aims*: (*i*) Education should help an individual to establish those principles and standards that are of immediate importance and value to him. (*ii*) To equip the individual to be able to test the truth and utility of these values and standards through experiments and examinations.
2. *Social Aims*: In order to bring about social efficiency the education should have the following qualities:
   - (*i*) *Economic efficiency:* It should be able to equip the child to earn his livelihood.
   - (*ii*) *Negative morality:* It should be capable of making a child leaving those standards and wishes whose satisfaction may hinder the economic efficiency of others.
   - (*iii*) *Positive morality*: It should be capable of stopping the children or individuals from trying to satisfy those desires and wishes whose fulfilment will directly or indirectly disturb social business.

Education is life

Dewey believed that education is not a preparation for life. It is life. The school is a miniature society facing problems similar to those faced in life. Children should, therefore, be made participators in the social and moral struggles of their communities. Since they are to live in a democratic society they should help to organise one and live in it. The basic purpose of the school is to train pupils in 'Co-operative living'. The child is to share the resources of a good society and to give back to that society, thus helping the development of other members. The school should thus serve to free society from its inherited evils by identifying itself with social and democratic life.

Education Should Combine Theory and Practice

The aim of education, said Dewey, should be to secure a balanced interaction of the practical and the theoretical attitudes.

Education is Experience: Dewey's was an education by, of and for experience. A conscious effort has to be made to make men more competent to take part in the activities and purposes of the human race. This effort is education. Education, he said, helps, "the process of the reconstruction of experience giving it a more socialised value through the medium of increased individual efficiency". Education, he says protects, sustains and directs growth.

Dewey's Concept of an Ideal School: He established the 'Experimental School' at Chicago in 1896. It was called Laboratory School because education was not imparted in the conventional sense of the term. No school subjects were prescribed. It was like a workshop where trades and other manual occupations that a man has t o undertake in his life were taught. It was an active School on which John Dewey has laid stress. Here learning by doing was the basic plan.

John Dewey believed that school is a socio-psychological necessity. It is psychological because it lays that the home-development may go on unhampered and social because it has to provide for the education of the child as a member of the society. Dewey believed that school is a society in miniature and so he also thought that in school all such activities that one has to face in society must be centralised. This helps the learner to face the bigger and more complicated problems of life.

School as an enlarged family—school should not be isolated from the family. It should preserve, continue and rebuild the activity with which the child is familiar at home. Schools provide better equipments and more scientific guidance.

Vocational Education: Dewey believed that in schools, children should be taught at least one vocation which may be helpful to them in their actual life in earning their livelihood.

Moral Education: Should not be in the form of a separate lesson but through 'social and conjoint activities'.

School should be the reflection of society: Dewey believed that there is no definiteness or unity in the requirements and needs of the society. They change according to the situations. The society is also not very definitely conscious of its needs and requirements. An ideal school should help the society to achieve this consciousness. The main aim of education is the development and presentation of democracy. This can happen only when people get education in the democratic way of life.

Dewey and Curriculum: Dewey believed that curriculum construction should be around the children's needs and their interests must be taken into consideration. The curriculum must grow out of child's interests, impulses and experiences. So it should consist of activities leading to reconstruction of experiences. The curriculum must be child-centred rather than subject-centred. It should be woven around the child's activities and not the subjects. Lesson should begin with social materials such as food-shelter, modes of social communication, speech, writing, reading, drawing, modelling etc. Only then the children will be able to take interest in learning the subjects. The mind of the child is a complete unit and is not divided into watertight compartments. Hence curriculum should be considered as a whole. He divides the total scheme of education into three stages. (1) Play period for 4 years duration (up to 8 years) (2) Period of spontaneous attention for 4 years (up to 12 years) (3) period of reflective attention from 12 years and above.

With the advent of this scheme Dewey has made his scheme of education as quite meaningful and purposive to all stages from Pre-Primary level. This scheme alone, he believes will realise the aim of education, namely making the learners acquire efficiency and become a meaningful and successful member of the society.

Method of Teaching: Dewey remarks, "All learnings must come as a by-product of actions and never as something learned directly for its own sake". This reveals his concept of the direct method and direct experience in teaching and learning. By this method the pupil learns to gain experience through participation. He wants the teachers to wait for the learning situation and to create interest in them for learning. For this he recommends the doctrine of natural interest, effort and motivation. He strongly recommends the methods of learning by living and learning by doing. Here it speaks about the 'Project Method' which deals with the problems, experiments, activities and interest of the learners.

Project Method: The project method was perfected by Dr. J.A. Stevenson. In this method the curriculum and technique of teaching are considered from the child's point of view. It lays emphasis on "learning by doing", and "learning by living". The teacher has no business to impose himself upon the unwilling children. The children select their own material and plan their own methods. Learning to be effective has to be the outcome of wholehearted purposeful activity and this is exactly the essence of the project method. The underlying idea of this method is that, all education should be purposeful and should be connected with real every day life.

Dr. Kilpatrik defines it as, "a wholehearted purposeful activity proceeding in a social environment." There are certain principles on which the project method is based. They are : Principle of (1) purpose, (2) activity, (3) experience, (4) reality, (5) freedom, and (6) utility.

Dewey's methods of teaching comprised three processes: (1) Continuance of psychological order in the curriculum, (2) Retention of problem method, and (3) Extension of social opportunity. While the project of problem method entails co-operative effort it is also possible through this to correlate all the subjects necessary for the child to know. But Dewey warns the teacher not to allow the projects to be too ambitious and beyond the pupil's capacity to accomplish as the children sometimes exaggerate their powers of execution.

Application of Project Method at the Pre-Primary School Level

As Dewey says the child learns in the natural setting rather than in a classroom, freedom is given to the child to learn whatever he wants to learn. Similarly projects on different topics such as the Animals, Birds, Transport, Food, Plants, Trees, Flowers, Community works, Inventions etc. are planned and introduced according to the capacity and interest of children, in the Pre-primary school. Children work individually as well as in group in Pre-primary schools to complete the project and learn while doing.

The Function of Teachers in Dewey's Scheme

Dewey gave a very important role to the teacher. A teacher should be more concerned with the child's impulses and interests rather than the inculcation of knowledge. Her function is to guide the young through the complexities of life, for this she should provide them opportunities to learn in the natural way without facing frustration and injury. The teacher should produce a race of young people, competent to cope with new experiences and new tasks which come before them.

John Dewey gave great freedom to the child. But this freedom has to be regulated and organised by the teacher. The teacher, "as a stage manager is more powerful than the teacher as a player strutting and fretting". She may not have the plasticity to adopt her own personality to new growth, but since she is ahead of her children in experience, she should survey the social heritage and look to a more distance and purpose than her children.

Instead of wasting her time in 'Chalk and talk', instruction and in the establishment of rigid discipline, the teacher must observe, plan and encourage. Dewey's child-centred curriculum gave to teacher a heavier responsibility and a greater opportunity for guiding the young not only into the habit of democratic co-operation but also towards the highest intellectual pursuits and the fullest aesthetic expérience.

Dewey wanted his teacher to indicate short-cuts and to persuade the pupils to engage in progressive activities. For this she must know the intelligence and temperament of each child. The teacher is a friend, philosopher and guide, "Every teacher should realise the divinity of the calling". The teachers should have sympathy for children.

Discipline: Dewey has said that if the activities in the school are organised according to the natural interest of the child, there will be no problem of discipline.

Dewey has laid stress on the social discipline. He was of the view that the individual capabilities of the child can develop properly only in the society and therefore, his conduct and discipline should be developed while keeping in view the requirements of the society. In order to maintain discipline the pre-school should try to create a social atmosphere. If children are allowed to take part in the collective and co-operative activities in the school, their impulses will get refined and a new type of discipline will come into being.

Dewey believed that all the activities of the child's intellectual, moral, social and physical can be disciplinary in effect if they are carried out with the co-operation and with a definite purpose.

The teacher has to provide the proper environment that will enrich the child's experience and encourage him to perform his activities purposefully and in a co-operative manner. This will have development of social attitude, social interest habits and social will.

Conclusion: Dewey is a source of inspiration to so many thinkers in every walk of life and especially in the field of education. He is responsible for the changing dynamic society. His philosophy is more of criticism than any things. He has made education utilitarian and practical. He is remembered not only for having made 'Education' real and useful but also for having introduced the slogan, "Education for here and now at the spot, on the times".

Dewey's contributions have influenced many educators of even today. The progressive education movements and progressive schools came out of Dewey's ideas on education and his influence among educationists. This has brought over changes in education in very many countries. Dewey is also remembered for his contribution to Pre-school education as he emphasised much on the child, its activities unfolding, his potentialities and learning by doing and playing.

8

Margaret McMillan Sisters

Margaret McMillan was a middle-aged woman at the dawn of the twentieth century. She lived until 1931, but her main work was accomplished during the first two decades. As a student of education and a leader of thought on child education, she deserves a place in the history of Early Childhood Education. Her approach to education of young children was intellectual as well as practical and that her convictions were derived from philosophy and psychology as well as from her social conscience.

Miss. McMillan first earned her living as a governess, but later joined her sister Rachaeel in London; both sisters becoming infected with an enthusiasm for social work and an interest in the new Socialist Movement. Margaret had a striking appearance and excellent voice, assets that gained her a course of stage training at the expense of a titled lady but even while engaged in these duties, the lady was taking an active part in socialist campaigns. She was teaching music to groups of factory girls and was continuing her already extensive leading of literature on education, philosophy and sociology.

Contribution of Education

Margaret McMillan won a place on the Bradford School Board and she had started her campaign on behalf of the hordes of dirty, adenoidal, undernourished children of the town. From this time onward she published writings on questions relating to education, not regular or prolific, but excellent in quality and relevance. Her knowledge of music and voice-production made her particularly conscious of the prevalence of faulty breathing habits among the young children. She wrote a pamphlet on this topic for distribution to mothers. As she fought her way towards the establishment of school baths, school meals and school clinics, she also pursued her studies of the latest theories and physical welfare. In 1896, she published a pamphlet, Child Labour and the Half-Time System and a new years later she completed her first book. Early Childhood, which reveals not only the depth of her sympathy for young children but also the width of her intellectual horizons.

Educational Theory

Miss. McMillan's kinship with Froebel may be traced in her assumption that emotion plays its part in child-development from the beginning. Only when the health of the child from birth has been recognised as a basic human responsibility and community concern, can the other aims of education be sought with any prospect of success. The human organism is a unity; the growth of feelings, sentiments and emotions depends on physical well-being and freedom from hunger and pain. She describes how sense impressions—through sight, sound, touch, and smell—cause feelings of wonder that she designates involuntary culture. Natural play activities give much experience of this kind of experiences which teachers might well aim to extend in school. There is a hint of Herbart in her contention that education aims to produce "the ethical man or woman", a process dependent on the early foundation of a healthy body and a rich emotional life.

Method of Teaching

Miss. McMillan elaborated her phiiosophy in a pamphlet, "The Ethical Aim of Education", a essay which reveals her growing interest in the science of psychology and in the actual process and methods of education. She regards current teaching methods as "a sin against the power of the emotions of children as a sustained of all vigorous mental and moral life". Her aim is to persuade teachers that they should study "spontaneous attention" in their pupils and should try "to build up the powers of voluntary attention from the involuntary."

"The creative power of the mind" is in her view the quality which every human-being should be enabled to develop and use in his personal life and work. The school methods and the factory system of her day achieved only the suppression of this power. The adjustment of school curriculum and methods to the psychological needs of the pupil should result in the production of an individual who will earn a living not merely by mechanical skill, but also with an intelligent, enterprising and interested attitude.

Her theory of education for young children requires the arrangement of contacts and experiences, both in play and in activities resembling play, so that each child may acquire and co-ordinate primary sensations. These eventually led to the refinement of perception and the development of those feelings and emotions on which expressive and creative imagination depends. She is the first to point out the problem of the day-dreaming child who has been denied those experiences which would have captured his attention for more real and creative mental effort.

Margaret McMillan stresses the individual nature of development and points out a problem that has not yet been solved—how to ensure that each youngster is streched to the utmost of his capacity. She is perturbed not only by the limitation of intellectual growth, but also because the child may express "only a fraction of his personality". The fault lies not only in the teacher with poor methods and in the industrial system with its mechanisation of humanity, but also in the mere physical stresses of social conditions which produce widely and rapidly in the child population myopia, faulty breathing, malnutrition and other weakness. These prevent full participation in experiences which develop the emotions—music, movement, drawing, poetry handicrafts and science. Many children in school cannot respond emotionally to such stimuli because their home life has not given them the early experience—joys, love, and beauty—which give the preliminary development of the feelings.

McMillan Sisters' Achievement in Pre-schools

During the ten years which followed the publication of 'Education Through the Imagination', the McMillan sisters achieved the foundation of clinics and remedial centres, night camps and camp schools for boys and girls in Deptford and an open-air pre-school. The pre-school was eventually moved from the camp site to a new location. Margaret wrote a book on nursery school and because she later effected the foundation of a nursery training college her name has become associated with infant education rather than with a much wiper theory and achievement.

Her aim was always the free and full development of the intellect and personality of the individual. In the nursery school she expresses some suscepticism of current trends in psychology, because it was developing as a separate science with the aloofness that spells failure. She hopes that the open-air pre-school will clear the decks not only for actions, but also for observations, so that a real knowledge of child development may be build up.

Margaret McMillan was instrumental in bringing remedial and preventive medicine into the orbit of national education. She provided proof positive of the power of doctors, dentists, nurses and even ordinary teachers, to improve the physical well-being of young children that learning difficulties and behaviour problems would remedy themselves.

9

Head Start Programme

With the Economic Act of 1964 the Head Start began in the United States under the economically deprived children of pre-school age to prepare them to enter the formal school system which will also enable them to deal more effectively with both their present environments and later responsibilities in school and community life. The Head Start Programme was designed mainly for the population of 3 to 5 years old children whose families were below the poverty line, through the pre-school programme, by providing adequate behaviour model. Since 1964 it has been providing rich experiments, demonstrations, increased quality, and expanded functions of Head Start. It is an attempt to break the poverty cycle in early years as these years are crucial in a child's life. From its conception Head Start was designed to prepare the disadvantaged and deprived children of pre-school age not only by offering pre-school experiences but also by providing health care and better nutritional standard and encouraging the parents to participate in the well being of the child.

History and Philosophy

The Head Start Programme grew from a 96 million dollar programme serving about 30,000 children in 1965 to a projected budget of over a billion dollars for 1984, serving half a million children in the United States. The programme serves children from ethnic minority groups as well as children from disadvantaged rural, urban and mountainous areas. Children from migrant families and children with some specific handicap are also included. The average cost per child is approximately US $ 1,600 in 1982.

While there have been a number of programme variations over the years, the essential philosophy of Head Start has remained the same. It is based on the recommendations of the Cooke Committee, chaired by Robert Cooke, which prepared a memorandum of recommendations for a Head Start Programme in early 1965. The recommendations included all the basic elements which persisted in the Head Start Programme as well as the philosophy of comprehensive services. They aimed at improving the total development of child physical, motor, emotional, social, mental and language development, by involving the families in the programme. It also aimed at developing a responsible attitude toward society; and increasing the sense of dignity and self-worth within the child and his or her family.

These basic elements reflect the philosophy of a comprehensive child development programme, which, in fact, was the original title for Head Start in the legislation. Head Start Programme for children from three to five years of age had clearly shown that environmentally caused developmental deficits will be difficult to over-come. Hence this programme gave attention to all the components.

Programme and Practice

Components of Programme

As a comprehensive child development programme Head Start provided a number of components in the curriculum. He also aimed at providing experience that will help children be successful in their formal schooling. The components require that : (*a*) educational experiences and activities to help children grow socially, emotionally and intellectually; (*b*) to provide each child a carefully planned and monitored health delivery system; (*c*) preventive medical and dental services to be provided; (*d*) a nutrition programme includes the provision of nutritious meals and snacks; (*e*) to involved parents in decision-making, as staff members or a volunteers; and (*f*) to provide the social service component which will help families to make maximum use of the community's services and resources. The programme emphasised learning language, healthy living, developing curiosity, building self-image, and respecting authority as a means to self- discipline.

Two more recent programme components are the enrolment of 10 percent of handicapped children in a mainstreamed setting (1972) and that bilingual/bicultural experiences are provided for children whose primary language is not English, so that they will be able to complete with English speaking children.

Quality control of the programme elements is maintained by a set of Head Start Programme Performance Standards which specify the basic requirements and standards for fostering the development of young children. Although Head Start is founded and quality control is directed by the federal government, it is a decentralized programme and is administered through 11 regional offices. There are about 1,300 grantees in about 10,000 Head Start centres in USA each consisting of several classrooms. Meanwhile, demands for extensive support for day care services for employed mothers resulted in mushroom growth of programmes for young children.

Organisation Pattern

Children for the Head Start Programme were selected on the basis of their parental income, those who were hailing from low income group or below the poverty line. Number of children in the family also was one of the criteria.

It used to be of small group with 15-20 children per teacher. These teachers were trained for a period of 8 weeks. They were selected from local areas.

Experimental Variations

While the Head Start Programme has continued with the major programme elements, there has been experimentation with different delivery systems, such as Home Start, which works directly in the home or in a combination of home and centre experiences. Similar programmes are experimented in Tamil Nadu which is called Home Stimulation. Head Start has also experimented with different emphasises, such as providing Basic Education Skills Programme which emphasises cognitive experiences, and with programme configurations, such as developmental continuity and follow through, which attempt to maintain the benefits of Head Start.

Problems and Issues

The problems and issues in Head Start were of internal, and from the evaluation of overall programme. The problems and issues internal to the programme was identified in a report in 1978 by the Department of Health and Human Services. The major problems and issues identified were:

(*a*) individualised planning for children is inconsistent and often limited to anecdotal rotations;
(*b*) most programmes experience difficulty in actively involving the majority of parents even when a variety of opportunities are created; and
(*c*) the narrow federal income eligibility requirement severely restrict the target population and frequently stigmatize Head Start as another form of welfare.

These problems and issues internal to the programme are addressed by changes in training emphasis to focus on individualised planning, experimenting with new relationships with parents to increase their involvement and pooling of other public money to reduce the problems.

Total Programme Impact

Evaluation of the impact of Head Start total programme was difficult to conduct. They are expensive, require sensitive and complex instruments, sophisticated field work and advanced statistical techniques were to be employed.

A total programme evaluation report by the Westinghouse Learning Corporation (1969) illustrates the problems. It concludes that full year Head Start Programmes had small effects on achievement and that summer Head Start Programmes had vegative effects. The report was given a great deal of publicity and its influence remained strong for a decade.

There was, little hard evidence even by 1975, that early intervention was effective for children from low income families or that Head Start was effective. The problems of assessing the immediate and long-term impact of Head Start and other early childhood programmes began to be resolved in 1976.

Programme Elements Impact

In 1973, Head Start began assessing the impact of specific programme elements as an alternative to the total programme impact. The rational was that there was a greater opportunity to improve programme elements when their specific role in the development of children could be evaluated.

Many specific programme elements have received evaluations. Mainstreaming and bilingual bilet cultural curricula are selected for discussion here because they represent the value of this approach and also the different implications of the findings for Head Start.

Firstly, Head Start is required to include 10 percent of all handicapped children in the programme in a mainstreamed setting; that is, in the regular classroom with non-handicapped children. An evaluation of the impact of mainstreaming reported in 1978 indicated that Head Start handicapped children show gain in motoric, self-help, social, academic, and communication skills, especially speech-impaired children.

Secondly, the Head Start bilingual bicultural curricula development effort was based on the assumption that one curriculum model would not meet the diverse needs of Head Start centers serving Spanish speaking communities. Further, children whose primary language is other than English, must receive Head Start experiences in the language they know best.

Four curricula were developed and tested followed by an assessment of their impact on the children. The findings indicated that regardless of the mix of English-speaking and Spanish-speaking children, those children with the least English background made the greatest gains in English. Overall gains in English were more a function of the amount of time spent using English than of the type of curriculum. Over time, English became the increasingly preferred language of the children Spanish did not improve as a result of curricula, the part of both the teachers and the children. The policy implications will be addressed for many lingualism.

Conclusion Statement

Head Start remains a viable, evolving programme. It is continually challenged to improve its performance by the findings from evaluations and the possing of new policy questions. It continues to be a model for comprehensive child development programmes around the world.

10

Rabindranath Tagore

INTRODUCTION

In the firmament of education two master-minds of India will remain outstanding—Rabindranath Tagore and Mahatma Gandhi. They were not only theorists, but also practitioners. Their results are epitomised in Shantiniketan and Basic Education. Tagore discovered the fundamental unities of our culture. He brought Indians together on the binding basis of all that is essential in our civilization and then showed the right path not only to Indians but also to the world.

Life Sketch of Rabindranath Tagore

Tagore was born in Calcutta on May 6th 1861. Maharishi Devendranath Tagore, the great Brahmo leader, was his father. Rabindranath Tagore was the youngest of his six brothers. He had his early education in home and went to England to study law. Tagore is a philosopher, poet, novelist, dramatist, actor, composer, educator, painter and prophet. By his writings he has enriched not only Bengali literature, but also English. The world recognised the merit of Tagore by awarding him the Nobel Prize for literature in November 1913, on the English version of his "Gitanjali".

Shantiniketan, the ideal school of Tagore's concept was established in 1901, Shantiniketan became Vishwabharati or International University in 1921 and since then it has been growing gradually. He died on the 7th August, 1914.

Tagore's General Philosophy

Naturalism, Idealism, Humanism, and Internationalism are the key notes of his philosophy.

Tagore's Naturalism

Tagore finds a fundamental unity between man and nature. So he wants that 'the *child's* education must be organized in natural surroundings. Thus the child can develop power of communication with the world. Tagore does not want that the natural senses of children should be debased in an urban atmosphere. Tagore puts more faith in the individual than in an institution. Children are more important than books and teacher. Tagore's naturalism paves the way to spiritualism, he considers music as an aid to it.

Tagore's Humanism

To Tagore man is the measure of everything. His conception of the universe is purely human. All values and virtues are to be realised through man; truth, good and beauty are felt as such by man. God is also human. He says that the teacher should regard himself as an elder brother of children. Tagore shuns all violence and force in the process of education.

Tagore's Internationalism

He wanted that East should give its best to the West and in turn it should assimilate the best that the west has to offer. He felt grateful to both the East and West and believed that the problem of the world could be solved only if a judicious synthesis was attained between the contributions of the East and West.

Tagore's Idealism

Tagore wants that the ancient ideal of Indian Education should come back in its essence though not in its entirety. Tagore believed in the ancient Indian Educational ideals and practices. To him education is not information nor does it consist in passing exams. He regards education as a preparation for a living in the world with a view to seek communion with the Divine power.

Tagore's Educational Philosophy

Tagore was dissatisfied with the existing system of education, because it ignored our own customs, traditions, conventions, manners, ideologies, morals and ideals. He felt that traditional schools gave information and not knowledge. He stressed only the intellectual side and ignored altogether, the other aspects of human growth. "Education", he said, is a permanent part of the adventure of life, it is not like a painful hospital treatment curing student's instincts. About the main object of education he said, "the best function of education is to enable us to realise that to live as a man is great, requiring profound philosophy for its ideal, poetry for its expression and heroism for its conduct."

MAIN PRINCIPLES OF HIS EDUCATIONAL PHILOSOPHY

The four main principles of Tagore's educational philosophy are:

(*a*) Freedom
(*b*) Creative self-expression
(*c*) Active communication with nature and man
(*d*) Internationalism

(*a*) *Freedom*: Tagore believed that children should be brought up and educated in an atmosphere singing with freedom and liberty. He was in favour of giving maximum freedom to children to display their emotional outbursts, feelings, impulses and instincts.

(*b*) *Creative self-expression*: Education should aim at the development of the creative tendencies of the child. Tagore laid great stress on self-expression through different forms of work like handicraft, music, art etc.

(*c*) *Active Communication with Nature and Man*: According to Tagore education should be in constant touch and active communion with nature and man. He said, "Next to nature the child should be brought into touch with the stream of social behaviour. He thought that the children should be given maximum opportunities for social conducts. This will help them to acquire socialised behaviour.

(*d*) *Internationalism*: Tagore had deep faith in the unity of man. Tagore was a true cosmpolitan. He believed in unity in diversity of races and nations. He opened Viswabharati to all the persons in the world irrespective of caste, creed, colour and sex.

Aim of Education

In accordance with his general philosophy Tagore emphasised spiritual, physical and intellectual aims.

(*a*) *Moral and Spiritual Aim*: The principal aim is to produce the moral and spiritual man, the whole man. He stressed inner development, attainment of an inner freedom, an inner power and enlightenment. Education should lead to satisfaction of mind and the peace of soul. It should guide for communion with God. Tagore emphasised moral training and development of character. This is possible through austere devotion (*Sadhana*) and development of inner discipline.

(*b*) *Intellectual Aim*: Education should cultivate the power of acquiring ideas through independent effort and develop the ability to learn directly from nature and life. It must aim at making the pupils familiar with the conditions of real life and habitual environments.

(*c*) *Physical Aim*: Tagore equally emphasised healthy physical development of children, specially in early years. This was possible through free movements and play in joyous natural surroundings.

Curriculum

Tagore was not satisfied with the existing curriculum which was purely academic and thus inadequate to the needs of the child. He envisaged many new ideas much ahead of others, and has tried to implement them into practice at Shantiniketan. He provided opportunities for the teaching of crafts, music, dance, painting, fine arts etc. in the curriculum at Shantiniketan. He welcomed the new movement of scientific thought and included scientific subjects in the curriculum specially experimental science. He pleaded universal outlook in history and a critical appraisal of national culture. Tagore emphasised teaching through the medium of mother tongue, but he was not against the teaching of English at the higher level. Like Gandhiji, Tagore pleaded for manual training.

In short Tagore recommended a curriculum for the full man satisfying the spiritual, the creative, the aesthetic and the vocational aims of education.

Methods of Teaching

Tagore was against the prevalent system of instructions which was mechanical and stereotyped. He strongly criticized the bookish and examination oriented teaching. To him education should be conducted on realistic lines, reflecting the actual surroundings and theortical life. Knowledge should be acquired through independent effort and thinking. History, Geography and many social subjects could be best taught through educational tours. He believed that there should be daily practice by pupils in expressing immediately what they are learning. Tagore loved tranquility and calm atmosphere. He followed the activity principle, and advocated constructive and creative activities. To cultivate observation and reasoning among children Tagore emphasised the contact with real objects nearer to the children and the real experiences in handling the objects, in free atmosphere as he believed that only through freedom the child can have wholesome development.

On the Duty of a Teacher

"The greater part of our learning in the schools has been wasted because, for most of our teachers, their subjects are like dead specimens of one liking things, with which, they have a learned acquaintance, but no communication of life and love", Tagore said. Tagore wants that the teacher should try to understand the relationship between their subjects and human life and the same should be brought home to the students as well. This can be possible only when the teacher continues learning and does not stop his growth by suffering their minds with that matter. A teacher can never truly teach unless he is still learning himself. "A lamp can never light another lamp unless it continues to burn its own flame".

Discipline

Tagore wanted to give the maximum amount of freedom to children. Tagore convinced that, "the object of education is the freedom of mind which can only be achieved through the path of freedom—though freedom has its risk and responsibility as life has."

About the nature of school, he says, "It is not a school which is imposed upon the boys by authorities. It always tries to impress upon their minds that it is their own world, upon which their life thoughtfully and freely to react."

Shantiniketan is an excellent example of freedom in the world of emotion and abstraction. Tagore advocated self-Government by the students to maintain discipline.

Shantiniketan

Tagore created Shantiniketan, which realised his educational ideals. Originating with 10 boys in 1901 Shantiniketan became Vishwabharati or International University in 1921. The school was started with the following ideals in view:

1. To impart spiritual culture to the boys.
2. To provide a new approach to western science and culture.
3. To bring out an understanding between the East and the West by the study of their culture, philosophy, art and music, and then to promote unification of mankind.
4. To allow opportunities for the freedom of mind, heart and will.
5. To cater for the education of the wholeman of his emotions and senses as much as his intellect.
6. To strike a balance between spiritual, physical and intellectual education.

Conclusion

Vishwabharati, the ideal school of Tagore's concept is not only preserving and furthering the cultural beverage of India, but is also combining with it, the best of Western Culture, Science, Literature and Art. Tagore's unique contribution is in the form of rural reconstruction for the welfare of poor villagers. Arts, crafts and cottage industries receive special attention in this institute. Vishwabharati led to the formation of many Rural Institutes in India. Let us conclude in the words of Calcutta University Syndicate, 'Through Rabindranath Tagore, India has given her message to mankind and his unique achievements in the fields of literature, philosophy, education, art and have won imperishable fame for herself and have raised the status of India in the estimation of the world". And his love for children will remain a beckon-light in the system of education for going children.

11

The System of Pre-Basic Education of Mahatma Gandhi

The movement of pre-primary school education is a new endeavour in the educational system itself. Education for the children below five years of age, outside the home was not given much importance in the history of educational movement. It was the opinion of the people that it was the duty of the home to educate the young children and care for them. Mainly the custodial care was emphasised in this formative period when much learning takes place. Thus, the idea itself is that the education of young children outside home, in a pre-school is of a new and recent origin in the history of education.

We have many types of pre-schools in India such as Montessori Schools, Kindergartens and Nursery Schools. They are not the educational systems that were developed for our children or experimented with our children. These systems are the contributions of people from the West, with a different outlook, standard of living and culture. Though we have accepted these systems with some modifications and changes to suit Indian children, we cannot say that these are the best methods for our young children in the villages of India. After careful study and observation and practice of these systems in India, Mahatma Gandhi gave us a new system of education to experiment with Indian children in the Indian soil itself and develop a new national system of education best suited for our children, which is called the Basic Education on *Nai-Talim* or the Wardha Scheme of Education.

The purely literary education which was introduced by the British in India was merely aimed at producing the "White Collared Clerk" to work in their offices. This type of education neglected and destroyed the country and its culture mainly the villages, which form the backbone of our country. The so called educated looked upon their education as a mere means to their own advancement even at the cost of the poor. Gandhiji, while he was fighting for the political freedom of India, also thought of a new educational system based on Indian culture, and wanted to save and preserve it by reviving village economic life and by relating education to it.

He was of the opinion that education should be child oriented or child centred. He emphasised the harmonious development of the child. Gandhiji said, "by education I mean all round drawing out of the best in child and man—body, mind and spirit." According to him new education, is education for life and through life. He wanted education to be related to the very ideas of life itself. As many of us think Gandhiji was not against literary training. He wanted such literacy training as is useful in life and is to be attained in correlation to work.

1. "All education must be self-supporting that is to say, in the end it will pay its expenses excepting the capital which will remain intact.
2. In it the cunning of the hand will be utilised even upto the final stage, that is to say, hands of the pupils will be skillfully working at some industry for some period during the day.
3. All education must be imparted through the medium of the provincial language.
4. In this there is no room for giving sectional religious training. Fundamental universal ethics will have full scope.
5. This education, whether it is confined to children or adults, male or female, will find its way to the homes of the pupils.
6. Since millions of students receiving this education will consider themselves as of the whole of India, they must learn an inter-provincial language. This common inter-provincial speech can only be Hindustani written in Nagari or Urdu Script. Therefore, pupils have to master both the scripts".

Philosophy and Aims of Pre-Basic Education

Pre-Basic Education is not a separate system but is a part of Basic Education. Actually Pre-Basic Education is the second stage in the New Education. Every Basic School naturally has to be preceded by a Pre-Basic Course which keeps the young children busy and at the same time makes them happy.

According to Gandhiji, the education of the child actually starts from its conception in the form of adult education, where expectant mothers are educated in child rearing practices and to be wise parents. A child gets his first impression from his mother, father, siblings and other adults at home. A child is always active and all his movements are creative, and not destructive. He wanted especially to create a conducive atmosphere in the Pre-Basic School which will help the young minds to realise that their education is going to revive their old culture which has disappeared. Gandhiji wanted to bring a new life to the villages through *Nai-Talim*.

Pre-Basic Education emphasises that a child's education must be based on the mother's intelligence and her education, that is adult education. The home where the child is born and lives influence him and that becomes the first centre of his education and learning. There should not be a feeling of opposition between home influence and school influence because it creates a conflict in the child's mind and injures his life seriously. The teacher and the parents should be co-operative with each other in understanding this fact. We must educate the parents to co-operate in carrying out the education of young children successfully and effectively. This co-operation and friendship between parents and teachers, home and school, brings happiness and joy in the young child's life.

One of the main principles and philosophy of Pre-Basic Education is that it must be inexpensive so that it can reach the millions in the villages. It is expected at the higher level of Basic Education system that it must be self-supporting and the principle of self-sufficiency is followed through the medium of a useful craft or an activity. How can we expect the Pre-school child to be self-supporting at this young age? Can we expect him to earn something at this tender age? As it is said before, a child is creative, all his movements and actions are creative in nature. According to Gandhiji a child's play is also creative and his play means learning to do something. If the child, from the beginning learns to be active and creative, it will be easier for him to use his limbs along with his brain when he grows older. Work thus will not be a burden for him and he realises the dignity of labour. He learns the wise use of both his hands and head that is energy and intelligence. Though a child in a Pre-Basic School is not expected to be self-sufficient on self-supporting he makes a start, an attempt to develop this quality in future when he enters the Basic School. The child starts learning that he should not be a burden to the society and that every one in the society should shoulder the responsibility for a healthy and happy life. According to Mahatmaji self-sufficiency means that every one must learn to labour and to earn, intelligently, one must not be a parasite on the family whether he is a child or an adult, a girl or a boy; an ordinary person or an intellectual.

Programme of Instruction

As it has been told earlier, Pre-Basic Education is for the under sevens, that is from conception to seven years of age. This whole period has been divided into four main stages and the instructional programme has been framed accordingly. The first stage is from conception to birth, the second stage from birth to two and a half-years, the third stage from two and a half to four years—the junior group and the fourth stage is from four to seven years—the senior group. In the first two stages education involves both the mother and the child. Opportunities are provided for mothers to learn more about new trends and scientific methods of child rearing, health and hygiene, and mother craft. Children at this stage that is those below two and a half years, are given mainly the custodial care. The medical section of the Kasturba Trust took the lead in planning and implementing this. As they had the Maternity Centres attached to their welfare work centres, it was easier from them to carry out their plan. Now the Community Development Blocks, Panchayats, Pilot Health Projects, Social Welfare Board, Indian Council for Child Welfare and some private agencies and factories are also interested in these children as well as their mothers. As a result we see a number of creches, maternity centres and well Baby clinics where educational programme as well as the custodial care go hand in hand. The first two years of life are very important for building up the health of the child. Once he becomes physically strong and healthy the chances for better all round development are more. Hence, this programme stresses the need for some arrangement for Child Welfare Centres to be attached to pre-schools.

After two years of age the child can be weaned from his mother and he is then ready to live away from his mother for about one or two hours a day. However, it is necessary that the atmosphere in the Pre-Basic School is a lonely one. There must be some similarity between home and school: the school and the teacher should become substitute home and mother respectively for the children when they are away from home. The teacher in a Pre-Basic School should have close relationship with the parents, homes and community as a whole in order to run an effective programme in her school.

The children of two and a half years to seven years are divided into junior and senior groups. The first group consists of children from two and a half to four and the second group, from four to seven years of age. The programme and the syllabus for these two groups differ. While planning the programme for these two groups, children's abilities and interests are taken into consideration. The children below four are more individualistic in nature and like to play and work alone. They are less interested in group play or group activities. During this period children are left free, though such an atmosphere is created for them in the classroom that it motivates them to do something. Therefore, the main principle to be followed in this classroom situation is to give complete freedom to act, to move about and to choose their own activities. A teacher must take very good care in arranging the materials around the child. The classroom should be so arranged that the child's approach to the activities is correct and easy: the purpose of each bit of article must be obvious, so that they will act exactly as he should be in the situation. A teacher's work is mainly to show the child the correct way to handle an equipment. The child through repetition will learn to use it effectively.

A child, after his fourth birth day can do some definite work. Hence, useful and purposeful activities such as cleaning the classroom, washing small vessels, watering the plants, measuring and weighing things, ginning cotton with a small iron rod and wooden plank, bringing water, drawing, painting etc., are introduced to the children above four years of age. Here, the teacher has to make a start in these activities. In the beginning it becomes her responsibility to distribute the work to the children. Then, gradually children themselves will take up leadership and supervise the work. Though this type of creative and useful work and activities are provided for the children, doing work is not the main objective of education; the teacher has to see that while doing some work, the child must feel happy and that the child gets the opportunity to develop his natural potentialities. A teacher must be in a position to understand the child's likes and dislikes, based on which she should carefully change the activities and thus create interest in them.

In framing the time table for Pre-Basic Schools we have to consider many things. In other Pre-Schools children come and go at a particular time. Hence, the question of time-table is for a few hours, but in a Pre-Basic School, a child's home is connected with the school, his home life with his school life. We expect the school to be the community centre. So, the school begins early in the morning and ends in the evening. A teacher's work in a Pre-Basic School starts at dawn when the children get up from their beds. She starts visiting the homes and takes this opportunity to instruct the parents on health and hygiene. According to Mrs. Shanta Narulkar the actual school hours for Pre-Basic children should be from 8.30 a.m. to 10.30 a.m. Of course children are there in the Pre-Basic Schools till the evening. There two hours must be fully utilized by introducing various activities which have educative value. Time table is planned for the teacher's guidance. We must keep in mind the child, his interest, the needs of the people and the expectations of the village.

Equipment for the Pre-Basic School

Pre-Basic School should be inexpensive and related to the life in the village for it to succeed and to be of full benefit to children. We must provide them with equipment and materials which unite the home and school, which do not create any disparity between home and school, do not create a conflict in the child's mind which have educative value and which help in developing the child's personality. Everything in nature, such as trees, sand, clay, water, stones and pebbles in the river etc., should become his play materials and equipments, these equipments and materials are not available from the shops in the big cities. These are inexpensive materials from nature for which a teacher has to go to nature, to the village life. Though these materials are inexpensive and available from nature they must have educative and aesthetic values and create interest and aesthetic appreciation in the child. Whatever material the teacher may collect or prepare, it should not bring an artificial atmosphere into the school. These suggestions made above for materials for education should be of interest to any child, rich or poor, and at the same time should serve the purpose for which it is meant.

The curriculum for the Pre-Basic School is based on subjects such as health, and sanitation, food and water, creative activity and gardening. All these activities are connected with play. The material and equipments needed are also connected with these activities. For example, materials such as combs, towel, soap, bucket, brushes, brooms, baskets etc., are used for environment, sanitation and personal hygiene; paints; crayons, clay, colours, chalks, pencils, slates, takli etc., are for creative art activities; small gardening equipments such as buckets, water cans, spades etc., are for gardening activities; plates, small cooking utensils, spoons, stoves, chulhas, knife etc., are for cooking of house-keeping activities. These are very simple and inexpensive and at the same time educative, creative and are used in daily life by the village people. It does not mean that in Pre-Basic Schools there is no place for the equipments such as slide, jungle gym, swing, rocking horse etc. It is possible to make these equipments, in the village itself by the village artisans, they are of great help. These can also be inexpensive and simple if they are made in the village itself.

Materials and equipments should not be a problem in Pre-Basic Schools. What is important is to learn the method to use the equipment properly.

Teacher in a Pre-Basic School

A teacher in a Pre-Basic School is different from teachers in other types of Pre-Schools. She is not only a teacher but also social, village level worker. Hence, her academic qualification is not of much importance. She must have an aptitude and liking for village work and the welfare of women and children. It is very difficult to expect a Pre-Basic School in a village to be fully equipped and housed in a good building. A Pre-Basic School depends more on the skill of the teacher in understanding the child than on the material collected by her on the building which she has to go to the village for social reconstruction through building up good relationship with every one in the village so that she will be successful in her work.

A standard academic qualification as such is not prescribed for a Pre-Basic teacher. Even completion of primary school education or pass in vernacular is recognised (with a special training in Pre-Basic education). The first and most important qualification which is prescribed and to be attained is the genuine love for and interest in young children, below seven years of age. As she has to give more individual attention the teacher child ratio should not exceed 1:25. Then only she can do full justice to her work.

Highlights and a Critical Appraisal of Pre-Basic Education in Comparison with the Other Systems of Pre-school Education

A remarkable change has come over in educational theory and practice during recent years. With the Renaissance, and Industrial Revolution in West there was a protest against abstract and formal education. There was a revolution against the present system of education during the recent years. They demanded that the child should be taken into consideration while teaching. No learning will be effective unless the receiver, the child, is capable and interested in the learning process. It will be a waste of time and energy if we force a child who is not willing and not capable of learning. According to Rousseau "the child has his own ways of saying, of thinking and of feeling; nothing can be more unreasonable for us than to substitute our own way." He emphasised that the child's nature of growth and development should be considered first before we start teaching or expecting him to learn something. That is to say, Rousseau kept the child at the centre of the educative process.

In the same way Dr. Montessori has given importance to the child. She has carefully paid attention to the physical and psychological needs of the children. She stressed the point that the young child should be given complete freedom. She too emphasised that the environment must be according to the culture of the community and nations. Dr. Montessori has borrowed the principles of Rousseau, Pestalozzi and Froebel and modified them to suit her own nation and the standard of living and evolved her own principles of teaching the young children. She was very particular that the teacher should keep herself in the background and that her duty is to guide the child. The child in her school was to be brought into direct contact with didactic materials and not with teacher. Dr. Montessori is of opinion that the child is with full potentialities to learn and acquire knowledge; so when he is left alone without the interference of the adult and teacher, he will learn better and learning will be more effective. She emphasised that the child's senses should be involved in the learning process and so gave importance to the sense training and self-correction. The individualized instruction is another important principle which Dr. Montessori introduced in her school.

Froebel was one of the educators who contributed a lot to pre-school education. He advocated the idea that instruction and knowledge can best be imparted and assimilated, and the child's capacities made to develop through practical work done by him in the school. Hence, he introduced play way technique in his Kindergarten Schools, through a set of apparatus which he developed.

After Pestalozzi, Froebel further elaborated and emphasised the needs for taking into consideration the child's needs and capacities in educating him.

John Dewey, a Socialist, emphasised the social aspect in education. He wanted education to be related to the society in which the child lives. His main contribution to the progressive method stresses upon close relationship between home and school, and parent and teacher. it was his opinion that every individual should work and be independent, and should not depend upon others and at the same time should have close relationship with the culture, the society and his nation. "We must use all work in wood and metal, of weaving, sewing and cooking as methods of living and learning not as distinct studies."

Just like all these educationists from the West Gandhiji too put the child at the centre and stressed the child's harmonious development as the end of education, by which he means the development of Head, Heart and Hands—3 Hs. The exercise of the hands has a vital part in the development of the human brain. Human life is a composite whole, in which the development of the mind and body should go together and this is a pre-requisite for good intellectual development and for proper exercise of the senses. The vitality and curiosity of the child should be provided with an outlet. Gandhiji's New Education provides opportunity for a wiser outlet for this building energy and to canalise it to better purposes by providing handicrafts. This principle of learning by doing or playing is an accepted theory in the western progressive countries. But the special contribution of Gandhiji has been that whatever activities provided should be purposeful and directed towards a social end. Whereas other educational thinkers of the West accepted the craft or work as an instrument of education. Gandhiji made the educational process not only creative but productive too. This is the unique contribution by Gandhiji to the modern educational principles and practices through his Basic Education. He believed that using creative urges of the child just for temporary purposes and to waste their activities is both morally and economically unsound. He wanted to reconstruct the society by introducing a productive activity as a medium of instruction. Gandhiji recommended the "Why" and "Wherefore", "How" of the processes of a craft and other manual activities when they were introduced. In this manner the scientific and the social aspects are stressed in his approach to education. As Dr. Montessori and Froebel did, Gandhiji did not neglect and keep the teacher at the background. He gave importance to the teacher and expected the child to be inspired in the presence of teachers. Gandhiji wanted the child to achieve discipline and social consciousness through craft and group activities.

Of course, we cannot expect a child in the Pre-Basic school to be self-sufficient and self-supporting. Gandhiji wanted the child to develop a desire for work and dignity of labour from the beginning when they are very young and are at a formative period. When they develop these qualities in their young age automatically the above mentioned qualities will develop as they grow older and enter the Basic School. But many of us without understanding Gandhiji's principles properly in the right sense apply them. As it is not properly understood, it is criticised and condemned. Many people say that principles of Basic Education are unsound and impracticable. If Gandhiji's principles and methods are properly understood, taken in the right sense and are modified to suit the present situation and applied, then this is the best system for our rural India.

12

Tarabai Modak

Tarabai Modak, rightly called as the 'Montessori Mother' has made a significant contribution to pre-school education in India. Her method brought in a 'silent revolution' in the tribal community of Kosbad.

Life-Sketch of Tarabai Modak

Tarabai Modak was born in April 1892. She graduated from the University of Bombay. In 1921, she became the first Indian Principal of Barten Female College of Education at Rajkot. She came across Maria Montessori's writings and decided to educate her own daughter accordingly. In 1923, she resigned from college and joined Shri Gijubhai Badheka who conducted a pre-primary school in Bhavnagar and propagated Montessori's theories. In 1926, she helped him establish the Nutan Bal Shikshan Sangh (the new Child Education Association) for the spread and development of pre-primary education. In 1936, she opened a pre-primary school and teacher training centre at Dadar in North Bombay. She started the Gram Bal Shiksha Kendra at Bordi in 1945. From 1946 to 1952 she was a member of the Bombay Legislative Assembly. She visited Europe in 1949 to attend the Montessori Conference held in Italy and to observe pre-primary institutions in the European Countries. In 1957 she shifted the GBSK from Bordi to Kosbad. The Vikaswadi Project was launched and conducted at Kosbad under her constant guidance. She devoted the last 27 years of her life to this project which was the core of the GBSK activities. She was the General Secretary of the Nutan Bal Shikshan Sangh for over 25 years and subsequently become its vice-president. She wrote a number of books for children and parents in Marathi and Gujarathi. She also wrote books on Child Education in English.

In 1962, the Government of India honoured her with the title of "Padma Bhushan."

She passed away on 31st August, 1973 at the age of 81.

Tarabai's Contribution to Pre-Primary Education

The concept and practice organized and formal child education are imported into India from the industrialized West. Madam Montessori gave a big jolt to the theory of "moulding" children through education. The transmit of her ideas from Europe to India was unbelievably quick. Fascinated by the theories of Montessori, Gijubhai Badheka started his Bal Mandir at Bhavnagar and began to Indianise Montessori Method. By this time Tarabai also joined him. The Nutan Bal Shikshan Sangh was thus started in 1926 by these two people.

Objectives of the Nutan Bal Shikshan Sangh (NBSS)

The objectives of NBSS are as follows:

1. To promote in India the study and practical work, research work and spread of the new education theories bearing on child education and adoption of new methods on child education suited to Indian conditions.
2. To encourage those who have worked in and thought about child education, to write original books based on their experience, study and thought.
3. To encourage translations from other language of standard works on new child education, into the national language and regional languages.
4. To prepare small pamphlets in such easy style that the theory of new education could be understood by parents and to either distribute them free or sell at a nominal price.
5. To arrange popular lectures for parents and teachers.
6. To run a magazine for teachers and parents, enlightening them on new theories, in child education and recording the experiences of workers in this field.
7. To run as a beginning Training Colleges or classes for teachers to be trained in the new methods in order to have trained teachers for such schools.

8. To start Training Colleges and classes for teachers who are already working in the present day primary schools for training them in the new education with special emphasis on the necessary changes they will introduce in the light of new child education.
9. To promote efficiency and welfare of teachers who are a vital factor in the movement of the new child education.
10. To start an information bureau to supply up-to-date news regarding various activities in child education in foreign countries and in our country regarding new books written and the new apparatus designed for the use of such schools.
11. To manufacture and to encourage manufacturing in India, educational apparatus which should be scientifically correct, yet economic enough to meet the requirements of our country and facilitate its spread.
12. To advise, direct, supervise, inspect and to appoint inspecting bodies to inspect schools run on such lines.
13. To have a circulating library of books on child education and child literature in India and foreign languages.
14. To start a psychological research institute to study and experiment or to help such children under twelve regarding their mental development or to help such institutions already in existence.

    To establish, equip and run laboratories for such research.
15. To hold educational conferences to further and spread the cause of new child education.
16. To co-operate with other bodies having for their aims and objects the spread of child education on similar lines.
17. To establish Balwadis, Creches, Balmandirs, centres for parental education, children's clubs, libraries, museums, clinics, stores, and offices to achieve the objectives of the Sangh.
18. To take such steps to collect funds for the sangh in the shape of donations, gifts, annual subscription etc.
19. To print and publish magazines, newspapers, monographs, books or leaflets for the promotion of its objects.
20. To have a printing press or presses to print or otherwise undertake the printing of the papers, journals and magazines.
21. To have and maintain book clubs, book associations, libraries and reading rooms for the convenience of the members of the Sangh.

22. To establish, conduct, manage, guide, look after, superwise or support and to aid the establishment, conduct and management of any other association or institution with all or any objects of the Sangh.
23. To provide for holding of exhibitions meetings or classes, calculated directly or indirectly to advance the objectives of Sangh.
24. To cooperate with local, regional, state or national, appropriate education authorities and other organizations interested in any of the objects of the Sangh.
25. To merge with an institution, society or association having objects altogether or in part similar to the objects of the Sangh.

Tarabai thus designed child education which would help Indian children grow up joyfully and intelligently through self-learning activities. Tarabai and Gijubai went on propagating their ideas through '*Shikshan Patrika*', the mouthpeice of NBSS, prepared literature to orient parent and teachers and stimulate a kind of child education movement. In 1936, Tarabai established the Shishu Vihar Mandal in Bombay. Conducting pre-school centres and organising the training of teachers were the main activities of Shishu Vihar Mandal.

Pre-Primary Education for Rural Children

Acceptance for the new method readily came forth in the urban areas where institutions were in a position to provide the requisite accomodation, learning equipment, play space and trained teachers. Urban parents gladly paid fees and supported the *Bal-Mandirs* (children's Temples) and *Shishu Vihars* (children's play centres) springing up in their localities. They appreciated the activities which the children seemed to enjoy. Several parents who enrolled their children in these centres treated them as if they were primary schools and insisted that the primary curriculum be implemented so that the children might ultimately pass the Matriculation examination at a much younger age than normally expected. Tarabai, therefore had to make a very strenuous effort to educate the parents and orient them towards the new concepts of child education.

By this time Gandhiji's Basic Education received nationwide attention in 1936. Tarabai too started writing Shikshan Patrika about the need to pre-school education in rural areas. The rise in the cost of

Montessori's sensory training method, influence of Gandhiji's Basic Education system, and the experience of Tarabai in conducting a pre-school centre in a scheduled caste locality in Bombay (1936) convinced her that the poor and deprived children not only needed pre-school education more than any body else, but they would also need a methodology of learning somewhat different from what was being generally practiced in the middle-class situation. Tarabai found Basic Education to be more economical and hence she made up her mind to move out to some rural place where this amalgam of Montessori, Gandhiji and some of her own insights should be tried out. She moved to Bordi, a small coastal town about 160 km from Bombay and started her Gram Bal Shiksha Kendra—centre for the Education of Rural children a novel experiment in pre-school education in which not more than a handful of people took interest in those days.

The Gram Bal Shiksha Kendra, Bordi

A bungalow, its out-house, an abandoned shed originally constructed for setting up a rice-husking plant, a well and a spacious compound where children could play were all hired for Rs. 150/- per month. Next door to this place there was a scheduled caste locality. The entry of Anutai Vagh into Tarabai Modak's scheme had come about by sheer chance but led to a life long partnership in the GBSK experiment.

Entry of Children into GBSK

One fine morning Anutai Vagh and Gijubhai's disciple Bhagwati Prasad Shelat went out singing Gandhiji's favourite song '*Raghupati-Raghav-Rajaram*' to the accompainment of cymbals and walked into Harijanweda. Children gathered around them. They drew water from a well and washed their hands. The children did the same. The procession went to a hall, Anutai taught them songs. At the end of the session, sweets and jaggery was given to children. Home visits were also made. It was decided not to charge any fees to children. But donations were welcomed. On 24th December 1945 the GBSK was inagurated at Bordi by Shri B.G. Kher.

Work Education at GBSK

When children began to gather in and around the GBSK in sufficient numbers, Shelat and Anutai started another unusual routine. A lot of grass and weeds had grown in the compound. They began clearing it with *Khurpis* (small sickles) and the children would stop by to watch them. A supply of child-size *Khurpis* had already been, acquired by these astute educators. The young by standards would be offered these and asked if they wanted to join in the weeding operation. Eager volunteers came forward and the activity became popular. Gradually, clay work, drawing-painting and playing with learning materials appeared on the scene.

GBSK and Gram-Sevikas Training

Fortunately for the GBSK, the Kasturba Trust asked in 1946 to organise training courses for Gram-Sevikas (Village Workers). Batches of trainees conducted the Anganwadis (courtyard centres) in different parts of Bordi and got to know at first hand what it meant to grapple with prejudice, poverty and ignorance of childcare. They took out processions, undertook clean-up campaigns, improvised inexpensive teaching-learning equipment and kept the pre-school spirit alive in Bordi. A routine was evolved for them: clean-up, prayer, songs and stories, dramatisation, games, sensory training, free activity, orderly behaviour while having snacks together and going out to observation trips for nature-study. A day came when the number of children enrolled went up to 101. The pre-school of the GBSK had thus arrived. Wherever a few children could play and gather, Anganwadi was conducted.

Anganwadi: The Open Pre-School

The admission of Harijan Children into the GBSK's Pre-school centre has turned the caste Hindus hostile. A separate Balwadi for Harijan children alone was the idea put forth. But this idea remained as the negation of the basic purpose. Hence, a Gandhian solution was mooted. The teachers started going to the parents to show them the necessity of Pre-school education.

Working on the assumption that it would be more appropriate to conduct their special Anganwadi in harmony with their ways of living, the tribal Anganwadi programme began to be planned for about a week in advance and carried out daily for not more than 2½ hours. The routines were more or less like the following:

1. Collecting the children for cleaning the open space.
2. Individual cleanliness activities.
3. Prayer.
4. Songs, stories, dances, dramatisation, and games.
5. Going out on sandals for nature-study.
6. Engaging in crafts like paper work, drawing, painting, clay work.
7. Free activities by using whatever material was available in the environment feathers, empty nests, sticks, colourful seeds, shells, big and small stories, clay, dry, leaves etc.
8. Sensory training by using natural objects.
9. Exhibitions of playthings, specimens and natural objects collected by the children.
10. Planned excursions for observation of particular activities and plans.
11. Systematically distributing and eating simple snacks like roasted gram, parched rice etc.

An important aspect of the Anganwadi Programme was the informal education of the parents and older children in proper practice of child-care.

Experiments in Primary Education

On its establishment at Bordi, the GBSK requested the District School Board to allow it to conduct the Primary School for Harijan children. The garden, crafts and the enclosed playground of this school were of great attraction to children. Then the school was renamed as Primary School No. 2 so that children from other communities would also be enrolled in it. The GBSK then prepared its own primary education plan for the tribal children. A programme of story-telling, recitation, songs, games and a little formal education was drawn up to arouse their interest. Gradually this experiment was divided into three types of activities: (*a*) creche, (*b*) pre-school, and (*c*) Primary school. Tarabai, put forward a new name for this teaching learning process; Vikaswadi Vikas is development or growth. This 'Development Centre' was a good arrangement for the incidental education of parents too.

Development of the Vikaswadi

The first Vikaswadi was started in June 1954 at a place called Darjiwadi, about 3 kms from Bordi. For Tarabai Modak, educating the tribals basically meant diminishing the wide gap between the two extremes of Indian Society; on one hand, a highly educated and sophisticated class and, on the other, the class which had remained untouched by the benefits of civilization and scientific progress. Therefore, while training the tribal community in health, hygiene and scientific attitudes, the education devised for the children should make them economically competent, independent and self-respecting. The aim of tribal education is to preserve and promote the cultural highlights of the tribal community. The education should not make the tribals feel inferior but instead generate in them consciousness of their true capabilities.

The Single Teacher School and the Meadow School

In tribal and backward rural areas where small and scattered hamlets abound, the single-teacher school is the only educational service normally possible. The pre-school techniques were utilised for these primary school.

The other experimental intervention was to closely observe how the non-attending children spent their time and to evolve a relevant learning plan which would help the children to educate themselves without attending a formal school but with adequate guidance and stimulus from teachers. This arrangement of working with the children when they took the cattle out to graze in the meadows was subsequently called "the Meadow School."

The Earn and Learn Experiments

Tarabai evolved some principles of her own for combining remunerative work and academic learning:

1. The work to be provided to the children should be familiar to them.
2. Unfamiliar work creates confusion in their minds.
3. Children should not be made to work beyond their capacity.

4. The work should not be tiresome; it should be creative.
5. It should not come in the way of the tribal child's habit of roaming the woods and learning from nature at first hand.
6. The raw materials necessary for the work should be available locally in sufficient quantities.
7. There should be a ready market for the product and it should be sold at a price would cover the cost of production including labour.
8. Each child should get at least four annas a day.

The children were given training in carpentary, with the help of the GBSK, they set up a workshop on the camps. This was meant not only for production but for training other boys as well. Equipment was obtained and markets were canvassed for the product of the workshop. It began to manufacture painted wooden toys and pre-school equipment.

Tarabai's streneous work for Tribal education and the upliftment of Tribal children made them look at 'education—the sun' not as the dusk but as the dawn.

13

Objectives of Pre-Primary Education

Dr. S. Radhakrishnan, the great educationist and philosopher of our country once said "Children are the hope of the future and a special measure of responsibility rests on us, elders to ensure that every child in the country irrespective of the circumstances of birth, parentage, social and other environments has equal and full opportunities of development". Children are the principal assets of any country and it is the duty of elders to take care of them so that they grow into responsible adults with character and calibre and with culture and knowledge.

Having fully realised the importance of early years in the child's life, provision is made in the Constitution of India, under Article 45 "The state shall endeavour to provide within a period of ten years from the commencement of this Constitution, free and compulsory education for all children until they complete the age of 14 years". This goal could be achieved only when a proper foundation is laid at the early in the form of pre-school education which provides an enriched environment.

What is Pre-Primary Education?

Pre-primary education for early childhood years can be conceived as an extension of parental child rearing or a way of preparing children to fit into a social order or role, that they have to assume as they grow up. Pre-primary education is therefore, an integral part of child rearing experiences provided by any agency for all children irrespective of their parentage and socio-economic conditions. Hence, Pre-primary education is always viewed as an extension of home and the pre-primary teacher as a substitute mother.

Why Do We Need Pre-Primary Education?

Our understanding of human ecology, the advancement in technology and the recognition of the importance of the growth and development during this early impressionable, plastic period force us to realise that the choice for educating the young children is not between a continued or artificial and a natural environment, but between a planned and a haphazard programme for learning. If the pre-school is planned and conducted in a proper way it can be an ideal centre where natural human interaction between the children and the teacher, the children and the parents, and their peer group can effectively take place. Though it is a created and man made environment, the child gets such opportunities here which he might not always get at home. India is described as an under developed and economically poor country. We have plenty of natural resources but we have not developed and utilized them properly. Millions of children are born in Indian villages and slums and millions of them die neglected and uncared for, perhaps due to poverty, lack of knowledge and lack of welfare services needed for them. Thus there is a considerable wastage of human potentiality in our country. Every child should get recognition and due care and share.

In a country like ours, where the backbone of our society lives, under most helpless conditions of life, in a scheme of education whether it is pre-primary or primary, is bound to be less effective and wasteful if it is not substantially supported by planned welfare services. Unless pre-primary education is regulated and properly organised the problem of wastage and stagnation cannot be solved effectively. We must not look at pre-primary education merely as a social welfare service that needs our sympathy and support. Pre-primary education in the fast changing world has become a necessity.

There are researchers to show the influence of effective pre-primary education on the later achievement of children. The term later achievement does not mean merely the scholastic achievements. But attending pre-primary schools helps in promoting the child's readiness for the scholastic achievement especially in the early years at the primary schools. There are evidences to show that the children who had attended the pre-primary have higher achievement in the cognitive work as well as in social adjustment compared to those who had not had pre-primary education.

Children from more affluent home are better equipped to learn and understand whereas children coming from deprived home lack opportunities for developing and promoting their potentiality. Hence, it should be possible to arrange institutional setting, where children now culturally, socially and economically deprived by the accident of the social class of their parents can be supplied with a set of encounters with circumstances which will provide an antidote for what they have missed at home.

Reasons for Starting Pre-Primary Schools

Reasons for starting pre-primary schools could be classified as social, economical and psychological reasons. It is difficult to draw a distinct line of demarcation between these reasons:

Socio-Economic Reasons

Since the socio-economic reasons are inter-related with one another, let us discuss both together here.

First Document on the Government Level

The Sargent Committee Report is partially the first document in which we find a very helpful reference to the problem of pre-primary education. One of the very bold recommendations in the report is as follow:

"The pre-primary schools should be free and no pains should be spared to make them as attractive as possible with the object of persuading parents to send their children voluntarily."

The report had visualised a special allocation to the extent of 1.2 per cent of the total expenditure on education for pre-primary education.

Industrialisation

Development of Science and Technology has resulted in the development and mushroom growth of industries. People became busy and had little time to be with their children. But they left the necessity for bringing up their child well, to promote its curiosity, to provide better care and education, which the working mothers find difficult to give. This resulted in the formation of day care centres, creches, pre-schools, Balwadis etc., which were ready to satisfy all the demands of the parents.

In India, the Factories Act demands that if a factory employs more than 50 women employees, it has to have a creche.

Joint Family System and Nuclear or Single Family System

To a great extent, industrialisation has resulted in the break-up of the joint family structure of the Indian Society. The gradual disappearance of the traditional joint family and with its in-built security system, made the problem of working mothers increasingly serious. Care and guidance of older generation are not available now as young couples have to stay away from their parent's home. Again it can be noted that the guidance from experienced older generation was restricted to physical care in some families. Modern development in psychology and child development have opened a new venue in parent guidance. Mental development as distinguished from physical care of a child started gaining attention. The responsibility in achieving these goals was taken up by the pre-primary schools.

Women's Education and Employment

With increasing economic pressures, more and more women have to take 'out of home' jobs. Although it is mainly an urban phenomenon, rural India is also beginning to experience this. Rural mothers struggle hard not only in the fields but also to collect fuel, fodder and water. Thus their time 'out of home' is much more and the majority of them are forced to either take their infants along or to leave them under the "supervision" of elder children who stay at home, or even alone. This situation not only keeps older children away from the educational system, but endangers the health of infants and small children. Thus, the child care programmes were to be accepted and implemented by the Government and non-Governmental agencies.

Programmes Implemented

1. In 1950, creches were run by four national level voluntary organizations the Indian Council for Child Welfare, Bhartiya

Grameen Mahila Sangh, Bhartiya Adimjati Sevak Sangh and Harijan Sevak Sangh.

2. The Balwadi Nutrition Programme is another programme implemented since 1970-71 which looks after the social and emotional development of children in the age group of 3-5 years, apart from providing supplementary nutrition to them.
3. The Integrated Child Development Services Scheme launched by the Government in 1975 is the largest scheme providing creches facilities and Anganwadies to children in rural and tribal areas and in slums.
4. The National Policy of Education, 1986, laid special emphasis on child care and pre-school education.

Urbanisation

Urbanisation in India, coupled with large scale migration of people into the metropolitan cities, has created a tremendous pressure on the housing situation in the country. The ever increasing shortage of housing and the steep cost of urban housing, made the urban dwellers live in rented plots in multi-storeyed buildings. This resulted in the lack of proper places for the little children to play and enjoy. Hence, it was greatly felt that there should be a place where the child could play freely. This resulted in the formation of creches and pre-schools.

Psychological Reasons

In order to enable our growing generation develop into fullfledged citizens, we must give them enriched environment from carly childhood when their potentialities begin to develop at a faster rate. The wide spread literacy of the parents has made them realise that the psychological development of a child is as important as his physical development. They felt that the physical, motor, social, emotional, language, intellectual and aesthetic development of the child accelerates greatly during this period. A child could be moulded as we desire only during this age. Because of these reasons, this period is called as the 'Plastic period of a child's life'. Good habit formation also occurs during this period.

This knowledge and attitude of parents resulted in the increase in the number of children enrolled in pre-schools.

Political Reason

In many western countries, they felt a sudden need for accommodating large number of young children in pre-schools and creches during and after the second world war. This situation focussed the attention on providing good pre-primary schools and creches to look after the children of the sufferers of the war. Especially in England this problem was very accute. They also provided medical facilities to these children.

Objectives of Pre-Primary Schools

As the name itself suggests, the prime function of pre-primary school is of course, to prepare the child for the next stage. This goal could easily be achieved if the needs of the particular stage be met properly. Children between 2½ to 5 years of age are actually not matured and ready for the formal instruction in reading, writing and arithmetic. Initiating them into the formal education at this stage may lead to the improper development and malformation of their brain for their future work. So pre-primary education should aim at the integrated growth and development of children by providing the suitable and conducive atmosphere and satisfy their basic needs. The Education Commission in its report of 1964-66 has pointed out the following as the objectives of pre-primary education in India.

The objectives of pre-primary education may be stated as follows:

- to develop in the child good health habits and to build up basic skills necessary for personal adjustment, such as dressing, toileting habits, eating, washing, cleaning, etc.;
- to develop desirable social attitudes and manners to encourage healthy group participation, making the child sensitive to the rights and privileges of others;
- to develop emotional maturity by guiding the child to express, understand, accept and control his feelings and emotions;
- to encourage aesthetic appreciation;
- to stimulate the beginnings of his intellectual curiosity concerning the environment and to help him understand world in which he lives and to foster new interest through opportunities to explore, investigate and experiment;
- to encourage independence and creativity by providing the child with sufficient opportunities for self-expressions;

— to develop the child's ability to express his thoughts and feelings influent, correct and clear speech; and
— to develop in the child a good physique, adequate muscle co-ordination and basic motor skills.

The Recent Trends in Pre-school Education in India

Prior to Independence only churches, temples and some private agencies took keen interest in the development and promotion of pre-school education in India, and not the Government. Now Government also takes interest in this movement, though private agencies still have an equal role to play both in urban and rural areas. Central Social Welfare Board, Indian Council for Child Welfare, Community Development Programme, Nutrition Programme, Integrated Child Development Scheme, Indian Association for Pre-school Education are some of the agencies which are involved in this programme at the national level. Tamil Nadu has done much pioneer work in this field by training the local women for a period of 3 months and appointing them as the 'Balasevikas' in pre-school centres which are called 'Kaappagangal'.

There are balwadies run by welfare agencies in rual areas and in slums which cater to the needs of the children of 2 to 5 years of age. A few foreign agencies like CARE, CASA, FAO, etc,. also help in running the balwadies. In the fifth five year plan as an experimental, pilot project they started integrated child development scheme which has a pre-primary education component called Non-formal Pre-primary Education. Under this scheme Anganwadies are run in every block. Number of pre-primary schools run by private agencies in the name English medium Nursery Schools, Kindergarten or Montessori Schools are a mokery today. Such type of mushroom growth of pre-primary schools, especially in cities has become a business today. Unless a proper strategy is framed and imposed on all these pre-primary schools the future growth and development of children will be at jeopardy.

The Committee on the Study Group on development of the pre-primary school child recommended the following operational models and cover atleast 50 per cent of pre-primary school age children in urban slum areas, tribal areas and under privileged groups in rural areas.

(*a*) Comprehensive day care centres for age group 3-5 years meant primarily for urban slums.

(*b*) Half day balwadies.
(*c*) First stare centres.
(*d*) Anganwadies meant primarily for rural areas.
(*e*) Primary school based centres.

As India is a country with variations in every aspect, we cannot have a uniform pattern of pre-primary education throughout India. Depending on the locality, needs of the people, purpose of the school, and the availability of resources including the teaching personnels, we should develop curriculum and methodology for pre-primary education in India, keeping in mind the objectives for which they are set up.

Pre-primary Education in National Policy of Education (1986)

Realising the importance of early childhood years, the Government of India, in its National Policy of Education (NEP) has given importance to Early Childhood Care and Education (ECCE). NEP has considered ECCE as an essential input for human development, as a feeder and support programme for primary education and also a support service to working women and to deprived and disadvantaged children.

NEP has emphasised the importance of play and activity method, child-centred programme and has cautioned against the dangers of using formal methods of teaching and early introduction of the 3 Rs, at the pre-primary level. It also has suggested along with Anganwadies of ICDS, other day care centres should be assigned to care the young children. There are also a focus on providing early care and stimulation for children who come from poor homes, for a wholesome development of children.

The Strategy of Implementation of ECCE Programme

The ECCE aims at physical, motor emotional, cognitive, language, social and moral development of children from conception to 6 years of age. NEP has included a comprehensive programme of care of expectant mothers, hygienic and skilled birth attendance, nutritional care of mother during lactation, proper infant feeding practices, immunization, mothers education in child care, early childhood stimulation and health and nutritional support. It needs integrated ECCE training and ECCE centres. There is a shift from earlier child welfare programme, towards strengthening the ECCE programmes and make them developmental rather than providing more custodial care.

Workers in ECCE centres are to be trained for this multiple roles they have to play. It is also suggested in NEP that the full time ECCE workers are to be brought on per with the primary school teachers with regard to remuneration. It is also proposed to have proper supervisory system by increasing the number of supervisors and they should invariable be women.

Keeping in view the role of ECCE as a support service in universalisation of elementary education, ECCE programme will concentrate on underprivileged groups such as very poor urban slum communities, where children are required to do household activities, child labourers in unorganised sector, children of mobile workers, construction workers, nomadic communities, tribals etc. Efforts will also be taken to upgrade, expand and strengthen the existing programmes like ICDS, ECCE centres (Department of Education, Balwadies run by voluntary agencies, Pre-primary schools of the State Governments and Muncipalities, Day Care Centres etc.)

Attempt will also be made to evolve low cost and context specific models with the help of appropriate agencies. These models include Home-Based Model (from conception to 6 years), Family Day Care Centres (from birth to 6 years). In all these models early stimulation at home by trained women will be attempted. Mobile creches will also be encouraged to strengthen the ECCE programme in construction sites and other work centres.

Training: In all the models the training component will be strengthened by introducing strong component of field placement under supervision. The NEP suggested that there can be a two year Vocational Course in ECCE at +2 level with job training for specific situations, strengthening the educational component ICDS functionaries at all levels including supervisors, creating a system of accredited training institutions dealing with ECCE, and working out appropriate, task specific and flexible models for day care training at field level in rural areas.

Mass media will also be made use to convey to the parents and community the need for ECCE and the techniques of creating stimulating environment at home. Organisations such as Doordarashan, AIR, NCERT, NIPCCD will be encouraged to develop software in regional languages to propagate ECCE programme.

Monitoring and Evaluation: Monitoring and evaluation will be strengthened through Management Information Systems. Information will be collected, compiled, analysed and acted upon at the block/ local level. Flow of information at all levels will be attempted without any delay. Professional institutions and expert bodies will be approached for assistance to evaluate and to identify gaps and problems; and feasible view alternatives will be suggested as remedial action. Efforts will be taken to evaluate the ECCE programmes by independent agencies once in five years to provide quality services. In order to assess the contributions of ECCE an index of Human Development will be worked out which will include infant mortality rate, incidence of malnutrition in the second year of life; access to early stimulation and education and female literacy level.

When ECCE programme as visualised by NEP is implemented with true spirit it will certainly improve the quality of education at the elementary, secondary and higher education leading to better human resource development.

14

Activities

1. Visit pre-primary centres and identify the principles and philosophies of Comenius followed there.
2. Identify Plato's contributions to pre-primary education and justify their relevance today.
3. Find out the relevance of Rousseau's stages of education in the present context at the pre-primary level.
4. Visit the pre-primary schools of different types and identify the principles and practices of Kindergarten in those schools.
5. Modify the gifts suggested by Froebel to suit the local needs and write the values of each gift.
6. Improvise Didactic apparatus to suit local needs.
7. Plan activities to promote sensory, motor and language development of children.
8. Observe different types of pre-primary schools and identify Dewey's principles and practice of education if any.
9. Visit one pre-primary school centre in a city another one in a rural area and find out whether the principles of McMillan Sisters are followed.
10. Identify an area in your district and plan a programme for deprived children.
11. Measure the retention of the value of such programme among children.
12. Identify Tagore's principles and practices of education at the pre-primary level.
13. Visit pre-primary schools and observe the principles and practices of Pre-Basic System of education in those centres.
14. Find out whether any one in your area is working in Tribal areas especially for young children.

15. If you have to identify a place in a Tribal area for organizing Pre-primary education what programme will you provide?
16. Visit a Pre-primary school centre and find out the reason for starting the centre.
17. Interview few parents and find out why do they send their children to Pre-primary school.
18. Take a survey of Pre-primary age children in your locality and find out how many are attending Pre-primary schools and why others are not attending.

Part II

Curriculum Planning and Programme in Pre-Primary School

15

Pre-Primary Curriculum

Children in a pre-primary school are engaged in interesting and stimulating activities. So the prime responsibility of a pre-primary school programme is to create an environment that is appropriate and conducive for young children. Learning environment are provided to enable children to imitate, create and learn than merely to respond and reproduce. In planning programme or curriculum there should be consideration for long range values of strategies and approaches on learning and achievement of children of age group 2½ to 5 plus. So, the programme for young children should be guided by sound principles of learning and development.

Generally the term curriculum is defined as academic activity inside a school. At the pre-primary level the programme is used interchangeably with or in the place of curriculum. Programme for pre-primary school includes the activities for the wholesome development of children not only inside the classroom but also extended to the home environment. Programme for the young children is therefore, be adopted to the growth needs and interest of children of specific age group, as well as individual children. This will satisfy the rights of every child to learn and to be benefitted by what is provided in the pre-primary school.

The curriculum for young children should be based on the enrichment of the human resources by helping them learn to perceive, communicate, love, decide, know, organise, create and invent. Some children may have all these rich experiences at home and some children may not have these experiences and environment at home. Thus the pre-primary school takes up the responsibility of enriching its experiences and should become an antidote for the deprivation the children have at home. Pre-primary school curriculum should be an experience curriculum.

Planning the Programme

Good planning is essential for effective teaching and learning. Without well formulated plans confusion and aimless efforts may result on the part of both the teacher and the children which may also lead to frustration on the part of children.

In general planning the programme should consider that the school atmosphere provides feeling of security, sense of belonging and affections for achievement, creativity recognition for social interaction, motor manipulation, language exploration and for emotional release of children. The planning should also consider the types of activities to be organised in the pre-primary school, and how to organise them. The annual programmes, short-term programmes, weekly programmes and daily programmes include different activities which need advanced planning. To achieve the overall goal of child development, the planning should concentrate on the concrete purposes of specific activities and experiences, the teaching materials and equipments required, festivals to be celebrated, field trips to be undertaken, parent education programmes to be conducted availability of finance etc.

Teacher's planning of the total programme must be carefully ordered and maintained as the environment demands. Stability and consistency will enrich the programme.

Strategies of Programme Planning

Be Flexible

The growth of the children is dynamic. Hence, the programme should not be rigid with separate periods. It should be flexible and centred around to activities of the children. Flexibility on the bases of individual differences, seasons, availability of resources, teacher's resourcefulness etc. At the same time programme should be challenging simple and stimulating.

Balance between Group and Individual Activities

The pre-primary school programme should be balanced between group and individual activities. The teacher should keep an eye on children to ensure that each child gets an opportunity for individual work as well as group work. If she finds that a child indulges in only solitary play, she should gradually bring him to the group play.

Balance between Free Play and Guided Activities

Balance between free play and guided activities is also very important in the pre-primary school programme. Each day for a certain amount of time children should be allowed to play on their own. It gives the opportunity to explore, investigate and find out the different possibilities of using the different types of play materials. The guided activities are teacher-initiated activities where planning is done by the teacher before presenting them to the whole group.

Active Play to Follow Quiet Play

The pre-primary school programme should alternate between active play and quiet play. If the children are taken outdoors for free play then this activity should be followed by a quiet indoor activity as too much physical activities make the children exhausted, same with the sedentary activities; too much of them make the children restless.

Be Functional and Meaningful

The programme should be functional and meaningful. The teacher should always think why should she introduce certain activities before she introduces them. Similarly the programme should be related to the life in the community and the society and should inculcate those social values and skills in the children which are approved by the community and the society.

Principles of Programme Planning

The type of experience a child has in a pre-primary school depends upon many factors such as (1) number of children or strength of a group, (2) the teacher-child ratio, (3) the age range of children within a group, (4) the duration of the school day, (5) infrastructural facilities of the school, (6) the philosophy aims and objectives of the school, (7) location of the school—urban and rural areas, (8) financial position of the school, (9) expectations of the parents and the community, and (10) the staff—their training and experience.

The Number of Children in a Group

In a good pre-primary school the number of children in any group should not be large. Space arrangements, the age structure of the children, the experience of the staff etc., will be the other factors which determine the exact number of children in a group. There should be only 20 children in a group, for large groups creates strain and reduce the contribution which the school can make to individuals. Young children profit from group experiences only if they can receive individual care and attention when they need it. The school makes a significant contribution to parents and children only when it is adequately staffed. If the pre-primary school is not adequately staffed the children will be deprived of adequate experiences.

Teacher-Child Ratio

In a pre-primary school every child is unique with different needs, interests, capacities and from different family background. It is the duty of the teacher to provide individual attention so that every child feels secured and wanted. This is possible only when the ratio between the teacher and child is very small. Group instructional strategies will be of very little use at the pre-primary school level. All possible attention should be made to individualise the instruction and provide individual experiences, by making the teacher-child ratio as 1:20—an ideal number in the Indian context.

Ages and Range in a Group

The age range in a pre-primary school is difficult to decide because chronological age is not variety of experiences with which a child's will effect his readiness to attend a pre-primary school. Most of the children are ready for pre-primary school when they are around the age of 3 years. They seem to need 3 years in which to 'live out' the period of dependency on parents, to achieve sufficient security in the home and with their parents to be ready to away in a pre-primary school group and to identify with other adults outside the home.

Every mother will, of course, see in her child an eagerness to be with other children long before the child is 3. This readiness can be met by informal experiences with children of the same age, by visiting or having a visitor for an hour or more. This informed experiences prepare the child for regular, sustained group experiences latter. The small size of the group into which a 2 year old can fit himself, the short day and the amount of individual care he needs, make the programme an expensive one if it is to be good one.

The real satisfaction the children feel in playing beside other children of the same age and the benefits of the experiences of physical contacts with others, sharing with them, and exploring a rich environment are great.

In pre-primary schools the age range within the group should be relatively limited and homogeneous so that the programme can be more easily adapted to the needs of the children who constitute the group. When children of widely different ages are together, and interests of the needs of one age level are likely to be sacrificed to the other although individual members may profit from occasional contacts with children of other ages. If the 2 and 3 years olds are in separate groups with flexibility it is easier to satisfy their interested needs. Development is so rapid during the pre-primary school period that difference of even a few months makes a significant difference in the maturity level, needs and interests pattern among these children.

Narrow age range in a group may increase competitiveness among the children and offer them less chance for learnings. Which come from being with children who are younger and older.

The 4½ to 5 year old child's interests become more sustained and his capacity for group play increases. He is ready for formal instruction.

Duration of the School Day

It varies in different pre-primary schools. The child gains most from pre-primary school experience when it supplements his home experience. Three or four hours a day spent in school serves this purpose in case of most pre-primary school children. Some spend a longer time in a pre-primary school because their mothers are employed and go out. In such cases the pre-primary school must plan to provide more experiences which we would like to see children find in their own homes. Type and number of activities provided in the school will also vary depending on the duration of the school day.

Infrastructural Facilities

The programme or curriculum provided at the pre-primary school depends on the infrastructural facilities available for conducting pre-primary school. Good spacious building, playground and equipment facilitate variety of programme in the pre-primary school. If there is no outdoor space to play there will be less importance to outdoor activities. Play equipments both outdoor and indoor will make the teacher plan for number of activities in the playground as well as inside the class room.

Philosophy and Objectives of Pre-primary Schools

It is another important aspect which influences the planning of a programme for pre-school. Montessori method insists on providing more importance to sense training and individual development; Froebel's Kindergarten social activities with gifts are emphasised; Mahatma Gandhi's Pre-Basic system insists of learning by doing and child centred approach; Piaget's theory of cognitive development emphasises on giving activities to the children on the basis of developmental task. If a teacher wants to adopt any specific system and follows their philosophy and objective she has to formulate a curriculum which will help to attain their goal.

Location of the School

Depending upon the location of the school the programme also varies. Urban pre-school may be in a position to provide rich experiences due to their easy accessibility. For example while talking about transport, animals etc. They can relate the children to Railway Station, Airport, Zoo etc. Whereas the rural pre-school may not be able to expose the children to such type of experiences, experimental content provided will be more in the urban pre-school than in rural pre-school. At the same time if a teacher is resourceful and has real interest can create at least, model situations and provide if not same environment, to certain extend similar environment.

Financial Position of the Pre-primary School

Availability of fund for organising programme is another important aspect which decides the type of programme. If more resources are available rich experiences should be provided to the children. If there is constraint the teacher may not be able to provide variety of experiences. If there is fund and facilities, children could be taken out to various places as field trips for first hand experiences. Similarly, more equipment and materials for other activities could be made available in the pre-primary school if fund is made available without any difficulty.

Expectations of the Parents and the Community

Well educated parents, cultured and developed societies expect high standard in the education. They would like their children learn more. Their way of providing experiences at home will be strengthening the child's learning. Whereas if it is a poor family with illiterate parents their expectations will be different. It is observed in many villages that the young ones are sent to the pre-primary schools just to have custodial care. A teacher should therefore, understand the needs and expectations of the parents and the community too that she could plan her programme accordingly.

The Staff—Their Training and Experience

Staff play a vital role in planning the curriculum as well as implementing what is planned. Proper training of pre-primary school teacher increase her competence to deal with the children and plan the programme to promote the total development of her children. A well trained and experienced teacher will be able to diagnose the difficulties of children and provide remedial programme. A committed teacher knows how to satisfy the needs of her children, provide security and affection to the children. She will also understand the expectations of the parents and community and will seek their co-operation to satisfy their expectations.

CHARACTERISTICS OF A BALANCED CURRICULUM FOR PRE-PRIMARY SCHOOL

1. A good curriculum for pre-primary schooler provides many opportunities for developing social adjustment and developing effective and cognitive skills. The experiences provided will build positive self image and gain confidences in themselves.
2. A good pre-primary school programme emerges out of the immediate environment of the children. It is need based, and women around the environment around the child is explored and fully utilised.
3. A good programme provides plenty of opportunities and time for self-expression of children. They are encouraged to express through any media-spoken, dance, dramatisation, paint, clay, paper, water, sand, music, story etc.

4. A good programme for pre-schoolers makes them use their whole body and develop wholesome attitude towards it. Through various activities children learn to use their body. A rhythmic functioning of body is possible through action songs, dance, good food, rest, elimination and vigorious play.
5. A good programme makes use of the experiences of children and meets the needs of children of various age group and builds a strong foundation for future experiences of formal learning through readiness programme.
6. A good programme takes into account the needs of parents and plan with them, through parent education programmes.

Types of Programme Planning

Planning the curriculum may be of Long-term, Short-term, Weekly and Daily, each type of planning leads to the other.

Long-Term Planning

This is also called as yearly planning. This type of planning for the year is helpful in giving perspective to daily planning. What a 3 to 4 years old child should learn and achieve during the whole year is thought of in the yearly or annual plan. The objectives, concepts to be developed, the learning experiences to be provided, the trips to be organised, the vacation period, the parent education programme and other activities such as celebration of festivals, nature walk etc. are noted down for the whole year.

Annual plan also includes the date of re-opening of the school, date of admission, criteria for admission, fees structure, expansion of programme of any additional facilities required, equipment needed etc. If the administrator plans all these ahead of time confusion, uncertainty and other problems could be avoided.

Short Term Plans

The teacher on the basis of the curriculum given for the whole year breaks up the curriculum into different units and decides the programme to be covered for the term, may be of 3 months or 4 months duration. This can be further divided into monthly programme. This will contain little more details of different activities to be undertaken during the month. Teacher could collect materials required in advance to have a smooth running of the programme giving maximum satisfaction to children.

Weekly Planning: On the basis of the programme planned for the month, the teacher plans the activities for the week, even before the commencement of the week. She looks back to the previous week to see whether she has left out anything during the past week so that she could compensate for the loss. She may have different themes for either the month or for the week and organise the programme according to the specified theme or project. The whole week she may concentrate on the theme with various activities relating to the theme or the project assigned to the week.

Daily Planning: It is the duty of the teacher to plan every day all the activities which she will introduce to the children. It is not only writing what she is going to do for the day but also getting ready with the materials every day. Doing the activities herself before introducing them to the children to avoid frustration is an essential element of the daily planning.

Arranging the Learning Experiences: The following should be borne in mind while planning the sequence of the pre-primary school programme:

(1) Alternating periods of activity and rest,
(2) Keeping short those periods where in children are expected to sit in one place,
(3) Avoidance of vigorous activity immediately before or directly after lunch,
(4) Arranging a sequence which will provide for easy transaction from one kind of activity to another, and
(5) Avoiding continual rearrangement of the room for successive periods.

A Day in a Pre-Primary School

Though the pre-primary school programme is to be a flexible one there should be some learning experiences provided to children. On their arrival the children are received and greeted by the teachers and the children learn to greet both teacher and the peers. Then the teacher does physical check up. She talks to the children to find out whether they had their bath, cut the nails etc. and also see whether they are suffering from any illness. This is followed by assembly. Children assembly for a prayer, sing songs together. Free conversation on any theme follows. Children play outdoor, go to toilet, wash their hands and legs, enter the classroom for a mid-morning drink. Now the teacher can tell stories; teach rhymes, provide opportunities for creative activities, readiness programme or science and social science experiences. After about 3 hours of their arrival in the morning children are tired and go for lunch. Lunch is followed by rest and sleep which help get ready for afternoon session if the pre-primary school programme is a full day programme.

In the afternoon, children may be taught action songs, rhythmic exercises, engage in gardening, outdoor and indoor play, story telling or readiness programme depending upon the age of the children. Around 4 p.m. children assemble again to sing National Anthem or prayer before they are dismissed to go home in the evening.

All these activities which are provided in the pre-primary school should be able to meet the needs of children and the parents. Child's physical, motor, emotional, mental and social needs are to be satisfied so that there can be a balanced growth among the children.

Time Allotment

The duration of the pre-primary school may be 3 hours to 5 hours a day depending upon the location and the parental requirements. In some urban pre-primary schools where there will be someone else—a nurse or an Ayah to take care of children even if the parents go out for employment, they may prefer their children to be back home early. So, the duration of the pre-primary school can be 3 hours in the morning. When both the parents go out and there is no one at home to take care or the young children in rural areas parents may prefer their children to be under the custody of the teacher in the school till they return home. In that case the length of the pre-primary school programme can be extended to the afternoon session also.

Suggested Time Allotment in Minutes

Activity	*Length of the Day's Programme*		
	2 hrs.	*3 hrs.*	*4 hrs.*
Opening	10 minute	10 minute	10 minute
Outdoor Play	15	20	20
Story Telling	10	15	25
Indoor Play	15	20	25
Creative Activities	15	25	25
Readiness Programme	15	20	30
Cleaning	10	15	20
Toileting	5	5	10
Lunch (Mid-morning drink)	5	10	15
Rest	5	15	20
Rhymes	10	15	20
Group exercises	15	20	20
	130	**190**	**240**

Allotment of the time for various activities varies with the activities, age, ability, maturity and interest of children. Care should be taken that the children do not get tired or fatigued. Shorter duration for each activity will maintain the child's interest, in few activities. Whereas few activities like outdoor play, indoor play, nature walk etc. may be more interesting to children even if more time is allotted. So, the teacher has to decide at the particular moment by looking at the participation of children in the activities, whether to continue with it or to change to the activity. We may not have uniform pattern of activities attention and interest all the days. Climate, children's mood etc. will decide the time allotment to various activities. However, a schedule is suggested as a guideline for various activities according to the length of the pre-primary school programme.

The allotment of time for each one of these activities will vary with age range of children in the particular group. Younger children may not concentrate for a longer period, hence, the time allotted for each one of these activities should be shorter. Though there is allotment of time it need not be a rigid pattern, there can be flexibility. A resourceful teacher will be able to follow her own pattern according to the needs, interest and moods of children.

Another example of suggested daily schedule for a pre-primary school group of 3 to 4 years and 4 to 5 years is as follows. All these are only suggestive not a rigid one.

CURRICULUM FOR 3 TO 4 YEARS OLD PRE-PRIMARY SCHOOLERS

June

Social Habits: Creating interest in children to come to school regularly, help the children tell the name of their parents and their family members, learning to wish the teachers and peer group.

Health Habits: Learning good health habits. Personal hygiene, learning to wash their hands before and after eating. Importance of good food habits, good toilet training and sleeping habits.

Language Development: Learn to tell their names, name of parents, school and the place of location.

Songs: Teaching songs on healthful living, going to the school etc.

Story: Stories related to the health habits.

Creative Work: Scribbling in the black board, clay work, paper folding.

July

Human Body and Food: Parts of the body, keeping body clean, importance of air for breathing, prevention of diseases, name of food materials and their importance, milk and milk products and their uses, seedling.

Nature Walk: Make a visit to poultry and dairy farms, vegetable garden, park.

Language Development: Learn the names of teacher, other children in the class, name of their village and street, names of the parts of the body.

Songs: Songs related to the theme.

Creative Work: Drawing in black board, slate with chalk piece, in papers with colour pencils and crayons, clay work, threading the beads.

August

Animals: Make the children be familiar with names of animals, types of animals, difference between wild animals and domestic animals, their food habits, dwellings and their importance.

Nature Walk: Visits to Zoo, Sanctuary.

Independence Day: Importance of Independence Day; Learning colours in the flag, dharma chakra, names of national leaders.

Mathematical Concepts: Learning small and big.

Song: Songs related to animals, and the Independence Day.

Story: Related to the theme selected-*i.e.* animals.

Creative Work: Brush painting, pasting the pictures, colouring the pictures, paper folding.

September

Air and Water: Importance of air and its uses, and the importance of breathing fresh and pure air.

Water and its uses, how to keep the water clean.

Sun and Moon: The difference between sun and moon, rising time and uses of sunlight.

Mathematical Concept: Understanding the differences between one and many.

Song: Songs related to air, water, sun, moon and night.

Story: Stories related to the theme selected.

Nature Walk: Make a visit to rivers, ponds and canals.

Creative Work: Finger painting, printing, pasting, patting the clay.

October

Deepawali: Importance of deepawali, how to celebrate deepawali and celebration of the deepawali in the school.

Gandhi Jayanthi: Importance of Gandhi Jayanthi and stories about Gandhiji.

Readiness Activity: Identification of the different sizes and shapes.

Nature Walk: Visit to match factory, cracker's factory and shopping centres.

Science Experience: Differentiating different tastes, small and texture.

Method of handling crackers.

Songs: Songs related to deepawali and Gandhiji.

Story: Stories related to the theme selected.

Creative Work: Arrange the seed, on pre-drawn sketches, tears papers in a definite shape, separate things by length, collect sticks.

November

Trees, Plants and Creepers: Naming trees, plants and creepers collecting seeds.

—germination of seeds.

—importance of air, sun and water for germination.

Nehru's Birthday—Children's day: Story of Nehru, Celebration of Children's Day.

Readiness Activities: Joining dots, draw the square, rectangle by themselves.

Mathematical Concept: Differentiate square, triangle and circle.

Science Experiences: Collecting seeds and planting, watering and observing germination of seeds.

Language Development: Teacher writes words spoken by children in the blackboard children observe.

Songs: Songs related to trees, plants, rivers, ponds and mountains.

Story: Stories related to theme.

Nature Walk: Visits to fields, garden, ponds, rivers etc.

Creative Work: Draw different shapes, etc. Construct Train, but out of empty match-boxes, building blocks, separate things based on shapes, collage work with leaves and flowers.

December

Flowers, Vegetables and Fruits: Learning names of different flowers, vegetables, fruits, their colour, taste, texture and their uses.

Readiness Activity: Joining the dotted letters.

Mathematical Concept: Learning different shapes and length through play materials. Serial counting up to 50.

Nature Work: Make a visit to vegetable market, collecting flowers.

Creative Work: Make ink spray, thread painting, paper boat, make the shapes with match sticks, make a ball with waste cloth, spray the colour sand and wooden powder in particular shape.

Celebration of Christmas

January

Transports: Vehicles on roadways, rails, air and water, their names.

Pongal Celebration: Pongal celebration by preparing pongal, understand the importance and ways of celebrating Pongal.

Science Experience: Identifying things that floats and sink.

Nature Walk: Visits to bus stand, railway station, airport, and harbour.

Readiness Activity: Learning to write alphabets.

Number Concept: Serial counting from 1 to 100.

Songs: Songs related to theme.

Story: Stories related to theme.

Creative Work: Threading small beads, Carpentary work, make garland with colour paper, preparation of greeting cards.

February

Community Helpers: Learning the functions of post man, milkman, police man—their dresses, nature of their work, their role in the society.

Birds: Types of birds, their food habits, dwellings, their young ones and their usefulness to the human beings.

Science Experience: Collection of feathers and pasting.

Readiness Activity: Differentiate animals, birds, vehicles, vegetables, fruits, plants and trees.

Nature Walk: Visits to post office and police station.

Song: Songs related to the police man, post man, and birds.

Story: Stories related to the theme.

Creative Work: Thread painting, making different shapes with empty card board boxes, match boxes. Making post cards.

Number Concepts: Serial counting and writing from 20 to 50.

Letters: Stories over written.

Dhoby, Potter, Blacksmith, Construction Workers: Duties of dhoby, potters, blacksmith and building construction workers, materials used by those people, methods of washing clothes, pot-making process.

Types of Houses: Thatched houses, tiled houses, concrete houses type of materials used for construction.

Science Experience: Learning uses of soap, ingredients used to make soap, methods of washing clothes, soft water, hard water.

Nature Walk: Visits of places of washing clothes and pot-making.

Number Concepts: Writing upto 50.

Song: Songs related to Dhoby, potter also related to uses of soaps.

Story: Stories related to the theme.

Creative Works: Clay work, weaving, collecting different types of soils, wash clothes, clean vessels, play with soap-water.

April

Doctor and Hospital: Learning the role of doctor in the community hospital set up.

Science Experience: Learning common diseases, causes and importance of immunization.

Readiness Activity: Learning to write. Looking of pictures and telling story.

Number Concept: Serial counting and writing from 70-100.

Song: Songs related to the importance of both hospital and doctor.

Story: Related to the theme selected.

Nature Walk: Visits to hospital.

Creative Work: Arranging leaves based on their shapes and groups flowers based on colours, pasting.

CURRICULUM FOR 4 TO 5 YEARS OLD PRE-PRIMARY SCHOOLERS

June

Social Habits: Learning to come to school regularly and punctually. Recalling what was learnt the previous year. Learning to the earlier help others be through child to child programme.

Health Habits: Inculcating the habit of doing the work sincerely and punctually at a time. Next learning to keep clean the home, school, and environment.

Language Exercise: Learning the names and places from where materials and equipments required for cleaning are procured.

Rhymes: Rhymes on importance of being clean.

Story Telling: Stories about child to child programme and environmental cleanliness.

Creative Activities: Painting and collage work, learning to draw and write in the black board.

July

Human Body: The functions of the different parts of the body, the difficulties and problems that arises while the parts are not functioning properly, and the significance of keeping the skin, nail, eye, ear and nose clean.

Food: Functions of food or why do we eat?

Types of food, requirements of food, process of eating and methods of handling food.

Language Exercise: Learning the name of the part of human body names of the foodstuff and their requirements. The words like 'enough', 'some more' and 'not enough' should be practiced by the children.

Rhyme: Rhymes about body cleanliness and foods and nutrition.

Story Telling: Based on the lessons, the teacher can tell the stories.

Creative Activities: Collection of foodstuffs, fixing the body parts in appropriate places, drawing and finger painting.

Readiness Activities: Find out and fill up the missing parts of the body and differentiate the healthy and unhealthy children.

Mathematical Concept: Tracing on the numbers, arranging the stories and seeds on the numbers and counting the numbers from 1 to 50.

Child to Child Programme: Learning to bring the smaller children and helping them to wash, comb, eat etc.

August

Animals and Birds: The habitat, habits and uses of wild animals, domestic animals habits and their uses; common and rare birds and food habit and their habitat, the reproduction of animals and birds.

Field Trip: Visit to Zoo, dairy farm and poultry and bird watching and rearing of pet animals.

Language Exercise: The teacher writes the field trip experiences of children and reads. Learn the names of birds and animals, associate the birds and animals with their habitat. Learn the colours in the flag with their significance.

Rhymes: Rhymes about animals, birds and flag.

Creative Activities: Painting with brush, cutting and pasting of pictures and clay modelling.

Readiness Activities: Classifying the pictures of animals and birds according to their habitat and food habits; pasting the pictures on the book and writing the names with the help of teacher.

Celebration: Celebration of Independence Day. Stories of the great leaders like Gandhi, Nehru, Bharathi, V.O.C. Cultural programme.

Mathematical Concepts: Naming, arranging and matching the shapes, count the numbers from 50 to 100 and write the numbers from 1 to 50.

Writing and Reading Readiness: Matching the pictures with words and naming the pictures.

Child to Child Programme: Learn the reasons for diarrhoea and what to do when a child suffers from diarrhoea.

Science Experiences: Watching birds and animals commonly found, collecting pictures of animals and birds. Rearing pet animals, feeding etc.

September

Seasons: Learn the names of English months and names of months in mother tongue. The changes during the summer, winter, spring and autumn seasons, requirement of the garments and foods in the seasons.

Creative Activities: Spraying the colours, cutting and pasting the pictures, making mat with palm leaf and kite making.

Readiness Activities: Observation of the changes during the seasons, pasting the appropriate pictures on the picture book, or draw the picture and write the headlines and observe the shadow and draw.

Mathematical Concepts: Count the numbers from 50 to 100 and write the numbers from 1 to 50. Classify the articles according to their shape and size.

Science Experiences: Type of dress. Materials-Silk, Wool, Cotton. Their origin understanding their texture by touching.

Rhymes: Rhymes about weather and dresses.

Story Telling: Based on the theme.

Field Trip: Taking the children to weaving places, factories and nearby places.

Celebrate the 'Vinayaka Chaturthi' and 'Krishna Janmashtmi'.

Child to Child Programme: Continue the last month programme.

October

Trees, Shrubs, and Mountains: The difference between trees, shrub and mountains, their uses, reproduction, growth process, parts of the plants and seeds.

Pouring water. and manuring and their uses.

Creative Activities: Pencil drawing, pasting and pressing the leaves and flowers.

Readiness Activities: Collecting the leaves according to the shape and pasting the flowers according to the colour, collect the seeds and store them.

Mathematical Concepts: Write the numbers upto 100. Count the even numbers. Tracing the shapes.

Writing and Reading: The teacher writes the names of trees, shrubs, and mountains on the blackboard. The teacher writes about Gandhi on the blackboard and reads.

Science Experience: Sowing the seeds, watering and watching the germination, conditions for germination, parts of the plants.

Celebrate Gandhi Jayanthi and 'Navarathri": Learning about Gandhi. Arranging the 'Golu' and invite others to school.

Child to Child Programme: Help other children while eating food, teach the rhymes and play with them.

November

Diseases and Prevention: The symptoms, prevention of fever, cold, cough, measles and diarrhoea; immunisation.

Creative Activities: Drawing, making figures with sticks, and clay modelling.

Readiness Activities: Collect pictures of different figures, cut it and paste, draw the picture and write their names.

Mathematical Concepts: Write the number from 1 to 100. Count the even numbers till 50. Cut different shapes and paste them in an album.

Writing and Reading: The teacher writes the names of the diseases on the blackboard and read; children write those words on their slates.

Science Experience: Learn the causes of common illness, learn to keep their nails, hair, mouth neat, learn the need to keep surrounds clean.

Rhymes: Rhymes about health and sanitation and 'Deepavali'.

Story Telling: Based on the theme.

Field Trip: Visit to hospital, observing Doctors at work.

Child to Child Programme: Check the other children whether they have immunised.

Children's Day Celebration: Nehru's Birth Day—Children's Day. Sports activities, cultural programmes, stories and songs about Nehru.

December

Clothes: Significance of clothes; kinds and sources. Learning about cotton, wool, silk, synthetic fibres, nylon, nylex and rayon.

Readiness Programme: Collecting bits of dress materials of various type and pasting.

Mathematical Concepts: Writing till 60. Count the even numbers till 100.

Drawing different shapes and sizes and discriminating them.

Science Experiences: Learn why do people in different parts of the country wear different type of dress. Giving experiences of weaving dresses made of different fibres.

Creative Activities: Making mats with palm leaves and papers. Painting with colours; making garland, making greeting cards after preparing paper cover, and preparation of cloth ball and doll.

Celebration of Christmas: Decorate the school. Preparating gifts and greetings and exchanging them.

Child to Child Programme: Learn to identify diseases that are very common among the children—like cold, cough, itching etc.

January

Transports: Development of transport—Road transport, Sea transport and Air transport their structure, fuels, prevention of road accidents and road rules.

Creative Activities: Preparation of greeting cards, preparation of paper garland, and preparation of train, car and ship with match box and other boxes, making paper boats.

Science Experiences: The objects that float and sink and the reasons.

Readiness Activities: Classifying the vehicles according to the type of fuel used and the kinds (Air, Road and Sea). Pasting the pictures of vehicles according to the developmental process of vehicles. Learn to write their names.

Mathematical Concept: Continue the last month activity.

Child to Child Programme: Continue the last month activity.

Celebration of Festival: Celebrate Pongal. Decorate the school and prepare Pongal.

Celebrate Republic Day—flag hoisting, cultural programme. Learn the names of national leaders.

February

People Those Who Help Community: Learn the activities of Postman, Policeman, Milkman, Potter, Cobbler, Tailor, Weaver, Teacher and Doctor and our responsibilities.

Science Experiences: Learn the uses of milk, milk products, and functions of a post office.

Creative Activities: Drawing, stitching the wrapper (cover), collecting pasting the picture, spray painting with sand and saw dust. Clay work.

Readiness Activities: Reading and Writing.

The teachers writes about social worker on the blackboard and reads; children write that on the note book.

Mathematical Concepts: Writing upto 100 and the even numbers upto 20.

Rhymes: Rhymes on community helpers.

Story Telling: Stories about community helpers.

Child to Child Programme: Bring the children from home and take them back. Help whenever a child's needs.

Field Trip: Visiting post office, weaving shed, tailoring shop etc.

March

Electricity and Mass Media: The importance, functions, and how to use electricity, radio, T.V., cinema and newspapers.

Creative Activities: Making fan with paper, and making radio and T.V. with match boxes. Drawing and painting.

Science Experiences: Learning the importance of electricity and how to use it. Learn the role of radio, T.V., cinema and newspaper in learning.

Readiness Activities: Identify and classify the mass according to their functions. Learn that news paper gives information. Learn not to touch switches and wires when they are open.

Mathematical Concepts: Count the even numbers upto 100 and write upto 50. Learn the concepts—short and long, small and big, many and few little and more.

Rhymes: Rhymes about radio, electricity, newspapers and cinema.

Story Telling: Based on the theme.

Field Trip: Take the children to radio station, cinema and newspaper office if possible.

Child to Child Programme: See the height and weight of the observed children and continue the earlier programme.

April

Measurements: Lengthwise measurements—centimeter, meter, volume measurement—litre; weighing method and values of coins.

Science Experiences: Measurement of length and breadth of cloth and class. The measurement of amount of food stuffs.

Creative Activities: Clay modelling, classify the sticks, stones and seeds according to their sizes, making paper arrow, making coins with card board.

Readiness Activities: Creating a small shop in the classroom with various articles. Few children as shopkeepers measure and sell, others buy with coins-money.

Our Country Leaders: Gandhi, Nehru, Budhist, Kamaraj, Rajaji, Bharathi and Indira Gandhi—their social services.

Field Trip: Take the children to shop to know the measurements and the value of coins and how to buy things with coins.

May

Evaluation of Children's Development

Based on the curriculum, the children's physical, motor, emotional, social development, language, intellectual development, concept formation, health habits are evaluated. The progress of children is sent to the parents and to the next class teacher.

The evaluation method and the records to be maintained in pre-schools are given in detail in appropriate chapters.

Every month discussed above other than the programme the activities such as outdoor play, indoor play, cleaning the classrooms, schools, environment and gardening are encouraged among the children. It may very according to the seasons, philosophy of the pre-school, number of children to a school, the strength of the class, availability of infrastructural facilities including finance resourcefulness of teacher, expectation of the parents and the location of the school, rural and urban. There is no rigidity in following the suggested curriculum strictly. There can be flexibility. Teacher is the right person to decide what type of experiences to be provided each day. What is given is a guide-line only. A resourceful teacher modifies changes and adds according to the situations and the availability of time and other factors.

16

Routine Activities in a Pre-Primary School

Arrival

The children approach a new situation, new people, new locality and new activities when they come to pre-primary school. If their approach results in happiness, they will be encouraged to try other new situations. A pleasant morning leads them to look forward to other pleasant times with the peer group. A child wants friendly teacher who is really interested in him, an opportunity to explore his new situation safely, and familiar activities which he enjoys. This experience makes the child attracted to the school and routine arrival at correct time.

On arrival in the morning the child learns to be received by the teacher and wish them and the children wish back and also learn to wish others in the school time conscious, punctual and doing things in the appropriate time. At the time of child's arrival saying "Good Morning" or "Namasthe" to the pre-primary school teacher makes the child to be familiar with giving respect to the teacher and other elders. The teachers' warm and affectionate welcome to the child makes, the child feel secured, when he is away from his mother and home.

Assembly

The purpose of conducting Assembly and prayer in the pre-primary school is not to introduce religious thoughts in the minds of children, as the children at this age cannot understand. Prayer in the pre primary school is just to help the children to concentrate their mind for a few seconds. It also helps the child to develop discipline and promotes orderliness and ability to sing in a group. The songs selected for the prayer should be simple and easily sung by the children is appreciated.

Health Checkup

Pre-primary school children are so highly susceptible to illness. Several precautions are necessary in order to maintain the health of any such group of young children. Each child should be examined by a physician prior to admission. Both the doctor's report and a report of the health history of child should be on file for use as needed.

Each child should be inspected each day to be sure that he is free from any illness. At the sametime, provision must be made to care for the child who suddenly becomes ill or injures himself while playing. The pre-primary school group recognises the importance of good food in helping children to have good health. Careful attention is therefore be given to the serving of food and the sanitation of provisions for handling it. Personnel of pre-primary school groups are generally agreed that there should be a daily health inspection. A Nurse or a pre-primary school teacher carefully checks each child and looks into his throat, nose, his skin and eye conditions. She should check the state of health of each child quickly but carefully.

Pre-primary school children must be taught how to.

Care for themselves, especially how to

- — use bathroom
- — get a drink when thirsty
- — wash hands before eating
- — put on and take off outer clothing as needed and to change to dry clothing when wet.
- — stay at home when ill.

Free Conversation

One of the major developmental problems of the pre-primary school child is to establish effective verbal communication with the people around him. He must learn the language of his home and his community. The child will be able to do because he is skillful in imitation and uninhibited in expression. The pre-primary school teacher can help the children in several different ways. She can provide them with a clearly spoken pattern which is easy to hear and imitate accurately.

She should speak pleasantly, so that the child responding to her feels appreciated, and in no way criticised unfavourably. So, the teacher should make a point of providing pleasant and happy total patterns for the children to listen and imitate.

The teacher should stimulate a child to communicate by helping him have vivid experience. She can plan each experience in terms of key words which will add to a child's vocabulary and serve as a basis for further conversation. Conversation is an integral part of a child's activity. The teacher routinely does several things to make sure that even a shy or non-verbal child has an opportunity to talk by including the following activities in a pre-primary school:

- — by making the children to be good listeners.
- — by making them observe carefully the things around them.
- — providing a daily opportunity to share with the teacher about matters of importance to him.
- — Scheduling an opportunity for him to bring his parents to the school.
- — providing regular opportunities for him to talk with other elders in the pre-primary school who take an interest in him.
- — by enriching the pre-primary environment which will induce them to speak.

The pre-primary school group should provide enough experiences to give each child the talking opportunities he needs.

Toilet and Wash

Pre-primary school children have not yet started having regular habit of going to the toilet. In order to make the children develop bladder control the teacher must attain objectivity about her own toilet training and put aside any bad reaction to excretory products. Appropriate toilet training to the children by the pre-primary school teacher help children to have control over their bowel and bladder. Teacher might help them in washing hands after their creative activity and outdoor play so that they could develop the concept of cleanliness.

Story Telling

Story telling and listening is an integral part of a pre-primary school curriculum. In presenting a story to a pre-primary school child or a group of pre-primary school children, an adult should communicate with them as completely as possible. She should talk directly with the children, going from conversation into telling a story. To enrich the story telling, she can pantomime action, show pictures on a flannel board, or use a puppet. A child beginning to listen to stories may do well to hear one short story on the way through. Story telling promotes, language development, intellectual development, comprehension ability of the pre-primary school children. More vocabulary and new concepts are introduced into the child's world, which promotes creativity and imagination among children.

Rhymes

Rhymes for pre-primary school children have to be simple, clear, understandable and within the child's world, of action and concrete experience. Child enjoys the songs when the child has greater maturity. Simple and brief poetic expression and poetic comparison may be presented vividly and enjoyable to the pre-primary school child as an integral part of child's experience in the world around him.

Besides employment children also learn new words, finer muscle and large muscle co-ordination when they are involved in action songs. New words are easily remembered if they are learned in verse. Poetry helps in vocabulary building. Bits of rhyme and brief poetic couplets punctuate the day of the pre-primary school child delightfully. The teaching of a new song should be scheduled for a time when the children are eager for new activities. A familiar song can be sung at the end of the day, but a new song should be sung when the children are active in the morning. The teacher should teach new song, step by step with action which the children enjoy.

Creative Activities

Creative activities for a pre-primary school group serve to introduce the children to a variety of art media and help them develop aesthetic appreciation. Sometimes the children use their hands directly with such materials as clay, dough, paste finger paints, flowers and materials of different textures. At other times, they use brushes, scissors, and carpentry tools and gradually develop skill in manipulation. But teacher and the child have a feeling of an achievement with some completed painting or model. The teacher can point out to the child artistic relationships that he observes, introduce appropriate terms, or encourage the use of some bit of technical skill which make the child get perfection. Child develops sufficient interest and satisfaction in expressing himself through art media. Teacher should encourage every child to express himself in whatever way he wishes with the materials he has. All these creative expressions help the child to improve his imagination, creative thinking, intelligence and also finer muscular development.

Readiness Activities

Readiness is a term related with academic skill in the pre-primary school education. Learning 3Rs, namely reading, writing and arithmetic is possible only when the child has completed five years of age. The child of pre-primary school years is not ready to learn these three activities because his nervous system and muscles are not matured enough. But the teacher in the pre-primary school can prepare the child for learning the 3Rs indirectly by providing suitable play experiences. These experiences which prepare the child physically and mentally to learn 3Rs are called readiness activities.

Child will not be ready to read before he is 5+. The child should know how to hold a book, the appropriate distance to be kept between the book and the eyes, the direction of the movement of the eyes, correct pronunciation, etc. before he learns to read. The teacher provides suitable experiences to children to imitate and learn.

The child is not ready for writing as the finer muscles of children are not matured. But these muscles can be given exercise by giving experiences in drawing, clay modeling, collage work, threading the beads, cutting, paper tearing, pasting etc. Besides the muscular co-ordination in the hands, eye-hand co-ordination is also needed for writing. This can be achieved through creative activities mentioned above.

Learning abstract number concepts is a difficult task for the child. The child is not ready to get correct concepts of numbers until he is six years old. But he can be prepared for learning numbers indirectly through play, stories and songs.

While planning readiness activities, the teacher should keep in mind that every child has his own pace of development and that she has to plan accordingly. She should not insist all children to do the same type of activities.

Besides these routine activities, we can also take the children for nature walk, celebrate festivals, organise programme for parents etc. once in a while. Science and Social studies experiences can also be introduced as part of regular curriculum.

Details of values of each one of these activities and methods of introducing in the pre-primary school are given in different chapters.

LESSON PLAN FOR FULL DAY

Name of the School:		Subject: Animals
Name of the Teacher:		Topic: Domestic Animals
Standard:	Date	Time: 9 a.m. to 4 p.m.

Instructional Objectives:

1. To promote allround development of children
2. To inculcate good health habits among the children
3. To promote memory power and creativity of children
4. To develop aesthetic sense of the children
5. To help them learn about the names of different types of domestic animals and their colours, food pattern, shelter and the characteristics.

Previous Knowledge: Children may know the name of some domestic animals and they might have seen some animals.

Concepts to be developed: Make the children familiar with the names of the domestic animals such as cat, horse, rabbit, cow, dog and their characteristics, food pattern, life style, sounds produced by them.

Aids to be used: Flash cards, rollograph on animals, photographs, charts and model.

Content	*Specifications*	*Learning Experiences*
Arrival and Assembly (9.15 to 9.30 a.m.) (Guided activity)	Children learn to be punctual and give respect to the teachers and elders. Learning to be orderly and learn to sing together the prayer song.	Children come regularly to the school and wish the teachers and others in the school.
Health check-up (9.30 to 9.45 a.m.) (Guided activity)	Children learn the importance of health habits such as bathing, combing, cleaning the teeth, nail cutting and wearing clean clothes. They learn to practice those health habits in their day-to-day life.	Teacher does the health check-up in the pre-primary school as soon as children arrive to see whether they cut their nails, combed their hair, taken bath and whether they are affected by any disease.
Free conversation (9.45 to 10 a.m.) (Guided activity)	Children get exposure to domestic animals like dog, cat, cow, rabbit, horse and its food pattern, life style, parts of the body and sounds which they produce. It helps to develop interest in rearing pet animals. Promotes language development.	Teacher discusses various aspects of domestic animals through models, pictures, and photographs. According to their time availability she takes the children to poultry farm and dairy farm.
Outdoor play (10.00 to 10.30 a.m.) (Non-guided free play)	Promotes large and finer muscles developmental co-ordination. Group plays develop social attitudes like adjustment, waiting for one's turn, etc., and also promote the creative thinking and imagination. Play helps to release the emotional tension of the child.	Teacher encourages the children to play outside and teach them the rules of group play, children play freely in the sand, tub, swing, merry go round and slide.
Toilet and Washing (10.30 to 10.45 a.m.) (Non-guided activity)	Children develop sense of cleanliness, health and sanitation and also they develop regular toilet habit. It promotes bladder control.	Teacher helps the children if they need, to wash their hands. Children also learn proper toilet practices.

(*Contd.*)

(Contd.)

Content	*Specifications*	*Learning Experiences*
Creative Activity (10.45 to 11.00 a.m.) (Paper folding, painting) (Guided activity)	Finer muscular development imagination and creative talents are promoted among the children, concept of colour, shapes, size etc., are promoted. These activities promote readiness for writing.	Teacher distributes paper to the children, demonstrates folding papers and ask them to fold into various shapes and also she gives colour for painting and ask the children to paint as they like.
Story telling 'Who said Miya' (11.00 to 11.45 a.m.) (Guided activity)	Listening skill, language development, memory power, emotional development and imagination of children are promoted. Children also learn about various sounds produced by the domestic animals.	Teachers tells the story with puppets "Who said Miya". Children repeat and enact the story.
Indoor Free Play (11.15 to 11.30 a.m.) (Book corner, Block corner, Dolls corner) (Unguided activity)	Imagination, creativity, constructive ability and the language activities of children are promoted as they play in different areas.	Children play with blocks, dolls, and other materials freely. They also look at the picture books. When they ask the teacher reads for them.
Rhymes with action (11.30 to 11.45 a.m.) (Guided activity)	Children learn to sing a song in a group and express their emotions in a proper way. Songs act as a channel to express their inner feelings. Gross muscular co-ordination and balance take place while they do actions.	Teacher teaches the songs with rhythmic and actions to the children.
Toilet and Wash (11.45 to 12.00 p.m.) (Unguided activity)	Learn the importance of washing hands before eating, they practice this activity throughout the day.	Teacher helps the children to wash their hands.
Lunch (12.00-12.30 p.m.) (Guided activity)	Children learn to eat themselves. Sharing, waiting for their turns to come etc., are promoted among children. They learn the importance of nutritious food in relation to good health.	School provide good nutritious meal to the children. Teacher serves the food with the help of the children.

(Contd.)

Contents	Specifications	Learning Experiences
Washing hands and plates (12.45 p.m. to 1.00 p.m.)	Children learn to wash their own hands and plates themselves.	Teacher helps the children to wash their plates.
Rest (1.00 p.m. to 2.30 p.m.) (Unguided activity)	It helps to regain the energy and feel fresh after the nap.	Children sleep in a clean and calm environment.
Toilet and Wash (2.30 p.m. to 2.45 p.m.) (Unguided activity)	It develops good health habits.	Teacher helps the children to go out for toilet.
Exercise (2.45 p.m. to 3.15 p.m.) (Guided activity)	Exercise makes the children feel fresh and energetic.	Teacher demonstrates simple exercises to the children.
Free play (3.15 p.m. to 3.45 p.m.)	Promotes large muscle-co-ordination social adjustment and releases to emotion.	Children play on their own fleely. Teacher may also organise some games.
Going Room (3.45 p.m. to 4.00 p.m.)		

17

Story Telling

The child develops skill in the language arts as it participates in various experiences and activities. One activity can contribute to growth in several of the arts and for that reason, activities have not been labelled as appropriate for reading, speaking, listening or writing. Certain activities have not been labelled for pre-primary school or Kindergarten, because of the wide range of individual differences from group to group. Using information pertaining to development and experience of the children, the teacher can select and adapt the activity most appropriate to them.

Story telling is an activity of great interest to children everywhere. Due to structural changes in the family, the traditional responsibility from the grand mother's lap has been showered upon pre-primary school teacher. Although the content of story may vary from generation to generation the values and objectives may remain the same.

Values and Objectives of Story Telling

1. Story is a joyful activity and it is a source of enjoyment.
2. It promotes:
   (*a*) *Social development*—Observing group discipline while listening to story.
   (*b*) *Emotional development*—The child identifies itself with the character of the story as though it is happening to the child. (Feeling of sympathy, joy etc.)
   (*c*) *Intellectual development*—Abstract concepts are made more concrete through story telling; enriches vocabulary, provides opportunities for thinking and reasoning, concentration.
3. It serves as a good foundation for future reading.

4. It is a gateway for imagination, creativity and self-expression.
5. It aids personality development.

Selection of Stories

Stories which are desirable for the pre-primary school not only are about familiar, every day subjects, but should be short and written in simple, correct English with many clear illustrations in colour. Stories should be selected only in terms of the interests and maturity reached at each age level. The teacher who wants to have story books suitable to the children she teaches and the parents who want to pace their child's development should look for stories which are especially appropriate to a child at a particular age level.

In selecting stories for the three-year old child, the wise teacher takes into account a very important fact. At the age of three, a child is only at the threshold of abstraction. He must build a wise base of realistic experience and he must see relationship among these realistic experiences before he can go on to even the simplest abstraction. The stories of three year child should increase the span of interest in listening to it. Stories should be based on the familiar experiences of the child. It should be wovened by the information about nature transportation etc. Imaginative stories should be based on real people and real animal. The way that the three-year-old child thinks in concrete rather than abstract terms is observable in what he says.

A good picture book which interests a three-year-old child also interests a four-year-old child, but for a shorter period. A four-year-old child has more breadth of experience than a three-year-old and is able to assimilate ideas more rapidly. He is much interested in words, creating stories with simple language and play on words. He has high interest in poetry and finds delight in the humour in stories. The child shows much interest in stories telling the function and growth of things. He enjoys particularly information books answering his "Why"? about everything in the environment.

As a five-year-old, a child continues to enlarge his understanding of the widening world in which he lives. He can also venture far into the world of make believe. He has come a long way as a pre-primary school child. At five he consolidates his learnings and widens his horizons so that he will be ready for the new activity of beginning to read for himself in first grade.

We have to make the realistic stories as suitable for pre-primary school. Folk and fairy tales formerly constituted almost the entire literary fare available to children along with the moralistic tale. In selecting books today, we know more about children's development including such facts as that rousing fear in them is damaging, that there is a readiness factor in learning, that children need help in understanding the world around them rather than in having it confused by things that are fanciful.

It is better to omit frightening elements from stories until the child has had time to develop secure feelings and confidence in his ability to meet the real world and distinguish the possible from the impossible. This doesn't mean that stories for the child should lack action and suspense, but that terrifying elements should be left out.

Some children will be ready at an earlier age than others for folk tales, depending on their level of emotional development. Introducing such stories too early may lead to disturbed sleep and a child who is more timid will also be disturbed in facing something which is unusual. Fanciful unreal stories are better left until the child has had time to form a concept of what the real world is like. There are some delightful animal stories in which animal personalities fit into their own animal world.

There are imaginative stories on the young child's level. The fairy tale with a wish fulfilment element and a safe ending of being welcomed home after an adventure that will be appreciated by most four year olds. It constitutes a good beginning in the realm of the unreal where the child is still on safe ground.

Art of Story Telling

In presenting a story to a pre-primary school child or a group of pre-primary school children, an adult should communicate with them as completely as possible. She should talk directly with the children going from conversation into telling a story. To enrich the telling, she can pantomime action, show pictures on a flannel board, or use a puppet.

The teacher can read a picture book, showing each picture as she reads. In each of these situations she should be so familiar with the story that she and the children have excellent rapport with each other and communication is maximized. She should let the children dramatize one of their favourite stories. She should tell the story with action, so that it will create more interests.

The story teller should avoid over expectations about the attention of her audience and should keep in mind that the pre-primary school child is learning to listen stories. A good pre-primary school group has a teacher who is apt at any point to be reminded of a story and has dramatic play in keeping with the stories she has been reading. She can use a few simple gestures, as she does in talking. But neither the gestures nor the inflections of her voice should be distracting.

As the children become accustomed to hearing stories, she will be able to introduce more voice inflections into her telling. She can use slow, measured, and simple words as the elephant walks heavily; fast, light words with the patter of the mouse's feet, her voice can slow down as the train pulls into the station.

Emphasis and repetition should be placed on the key words. The story teller should be careful not to use incorrect language as children pick up a good deal of language from the story teller. Children should be motivated to listen to the story rather than imposing on them. The teacher shall be prepared with the story and her technique well in advance so as to make herself calm and relaxed while telling the story. Teacher can hold the book in front and slightly to the side always at the eye-level of the child, when she uses books to tell stories.

Sitting Arrangement

Children should be nearer to the teacher when she tells stories. This gives a feeling of security and comfort to the children. She can make the children sit in a semi-circle so that every child feels the nearness and can look at the teacher directly.

Media and Techniques of Story Telling

Stories can be told using many media and techniques. A resourceful teacher in a pre-school will be able to attract the attention of children very quickly and will be able to retain long by using the media. Her gesture and action, with a bit of dramatisation will be able to attract the children much better than a teacher who is inactive. She uses her facial expression and action by using appropriate sounds, music, repetition etc. Children enjoy repeating the rhythmic words.

Sand Tray Techniques

Cut-outs of the characters in the story can be prepared and sticks can be attached at the back of each cut-out. A tray can be filled with sand

and naturalistic situations can be created by using plants, pebbles, stones, grass etc. The cut-out characters can be made to move in the sand tray by moving the stick figures. Children enjoy as they could see the characters in the story move.

Flannel Board

Flannel board is the medium with the help of which we introduce different characters and their respective characteristics. Pictures are moved on the flannel board which has a plain background so that the picture may emerge out well. The flannel board should be placed in a slanting position within the visual reach of the children.

Puppets

Puppets play, not only has entertainment value but also has educational and therapeutic value by making children more lively and free. Making simple puppets is joyful activity in the balwadi. The puppets made should be light, and simple so that it could also be manipulated by the children as and when the need arises.

Rollograph or TV Model

The pictures of a story are sequence-wise fixed on long sheet of paper or cloth, then fixed on the rods which are inserted on the two ends of the four sides frame which could be rolled and unrolled as the story proceeds. Care should be taken while spacing the pictures as to avoid overlapping.

Flash Cards

Flash cards in which pictures of the story are pasted on a sturdy base and placed sequence-wise before the story is narrated. On the backside of the flash card the selected part of the story is written.

Files and slides are the other story telling techniques which can be made use of.

It does not matter whether a teacher provides experiences with music that is primarily classical, modern, folk, or some other kind of music. But it is highly important that these experiences become increasingly more musical.

The child who is interested in exploring a drum should be encouraged to use it for creating rhythm or a musical sound, not just noise. The child who is interested in moving to music should be encouraged to listen to the time and texture of the music and to bring his movements into relationship with them. The child's immediate interest in the music around him, should be guided into enlarging that interest in the direction of increasingly beautiful music.

18

Music for Children

Music is an integral part of the pre-primary school programme because it is an integral part of children. A child learns the total pattern of a phrase before she articulates the words within it. The child can learn to distinguish among sounds, to differentiate music and voice and among musical sounds, high tones from low, soft sounds from loud. The child can learn to enjoy the various kinds of experience with melody and rhythm which are part of its culture. The child can become acquainted with singing, with moving to music, with using musical instruments and with listening to different kinds of music.

Values of Teaching Music in Pre-Primary Schools

Music can contribute in many ways by offering opportunities for listening, creating, singing, rhythmical responses, and playing instruments. Through these activities, the child experiences pleasure, joy and creative expression, develops listening skills, and auditory discrimination. Young children can be encouraged to move freely to music, permitting the music to evoke emotions and ideas responding to words in them. It helps in promoting physical development, and increases the range and flexibility of his voice. Music enables the child to be in groups which in turn develops discipline and harmony in the child.

Music can be used to communicate ideas, but with pre-primary school children it is primarily a medium for communicating feeling. Children,while mother sings lullabies to them at bedtime relate their pleasant feelings about their mother to the lullabies they hear her sing.

Music experiences are an integral part of the child's school day, a part of many activities and learnings. Music can contribute to the development of each child, according to its individual pattern of growth and development.

Music offers an avenue of expression to children which is closely related to that of language. It is an avenue which is used by children every where. There is significant buck of the concept of a mother as a person who rocks and sings to her child. The sound of a mother's voice, the feeling tones expressed in it, the rhythm of rocking are important to a child very early in his life. The child in pre-primary school will respond to the tone of the teacher's voice as much as to the words she uses. The child will be re-assured if her tone is confident and friendly, without regard to what she says. The "music" of the voice is our important medium of communicating feeling.

Rhymes

Rhymes lay the foundation for music. The rhythmic pattern of the rhymes appeals to the child and gives the child a feeling of joy and makes it easy for memorizing. The child gets a sense of confidence and feels proud in its accomplishment. As the child memorizing rhymes, it picks and adds for his treasure of phrases, in order to gain mastery over the language.

Selection of Rhymes

Rhymes should suit the age level of the children so as to be interesting and understood. Children are fond of rhymes with fnny words which provokes laughter. Rhymes may be of :–

(*a*) Those concerning his day-to-day activities such as personal environmental hygiene, habit formation etc.
(*b*) Nature: Animals, birds, plants, flowers, rivers, mountains, sun, moon and stars etc.
(*c*) Concepts like space, time, colour, size, shape, number, seasons etc.
(*d*) Family relations.
(*e*) Community helpers: Doctors, nurse, cobbler, carpenter, dhobi, potter, painter, policeman, postman, etc;
(*f*) Household pets: Dog, cat, parrots, pigeons, rabbit, squirrels, pests.
(*g*) Festivals.
(*h*) Modes of transportation: By road, by air, by water etc.

Satisfying Activities Stimulate Singing

When children are happy and content, when they are engaged in satisfying activities, especially rhythmic activities, they will sing. We can encourage musical expression when we help them find satisfaction and see that they have plenty of opportunity for the kinds of rhythmic activities that they enjoy. These activities are such things as swinging, bouncing, pounding, running or peddling a tricycle. Two swings side by side make companionship possible under simple circumstances, so that the joy of having a friend may find expression along with the joy of movement through space. Swinging and singing go together without needing to depend on an adult.

Dancing as well as singing will occur in many areas when children are free to act spontaneously. The teacher who can sing on the spot and move freely to music will encourage spontaneous responses in the child. There should be plenty of singing by the children and the teachers on the playground and through all the areas of play activity in the pre-school. There should be an opportunity for dancing wherever there is space and music.

Action Song

When children model clay, one of them may start pounding it. The child may develop a rhythmic pounding which others soon imitate. The teacher will pick up the rhythm and fit some such phrase to it as "Pound the clay, Pound the clay", She may suggest another phrase in the same rhythm, rhyming with the first phase. Then she can put the two phrases together and lead the children in singing "Pound the clay, hear and play," The young pre-primary school children are less skilled both with words and with paying attention to more than one kind of activity at a time. She should lead the children into using the second phrase for a while then move them back into more modelling activity.

The teacher who likes to enrich activities with music will find many rhythmic motions which she can emphasize by composing a simple song on the spot.

Story and Song

A story can lead into a song. Often a teacher tells a story and then introduce the song that tells the same story in music. For instance, she may read the carrot seed. After the children are familiar with it, she may play the recorded musical version of the story as a means of helping the children learn to enjoy listening to music. They can follow alone by looking at the picture in the book as they hear the music.

Listening to Music

Important experience that the pre-primary can offer is that of listening to good music through records or music played on the piano, the violin, the flute or any other instrument. If the teacher herself is not a musician, she can often find someone who likes children and will enjoy sharing music with them. This adds to the variety of the children's experiences with music and increases their interest.

Using Musical Instruments

The child manipulates and experiments with instruments. It becomes aware of differences in sounds in relation to way in which the instruments are played. It comes to recognize sounds of various instruments. It learns names of several of the better known instruments, such as the violin or trumpet. Through a variety of experiences with different instruments, the children can learn that sound is result of vibration. They can have a simple introduction to the different groups of instruments which constitute an orchestra: the violins and other string instruments, the flutes and other woodwind instruments, the horns, drums and cymbals and other percussion instruments. Most children love to play the piano and many of them will go often to the piano to play and sing there, turning the pages of a favourite song book. Drums of all kinds and bells are fun for them. Wind instruments may have only restricted use because children cannot be expected to keep from passing them from mouth to mouth. But every pre-primary school should have plenty of all types of sound instruments and the children should experiment freely with sound, both indoors and outdoors.

Selection of Music and Musical Instruments

Music is the language of feeling, it is the inside voice and tune; for the beginners in music the start should be made from familiar note with simple tune to make the child feel one with the music. The tempo of the music should have a rhymic progression.

The musical instruments should be of child's size, light and easy to handle and carry, locally available, of pleasant tone, durable, safe and attractive.

The Role of Teachers in Teaching Music

The teacher should take into consideration, the difference in the developmental sequence of the children. To help children enjoy and learn more about music and other aspects of sound, the pre-primary school teacher should be as relaxed and comfortable as she is in helping the children enjoy and learn about other facets of their world. She should share with the children the music that she knows and enjoys, because her pleasure in it will make it a pleasurable experience for the children too.

Every teacher should seek to enlarge her musical repertoire as a means of enlarging the musical experience she can provide for the children. As a teacher enjoys more music, she can put more music into her teaching and find it increasingly pleasurable and rewarding.

The teacher who is always ready to listen to the song a child has made up or has learned sets a good example which the children are apt to follow as they learn to enjoy the role of a listener.

The teacher should know how to stimulate children so that they eagerly participate in musical activities. She should also know how to use music in helping them to move from activity into rest. If the children have been responding to music creatively and individually to the point where they have become fatigued, the teacher needs to draw them back together by having them work with her.

Not all children may wish to listen each time a music experience is offered. There should be no compulsion about listening, for this does not build desirable attitudes towards music. The child who does not wish to listen can respect the needs of the listening group for quiet by playing at the other end of the room. Many times curiosity about a new instrument will bring even a non-listener into the group for a time.

The teacher should be well prepared with the rhyme so that she can introduce it without jumbling for words. In order to avoid monotony the rhyme could be presented in many ways like acting out or with the help of musical instruments.

It does not matter whether a teacher provides experiences with music that is primarily classical, modern, folk or some other kind of music. But it is highly important that these experiences become increasingly more musical.

The child who is interested in moving to music should be encouraged to listen to the time and texture of the music and to bring his movements into relationship with them.

19

Creative Activities

Each individual perceives the situation in his own manner and reacts to it on the basis of his experiences, imaginations and original thoughts. On account of these qualities, man creates new horizons and sets new standards. Creativity actually involves something newer atleast rare and useful and is so complex and multi-dimensional that each thinker considers in different dimensions.

What is Creativity?

Guiford (1956) explained divergent thinking as the ability to go beyond the immediate solution, to redefine the problem or some part of it, to cope with ideas that are unusual and to change or having new approach to the problem.

Mc Kinon (1963) defined "creativity as process extended in time and characterised by originality, adaptiveness and realization".

Torrance (1962) points out that "the creative person is characterised by spontaneity, flexibility, adaptiveness and originality"

Components of Creativity

The components of creative thinking have the following characteristics:

(*i*) Attention
(*ii*) Curiosity
(*iii*) Determination
(*iv*) Imagination
(*v*) Ingenuity
(*vi*) Initiative
(*vii*) Interest

(*viii*) Judgement
(*ix*) Resistance to the ordinary
(*x*) Simplicity
(*xi*) Venture
(*xii*) Vision.

There should be sensitivity for memories and association in inventive thought. This sensitivity should be combined with keen observations of : (*i*) arrangement, (*ii*) combinations, (*iii*) interchange of factors, (*iv*) results, (*v*) substitutions.

Stimulating Creativity in the Classroom

Most educational programmes designed to cultivate creativity emphasize brainstorming techniques. The aim is to stir up many original solutions and to evaluate them only after very possible alternative has been expressed. Alex F. Osborn (1963) developed a five-step process of creative problem solving:

(*a*) Problem finding or the search for the nature of the real challenge from different perspectives;
(*b*) Fact finding in order to understand the situation better and to imagine what the solution might be;
(*c*) Idea finding, aimed at calling up ideas from the pre and sub-conscious and to defer judgement of their quality until they have all been flushed out;
(*d*) Solution finding, at which point the ideas are evaluated for their relevance and applicability and the best one is chosen in implementation; and
(*e*) Acceptance finding, or gaining an audience that is willing to support the idea and put it to practical use.

Types of Activities

Through a variety of well-planned activities in an environment where the child is free to explore and experiment, the child progressively becomes aware of his environment and is better able to communicate this awareness to others. Moving at one's own pace, they could develop and refine the large muscles, strengthen the smaller ones, increase eye-hand coordination, and gain shape and colour concepts which lead to reading and writing readiness. The child develops socially through sharing materials, taking turns and assuming increasing responsibilities for using these materials. As he gains skill in using materials, he grows in self-confidence.

Creative Dramatics

In creative dramatics an experience is acted out by the children, as they are guided in thinking, feeling and creating their own dialogue and action. There are no lines to be memorized, no formal audience, no customs or technical aids, creative dramatics contributes to language arts skills, as children speak, communicate and listen. Auditory discrimination may also be built. As children play out appropriate stories and verse, they enjoy and learn to appreciate good literature.

Lease and Siks offer suggestions for introducing creative dramatics to young children. They suggest that the teacher should begin with:

Rhythmic Movement

Create the mood by several statements before asking the question. "Let's pretend that we are going outside to pick up nuts. Let's see how many nuts we can find. What is one way you can look for the nuts?" Some may crawl on hands and knees, others walk slowly looking down on the ground some skip others run.

The children may also do characterizations in rhythmic movements. For instance, they may characterize animals by the way they walk and sound, the weather, the wind blowing, rain falling.

Songs

Many children's songs suggest action, pantomime or characterizations. The teachers may sing while the children do the actions.

Finger Plays

As children participate in finger plays vivid pictures may be formed in their minds and they may be guided to feel and act as characters felt in the finger play.

Dramatic Plays

Dramatization may take many forms, including dramatic play, creative dramatics, and role-playing. Dramatic play is spontaneous and free of teacher's direction or control. In dramatic play children identify themselves with persons or things with which they have had firsthand contact or about which they have learned vicariously.

The teacher's responsibility includes: (*i*) providing many interesting opportunities for the children since the child's creative efforts are limited to his experiences—trips, contacts with various people, books, pictures, recordings and films, and (*ii*) providing space, materials, and time for the activity. If a child does not participate readily, the teacher may help the child enter the group by suggesting some role the child can assume.

CREATIVE ACTIVITIES IN PRE-PRIMARY SCHOOL

Creativity is considered to be solely in the province of the fine arts; instead recent findings in creativity indicate that many aspects of the school programme can be learned more effectively in creative ways, through creative activities.

Values of Creative Activities

Creative activities are considered an important part of the pre-primary school programme. Most of the children enjoy art activities, but there are also other reasons for including them. Art for the young child is a means of self-expression in visual form. The child uses art to express what he does, sees, feels, thinks and talks about. Experiences in art provide him with opportunities to explore and experiment, to express ideas and feelings about himself and the world around him. They strengthen the child's ability to imagine and to observe, and increase his sensitiveness to himself and to others.

Art experiences have therapeutic values. Through art materials the child can express feelings that are otherwise unacceptable and can learn to handle such feelings in an acceptable manner. Since the young child's speech is limited, it can often express its strong feelings through art experiences which involve psychomotor activity. Materials such as clay for pounding, paper for tearing and nails for hammering offer opportunities for handling negative feelings through positive action.

Helping a child to turn its feelings into creative channels gives him an outlet he/she can use throughout his/her life. To offer the child patterns or models would block this means of expression and prevent future growth. Asking the child what he has drawn or telling him how to do it might also be detrminantal to the creativity of the child. By leaving the child free to use materials in his/her own way, the teacher can sometimes gain insight into a child's private world by observing how it uses such materials, the results she/he obtains, and the way he/she feels about these results.

Intellectual growth takes place through art experiences as the child invents new ways of using materials and refines methods he has previously used. As children participate in self-chosen, and form groups easily from common interests. They learn to share materials, tools, and ideas, to make decisions, and to experience the give and take of group living. They learn to respect the rights, property, opinions and feelings of others. As individuals interact with each other, group leadership qualities develop and children become aware of the importance of co-operation and self-control. These values are derived when children are free to choose materials and use them in their own way.

Waste paper, empty match boxes, egg shells, seed coats of pulses, tea waste, rags, old socks, clay, sand, discarded icecream cups and spoons, card board which are the daily waste materials in shops and households can be turned into excellent playthings which are at the same time teaching aids for the tiny-tots. One special advantage of waste materials and inexpensive things is that the same material can be put to various uses as the situation demands to trigger off the imagination of the children.

Waste Paper

Waste paper can be put to very entertaining and productive use in paper work. Bright colours being attractive to children, old magazine papers are best for serawling, tearing, cutting, folding and pasting. Folding is a good activity by which very simple or highly complicated foldings are possible, such as book, scarf, boat, mat, peacock, aeroplane etc. Toffee and butter wrappers are very good materials for making dolls, butterflies and many other decorative pieces.

Card Board

Card board covers of old exercise books, discarded cartons of tea or biscuits and used greeting cards are good materials for making labels, alphabets, numbers and picture cards. Old calendar dates are really useful for number work.

Pasting

It provides tactile experience and opportunities for manipulation and co-ordination. It offers emotional release and opportunity to acquire motor skill. Through this activity the child feels, manipulates, explores and creates new things.

Cutting and Tearing

Cutting and paper tearing build muscle control and eye-hand co-ordination. The child cuts and tears the paper aimlessly exploring possibilities of material. He/she practices for skill trying to control scissors and direction of tearing. After completing his work, he names his forms. It offers opportunities to grow creatively and in awareness of form concept. Teacher should teach the child proper safety rules when they handle scissors.

Finger Painting

The child would like to feel and experiment with paints. He uses fingers, hands and arms and mixes all colours. He experiments with patterns. Teacher should provide the child with free choice of paper or oil cloth. Child should be allowed to paint whatever he likes. He develops an appreciation for form and colour. Finger painting encourages creative expression through its direct contact between child and product and provides a chance for self-discovery.

Preparation of cheap paint for Finger Painting Materials required:

2 cups of Flour
2 tea spoon of Salt
3 cups of cold water
2 cups of hot water
Food colouring powder

Mix 2 cups of flour with two teaspoon of salt in 3 cups of cold water. Beat it till smooth. Add 2 cups of hot water and then boil it till clean. Beat it till smooth. Let the mixture cool down for some time then add food colouring. One tablespoon of food colouring to be mixed as to make 8 ounces of paint.

Using Blocks

Child plays with single blocks. He creates a building and then names it. Their flexibility and ease of handling make an excellent first medium for the child. The teacher should provide the child with ample space and materials. She should watch for ways of helping timid child to participate in the activity.

The pre-primary schools need not necessarily have costly equipments and play things. In fact, cheaper the plaything, the more experiences and satisfaction that the children derive out of it. It is not necessary to hunt far and wide for cheap playthings for pre-primary school children. The waste which we throw away daily can be turned into wealth by the pre-primary school teacher with the magic wand of imagination.

Pieces of wood are thrown away by carpenters can be profitably turned into beautiful building blocks, after sand-papering and painting them. Empty match boxes and cigarette cases can be put to similar use as building blocks, railway carriages, cars, buses or barges according to the child's imagination and to suit different situations.

Other Materials for Creative Activities

The nature around the child could be profitably exploited by the teacher to enhance the creativity of the child. Dried leaves, flowers, wasted pieces of cloth by the tailors could be collected and pasted on news paper. The child can create different designs of its own which is called collage work.

Dried tea waste or seed coat of pulse like black gram or green gram can be put to some use. First make designs on paper with home made starch paste and then sprinkle dried tea waste on it and see excellent designs of birds or animals design.

A paste clay preferably coloured can be easily substituted for costly colours for finger paint, coating of clay paste on waste colours is good for making designs with used match sticks, small seeds and small pebbles.

Multi-coloured paper heads can be made by cutting long triangular places of coloured paper from old magazines, smearing home made starch paste or gum on one surface and rolling them on smooth splinter or knitting needle, starting with the broad end of the paper. Dry them after removing from the needle and use for beading.

Instead of throwing egg shells into the dustbin, use them to provide amusement recreation and opportunity for creativity. Keep the egg shells in salt water for a little time, then wash and dry them. Stuff a little cotton wool and paint the shells. Invert them carefully on thick broom sticks fixed on a clay base or hang them from a string.

Puppets

Puppet show is one of the most important activities in a pre-primary school which children thoroughly enjoy either by seeing them or by taking part in them. To make a simple puppet stage get seven bamboo sticks. The three sticks together to use them as stands at either end and place one stick across them in a horizontal position. Hang one sheet of cloth on it and behind this screen children can stand and act the story with the help of rod puppets, paper bag puppets and glove puppets.

Doll's House

Ice cream cups and spoons are very good utensils for the doll's house. Empty cartons, tins, and wrappers can be used for making a miniature provision shop. Samples of cereals, pulse, and other household commodities can be arranged in bottle lids and paper plates. This will encourage the child to be more imaginative and creative to play different roles.

After this long enumeration it is quite obvious that to keep our young enthusiastic toddlers engaged and to impart knowledge and imprint correct concept, no one need complain of lack of costly materials and teaching aids.

Art experiences for the young child are basic to developing a happy, wholesome and creative personality. Through these early experiences in art he develops the ability to imagine, feel, explore and express ideas. He learns to share materials, to cooperate, assume responsibility and to grow in awareness of himself as an individual and of his relation to those around him. As the child works with materials he develops his sense of feeling and perception and becomes sensitive to the world around it and to its needs and the needs of others. The future scientists, artists, writers, inventors, and dramatists are thus created.

20

Creative Drama for Children

What is Creative Drama?

The word, 'Creative' gives us the clues to the fact that it belongs to the arts which are devoted to the development of the imagination, to the opportunity afforded to the participants, use their own ideas and ways of thinking. The other term 'Drama' means that it has something to do with the use of the creative imagination in the specific forms. It is something that involves speech, movement of the body and music may involve other arts or it develops. Creativity, action and interpretation are part of drama at the pre-primary school level.

The origin of creative drama which some call child drama is natural play which children indulge in. It is in the child's activity which begins very early, first of all with the body—in moving, kicking, moving his arms, rolling back and forth, crawling and walking and very soon it involves the use of sound—the making of sounds with the exercise of vocal cords which is naturally a prelude to language, speech, communication. But at the same time these purely physical activities often become included with something of imagination and the child imagines himself not to be just a child, but to be various kinds of things he will pretend to be mechanical things like automobiles, aeroplanes, engines, trains and, of course, in these modern days, rockets and the noises of these things will become a part of his play.

Difference Between Formal Drama and Creative Drama

Creative drama is very different from the kind of formal drama which we see in the theatre. When the child plays he does not think of an audience and he becomes engrossed in what he is doing. He is quite often completely unaware of other people around him—either playing by himself or a group of children playing by themselves, becomes very intent on what they are doing and they have no awareness that perhaps someone is watching. So there is no audience, no stage and there is free all round movement in whatever space available. In handling a Creative Drama one should avoid any suggestion of stage. Everybody is both audience and actor, if one may use the formal terms. Casting this person or that person permanently in a role should not be done for creative dramas. There should be some actors and listeners and they could take shifts. The purpose of Creative Drama is not to present a finished performance for an audience. The purpose of Creative Drama is to develop the resources, the individuality, the talent which may be hidden in the individual child. So the leader does not try, to choose the person who can play the part best. If there are too many volunteers to play the part, she perhaps chooses the one who seems most unlikely to do that part well because it may so happen that the one who volunteers may have been a non-participant and it may be the first time that he has shown any interest and has had courage enough to volunteer to do the part. The forward ones could be given special roles such as to watch certain things, to observe or could be given a chance later on.

There is no director for the creative drama. The teacher or leader, guides, tries to channel it into directions which are important, valuable and useful, provide motivation and be alert for opportunities which Creative Drama may be useful. It is not just wasted time or an aimless activity. It is a hard work for the teacher. The drama should be based on enjoyment both for the participant and the audience. It is designed to get one out of oneself for the moment.

Usefulness of Creative Drama

1. Children learn to try to adjust themselves to their environment (through sense—touching, seeing, hearing, smelling and tasting).
2. Helps to develop a kind of thinking or a kind of awareness which is the basis of all aesthetic appreciation.
3. Promotes aesthetic appreciation.
4. Promotes muscular co-ordination.
5. Helps the individual to develop himself and to adjust himself to the group (social adjustment).
6. Helps him learn how to behave in a group.

7. Develops creative imagination.
8. Strengthens visual impression (to recall experiences, re-living and re-enacting experiences and testing again the observation which the children have made in any situation).
9. Promotes language, self-expression—learning to talk and express through language and physical movement.
10. Helps to co-operate in a group and working-together for a common purpose.
11. Develops ability to use vocal cords in various ways—human beings talk to-personify animal character or other characters.
12. Develops all-round expressiveness to make them more interesting and entertaining.
13. It is a way of interpreting the literary heritage of a country—pulling together many different social elements into one basic activity.

Kinds of Play

1. Personal—child acting as the character.
2. Projected—Manipulating objects as characters.

Aims

1. It is an art which is primarily beneficial for freeing the individual mentally and physically.
2. To help the child develop poise, his ability, and to express himself through talking and the other arts.

Age

Only at 7-9 years of age he will be able to play successfully. Much could be done with 4-5 years old than that of infants but not as much as the 7-8 year olds.

3-4 Years Olds

Walk awkwardly and will therefore respond to the idea of movement and rhythm. It would help in their muscular co-ordination of legs and arms. They could also be stimulated by music. So simple nursery rhymes, poems, songs etc., can be used not merely for singing but to move the limbs 'Mother Goose' and 'Humpty Dumpty' and also own made up songs and rhymes could be made use of.

Basic Techniques

1. Have a sense of freedom for movement (sufficient space).
2. Actions must be varied (as attention span is short).
3. Do not force participation in a given exercise.
4. Do not criticize them. They would develop a critical attitude themselves.
5. Be close to the group without participating much. Give ideas if needed. Work from what they know to what they do not know.
6. Not much equipment—not elaborate or realistic equipment.
7. There is no particular age when children can face an audience. When they have built confidence and are used to doing it smoothly they are ready for an audience.
8. Time limit—does not count much for older children, short duration for younger ones.
9. Do not ask them to prepare for staging something for an audience.
10. Select a story that has an element of conflict—gives sense of completion.
11. Puppets are also useful in developing creative drama (children should be encouraged to make their own puppets).
12. Have more of action and less of dialogue.

CREATIVE ACTIVITIES

CREATIVE ACTIVITIES

READING PROGRAMME

READING PROGRAMME

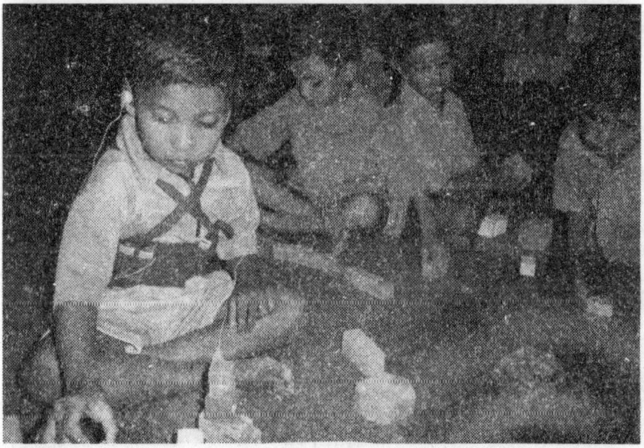

OUTDOOR ACTIVITIES IN A PRE-PRIMARY SCHOOL

OUT DOOR ACTIVITIES IN A PRE-PRIMARY SCHOOL

INDOOR PLAY

INDOOR PLAY

21

Science Experiences in Pre-Primary School

Experiences in science are important to the young child, as we are living in a scientific world. Now-a-days every action is based on science. The child raises so many questions like, Why is it happening? How does it grow? How is it rotating? How does it rise? How it comes? and so on. It is the duty of the teacher and the parent to answer the children very patiently. Raising questions by the child reflects its intellectual development and curiosity to know the world around. The parent and the teacher have to induce and encourage the child to ask questions related to science.

Giving science concepts at the Pre-primary school aims at helping the child develop the concepts which will keep it safe from the hazards of environment. The child watches, wonders, studies and questions as it experiences science as a part of its every day living. Science awakens and encourages child's curiosity, to know more about surroundings. Teaching science at the pre-school level so the needs for scientific attitude.

Objectives and Values of Science Experience

The objectives of science education have been divided into four sections by Mr. Sara Hament. They are:

1. Developing skill among the children to solve the problems through the use of method of science.
2. Developing scientific attitude among children.
3. Helping to learn new scientific concepts.
4. Developing in children an interest and appreciation in the science around them.

To attain these four objectives, the Pre-primary school teachers has to keep in mind the following points:

1. The teacher has to use the child's talents to a fullest possible extent.
2. Inducing the curiosity among children by asking them more and more questions.
3. Making the child skillful to express freely about what it thinks? What it wants to know? and What is requires?
4. Stressing the importance of observation and demonstration.
5. The teacher has to bear in mind the children's skill, intelligence and curiosity.
6. The children should be made to feel the similarities and differences between things and experiences.
7. Should use the methods to induce the curiosity of the children.
8. The teacher has to give them activities and experiences which pacifies the children.
9. It is essential to follow the methods which develop children's argument skill, and thinking power.
10. New experiences, new objects develop scientific attitude among children.

Strategis of Teaching Science

Incidental Approach

The teacher can utilize the incidents and yet provide a well-balanced science programme which is flexible and adaptable to the needs and interest of children. It is important to consider the requirements for an adequate science programme for young children. These include:

Planning Which is Both Definite and Flexible

There is a framework which is flexible enough for children and teachers to plan co-operatively for experiences that meet their particular needs. Such a framework often helps the teacher to utilize incidents more effectively because she sees in the situation possibilities for developing certain concepts. Without such planning many incidents may not be utilized or two many incidents of a similar nature may be emphasized, thereby the science programme may tend to be limited in scope.

Concepts from all major areas of Science

These areas include our earth and the universe, living things and their activities, man and his environment and matter and energy. Children of all ages are interested in all areas of science. Simple ideas which are introduced in pre-primary school lay a foundation for understanding more complex, one later as children grow through constantly enlarging experiences. At one time the belief that science for children should deal primarily with biological concepts was prevalent. Investigators have found that children are also interested in the physical sciences. They found that young children are able to generalize to some extent. This skill is not one which appears suddenly but one that develops steadily with maturation and experience, some of the areas and some generalisations appropriate for pre-primary school are listed below:

Matter and Energy: Under this heading we can talk about the following:

Air is around us.
Sounds travel a long distance.
Many things make sound.
Fire needs air to burn.
Electricity makes light.

Living Things and Their Activities: Under this the following concepts can be given to the children.

1. Living things needs air, water, warmth and food.
2. Animals eat different food.
3. Some plants grow on land, some plants grow in water.
4. Animals move about in different ways.

Our Earth and the Universe

1. Man has travelled in rockets into outer space.
2. Stars move in the sky.
3. The sun gives light and heat.
4. Man has put satellites in orbit around the earth.

Man and his Environment: Under this we can talk about the following:

1. Animals help man work.
2. Love and care the pet animals.
3. Man can travel in many ways.
4. Man uses plants and animals for food, clothing and shelter.
5. Grow more trees and plants.
6. Plants need water.
7. Man uses and controls heat.
8. Man likes animals.
9. There are different kind of soils.

Integration of Science Learning with other experience of Child

In studying 'living things and their activities', the science learnings may be closely related to health and social studies. Living things make adaptations to the cold or heat with the change in weather. Children may discuss the relation of proper clothing to health status. Experiences are needed which help the child sees how science is related to his own life; for example, electricity for lights, cooking, cooling and heating. The social implications of science in relation to community activities help children to understand why transportation is important and why the city provides water.

Variety and balance in the activities in which children participate

Field trips, experiments, educational media, observations and resource people can offer a wide variety of science experiences to children. This does not mean that every science experience will include a field trip or an experiment. The teacher will have to choose carefully the activities most appropriate for developing the basic generalization under study. Field trips may be made to nearby spots, within walking distance of the school, or to sites farther away which necessitates transportation.

Science Curriculum for Pre-primary Schoolers

Biology

(*a*) Human beings, animals, birds and plants grow.
(*b*) Name of the parts of human body and its functions.

(*c*) The importance of food, air and water in life.
(*d*) Food for plants.
(*e*) Kinds of food items.
(*f*) Tastes and smells.

Botany

(*a*) Seed and its growth.
(*b*) Importance of soil, water, sunlight for germination of seed.
(*c*) Parts of plants and their functions.
(*d*) Structure and shapes of different kinds of leaves.
(*e*) Flowers.
(*f*) Vegetables and fruits.

Zoology

(*a*) Animals—Pet animals, Wild animals,—their food habits and uses.
(*b*) Birds and their food habits.
(*c*) Animals—give birth; birds—lay eggs.
(*d*) Uses of milk.
(*e*) Vegetarian and non-vegetarian food.

Hygiene

(*a*) Importance of neatness.
(*b*) Clean body.
(*c*) Importance of taking bath.
(*d*) Clean dress.
(*e*) Symptoms of healthy persons.
(*f*) Common diseases—fever, cold, small pox.

Physics

(*a*) State of objects—solid, liquid and gas.
(*b*) Objects expand when they are heated.
(*c*) Mirror reflects.
(*d*) Uses of pulleys.
(*e*) Round objects—cylinders, rollers—can roll, others cannot roll.

(*f*) Wood resists transmission of heat.
(*g*) Metals transmit heat.
(*h*) Heavy object submerge in the water.
(*i*) Uses of electricity.
(*j*) Softness-roughness differentiation.

Chemistry

(*a*) Some chemicals dissolve in water.
(*b*) Soap—Foaming.
(*c*) Salt water—Soft water.
(*d*) Match box, crackers.
(*e*) Petrol—uses.
(*f*) Paper.

Introduction of different Sciences to Pre-schoolers

By the time a child is ready for elementary school, his pre-school experiences should have provided him with simple concepts basic to each of the sciences. Many of these learnings are a natural commitment of everyday activities during each of the seasons. Others must be consciously taught at some time during the pre-primary school children lay ideas in such physical sciences as chemistry and physics.

The beginning of physics in the mind of a pre-primary school child, like the beginning of any other science, are formed out of his first hand experience when that experience is interpreted for him in terms of basic physical concepts. In the scientific world of today, it is important for the pre-primary school child to develop an elementary understanding of the physical concepts on which he can build further appreciation of physical science.

The child may begin his mathematics with blocks. Two small blocks equal one big one. He can use one big one or two small ones to fill the same space. The small ones are half the size of the big one. But putting these relations into words, by making them explicit, the teacher gives him tools for thinking in the realm of number relations as he plays and solves problems in block building. In another situation she may say, "How many chairs do we need at the table? There are two boys and one girl". She counts the cups and plates as she puts them on the table, she provides measuring cups of different sizes, one cup, two cups or a quartz size and finds opportunities to show the child he can use these when he wants amounts of something.

The child has many opportunities to learn biology as he cares for plants and animals and watches them grow. A garden in the spring offers rich opportunities for learning and extending concepts about plant life. Watching and caring for pets teaches the children about the ways different animals iive, what and how they eat and how they sleep and reproduce. Experiences like these go to make up a background which is the basis for understanding what will be learned about biology later. Every school should offer a wide variety of experience in the natural science as possible.

Trips to places other than farmyards are a desirable part of the curriculum and help to broaden the children's concepts in the general area which we might call Social Studies. There are many opportunities for trips in city. Trips to the grocery store for needed supplies are always interesting. Other stores such as the feed store which supplies food for the chickens or rabbit may be a rich experience, especially if the store handles grain or hay in quantity.

Many of the most valuable experiences outside the school lead directly to more variety and richness in the play experiences within the school.

Developing a Scientific Attitude

The essence of a scientific attitude is curiosity. The scientific attitude stems from interaction of a pre-school child with his environment. Grown ups can enhance its development by their guidance, or they can interfere with its development. For instance, when construction activities are going on nearby, teachers and parents can express their own interest in the machinery and its use and can share their interest with the children. They can help each child find a safe place from which to watch what is going on. Their interest and enthusiasm are caught by the child to the point where he will notice similar construction activities and will find an adult to share the experience of watching with him again.

One of the important things that a pre-school child learns is what to be interested in and what not to be interested in. Some adults take children to new situations and let them explore those as a means of widening their interests. Other adults do not like to be bothered with their children and leave them with an unequipped backyard or with only a TV screen to watch. Thus they give their children only a fifty-fifty chance of discovering such wonders as the bugs and other insects which inhibit the yard. Only with adult assistance and guidance children can become interested in a wide gamut of scientific phenomena.

Especially with four and five-year-old children the grownups can aid the development of scientific attitude. A child who is building with blocks and attempts a different problem such as using centilevers to support a roof. He adds a block and the structure, off balance, topples. The frustrated child bursts into a emotional tantrum. The nearby adult then has a choice of paying attention to the child and his tantrum, or considering the problem which initiated it. The adult can calmly say, "Let's get a drink, and then I'll show you what happened". The adult thus takes care of the child's need to relax his concentration at the same time that, with calmness, she shows the child that failure is just part of an activity. Adult interest in solving the problem encourages the child in discovering facts.

Experiments

Experiments are planned to test, to try out ideas, and to help the child to come to accurate conclusions. Experiments are not arranged to provide a display of magic and arouse fears and doubts in the child's mind. If there is a problem to be solved, children may be helped to use an experiment, in finding the solution.

The role of the Teacher

The teacher has an important role as a reinforcer of learning through the attention she gives. The pre-school child is influenced by his teacher's response or lack of response to what he does. There is evidence that positive reinforcement of a response is an aid to learning. "That's right, "That's fine", reinforces what a child has discovered and confirms his own feeling. A glance and smile reinforce when words may not be needed. The teacher reserves attention for the times when the child makes a mistake or misbehaves.

The teacher serves as a model for the child. He imitates her behaviour and patterns himself after her in all kind of ways including speech, gesture, attitudes, interests and feelings. She may be the spark which starts him off on many different paths or turns his attention to many new things.

The child also learns more about relationships from what he experiences in his relationship with the teacher. One of the handicaps from which the culturally deprived child often suffers in school is that he has failed to perceive adults, at least those outside the family, as to whom one can turn for help in coping with problems.

The experienced teacher introduces only one science point at a time. She makes sure that the fire is a safe and happy experience for the children. She knows that during the next fire experience she can teach the children a little bit more, especially if they find the learning situation a pleasant and fascinating one.

The pre-primary school teacher should help the children become aware of different properties of wood, metal, plastic, and concrete and of everyday objects made of these substances. The teacher should guide the children in associating only obvious properties with different objects.

The teacher should supplement and consolidate the real experiences that the children have outdoors in their garden and one walks by telling them simple stories with her flannel board and with a suitable selection of children's picture books. She would arrange for the children to visit a nearby farm or a home where baby animals grow. It is the teacher in the pre-school who could create an atmosphere which will be conducive to the child to learn the scientific concepts and promote scientific attitude.

22

Social Studies Experiences

Social studies education, has the task of helping the young to grow in their understanding of the sensitivity to the physical and social forces at work around them so that they could develop the ability and skill to cope with and to manage their futures. Such education help children generate hope in the future and confidence in their ability to solve social problems.

Social studies experiences help children learn about people, how and where they live, how their communities are formed and governed, how do they meet their needs, how and why do they hate each other, how people use and misuse the resources on the earth and how to handle all these situation effectively so that children could adjust themselves to the changing social needs and expectations.

Social studies experiences help children to function as members of social groups such as family, community and the world. The aim and functions of social studies experiences are follows:

1. To develop understanding of importance of co-operative group living and other social values.
2. To broaden the child's social environment by providing opportunities to live, play and work with other children and adults.
3. To explore the child's interest in the environment at home, school and neighbourhood and their dependency.
4. To help the child understand the interdependence of parents, siblings, teachers, neighbours, community, helpers and how could he/she help others.
5. To expand the child's horizon of the world by understanding the home, community, state, nation and the world and the ways of living.

Social studies experiences are concerned with behaviour, goals, values, skill and the knowledge needed to bring about change. Children can easily change their character, behaviour and adjust with the changing environment when they come to know more about their family, their environment and the persons around them. This behaviour continues from childhood to adulthood. Social studies experiences are helpful in inculcating this ability.

What is social studies? How to teach social studies to pre-primary school children? Is it possible for the children to study History and Geography? How to teach the concepts clearly? Which method to adopt? Which activities are suitable to provide social studies experiences? Naturally such questions arise in the minds of the pre-school teacher, as the pre-primary school stage is like that.

Social studies means, normally the History and Geography will come into our mind. But during the pre-primary school stage, the aim of providing social studies experiences is to help the children understand themselves and to know the world around them. These opportunities help them to inculcate good habits, to understand others, to co-operate with others, to know their responsibilities and how to do their duties sincerely. It also develops the feelings of being a member of a family, member of a school, member of the society and prepares the child to be a good citizen. Thus inculcation of social feelings is one of the aims of providing social studies, experiences in pre-primary school.

Concepts to be Taught

Social study experiences for the young children should form on the immediate environment of experiences of the child. For the first time the pre-primary school children leave their mothers and the family and enter a new situation outside home to a pre-primary school. So, the first social study experience provided should help them understand the new environment. If they understand the situation, children can understand the need for changing their behaviour. Understanding oneself helps how he depends on others and how others depend on him for each other need fulfilment in school as well as in the society. It tends to inculcate the habit of mutual understanding, sharing and co-operation. When they participate in other activities, they develop duty consciousness and ready to take up and perform new responsibilities skillfully.

Learning social studies help the children to move with a new situation and with the children of the same age group of varied needs and interests. It develops the leadership quality. They also learn to be leaders as well as good followers. All these experiences help the child to become a good citizen in a democratic country. They also learn the value of dignity of labour and other value which are cherished by the world.

Topics that could be dealt with under the social studies experiences are given below. These are only suggestive. It is the teacher who has to decide how much information and concepts to be given to the children according to their age, maturity, experience and situation.

1. My family.
   (*a*) My name,
   (*b*) My parents' name,
   (*c*) My brother's and sister's name, and
   (*d*) My family name.
2. Name of the street where I live.
3. Name of my village/town.
4. Name of my school.
5. Name of my teacher.
6. Name of my friends.
7. Names of places where my friends live.
8. My duties in school.
9. What my friends do.
10. Community workers—They help us in many ways:
    (*a*) Doctor,
    (*b*) Policeman,
    (*c*) Watchman,
    (*d*) Postman,
    (*e*) Milkman,
    (*f*) Cobbler,
    (*g*) Tailor,
    (*h*) Dhobi,
    (*i*) Potter,
    (*j*) Weaver,
    (*k*) Carpenter, and
    (*l*) Driver.
11. Transports—People travel in different ways.
12. Communication—Messages are sent in different ways.
13. What are the duties of my parents.

14. City Town and the Village
15. National leaders.
16. Our Flag.
17. Independence day, Republic day.
18. Costumes of different countries.
19. Our food patterns and habits and others.
20. Types of houses.
21. Mountains
22. Sources of water—river, pond, lake and well.
23. People in the world.
24. The role of a child, as distinct from that of adults.

The curriculum and plan should be a flexible one. The teacher may change according to the situation and the needs of children and parents. The above titles can't give fully the social studies experiences. It may also change according to the social change; one should give new and novel concepts and it all depends on the teacher's competency and skills.

Teaching Methods

The teacher should not get exhausted when they see the above titles and concepts. All these concepts can easily be taught to the children through play way methods. Any concepts can be given to the children depending on the age experience and maturity of the children. Spiral method is one of the methods in planning the curriculum. It means the same concepts are expanded according to the age and experiences of the children. On the basis of the age and experiences of the children the social studies concepts are taught in the pre-primary school stage. It is possible to teach the social studies concepts to children through free conversation, outdoor play, stories, rhymes, outdoor play equipments and books. For example let us take the title of 'Our Country'. First the child learns the name of her residence then the place of location of school and the distance between them. And then about the houses of friends and neighbours, their places and the distances. The child learns the names of towns and villages her friends live and distance between the places. That is from micro level to macro level village to the district, state, country and the world. The teacher should give the opportunities to understand the concept of space, gradually through social studies experiences.

Social studies concepts can be introduced by involving the children in varied activities. The children can help their teachers while serving the lunch; cleaning, arranging the equipment etc. In doing the creative activities the children can distribute the materials and collect the materials after the activity is over and arrange them in order. They can also participate in cleaning their classroom and the school, and satisfy the needs of younger children through child to child programme. All these help the children understand their duties and responsibilities.

By celebrating national festivals like Independence day and Republic day children develop the respect for flag. It will promote the feelings of patriotism and democracy. Similarly celebrating the birthday of great leaders will help the children understand the importance of sacrifice and hard work.

Thus the pre-primary school teacher can reduce the distance between the children and their environment through social studies experiences. While decreasing this distance, the children can easily modify their behaviour according to the situation and expand their knowledge of world in which they live. This paves the way for the study history and geography of the country and world.

23

Children's Literature

An important part of the curriculum consists of experiences with language as well as communication with others. The pre-primary school teacher needs to talk with children and to give them opportunity to talk with her about their experiences. Children from culturally disadvantaged homes seems to be handicapped in school to a great extent because of their lack of language. In every pre-primary school whose children are lacking verbal experiences there should be a rich variety and a number of experiences with language. Singing, play with words, poetry and telling reading stories are part of language experience, that could be provided in a pre-primary school.

Aims

Literature is a major integrating experience in the elementary school language programme. It also has a value of its own because it provides new perspectives through vicarious experiences, develops insight into human behaviour and wisdom and provides beauty and inspiration. A good literature programme encourages the development of knowledge about our literary heritage, establishes skills of literary analysis, fosters language skills, enriches content of the curriculum and stimulates creative activities. The major goal is to promote the experiencing and enjoyment of literature as a means of developing children's taste for reading and lifetime appreciation of fine readiness materials.

Literature comes in many forms such as poetry, drama, fiction and non-fiction. A good literature programme will help children to become acquainted with the best of all forms of literature. Literature has the power to deepen and enrich the real and imaginative life of the child. It opens the doors for knowledge and widens horizon to the outside world.

Books can be friends and companions and create an awareness of fun and enjoyment besides being a source of information, joy to meet a child at his own level in literature and then help him explore and become acquainted with other kinds, so that he may find more towards the best. The reading of any story whatsoever to a child meets one of his basic needs for security. The pre-schooler should feel secure in his relationships to each member of his family.

Several stories show a young child taking on a real responsibility that is important in the adult world. The children identify with the character and think of themselves as similarly able to contribute to activities important in the community. Vicariously they enjoy thinking of being responsible and of being admired, not only for themselves, but also for what they can do.

A basic need of pre-school children is to have a feeling of belonging to the pre-school group as well as to the family. How their needs for security within the family is met, is interpreted for them through many picture books, some books interpret for them the human relationships within their pre-school group.

Components of a Literature Programme

Many different procedures and activities are used to encourage children to be knowledgeable about and delighted by literature. Background and knowledge for the teacher or pre-requisite to develop a good literature programme for young children includes:

(*a*) acquiring a repertoire of stories and poems that brings you pleasure;
(*b*) knowing the interests and reading levels of the children that you teach;
(*c*) knowing the books available in your library that meet the interests and reading levels of your children;
(*d*) establishing "reading-is-fun" environment;
(*e*) using some form of literature in your lesson plan every day;
(*f*) helping children understand the background of the literature they are reading; and
(*g*) providing time for free discussions on what you have read and what they read.

Oral Reading

One of the best ways of presenting literature to the pre-primary school children is to have the teacher read a story to the class. Teacher should make children sit around her and read the book for them. Teachers should read in natural tones and with expressions, but not dramatically. Time should be provided for sharing the illustrations with the children, exploring key words and phrases and evaluating reactions. It is better to read aloud stories when, children cannot easily read for themselves, the teacher personally likes and is thoroughly familiar with, possess the qualities assigned to the best in literature.

At times a child may ask to read his favourite story to the class or to a small group of children, and at other times the teacher should encourage children to share stories of general interest orally with the group. Older children reading stories to younger ones can be highly beneficial to both groups. No group should be compelled to listen to a poor reader. The teacher must help the reader be well prepared for the presentation of his material.

Criteria for Selecting Children Books

The contents of the story books and other books offered to the children should be:

1. Realistic, since children of young age have much difficulty in distinguishing between what is real and what is fantasy, the content should be realistic.
2. Should be interesting to the young children.
3. Entertaining with colourful pictures and an element of surprise are necessary.
4. Accurate in information.
5. With humour and with no element of terror.
6. Promote the child's learning by supporting his first-hand experience.
7. Interesting in words, sounds or play on words, with some repetition in the form of phrases, incidents and ideas.
8. Short in length. Three-year-olds may remain interested for 6 to 10 minutes; four-year-olds from 10 to 15 minutes.
9. Acceptable in terms of the effect on the child.

10. Simple in style, form and mannerism and well-developed. Unnecessary details should be eliminated.
11. Simple in words, descriptive with the appropriate language and with lot of.
12. Direct conversation.
13. Illustrations which closely represent the written text.
14. Book should be enough so that young children could easily handle.
15. It should be printed in bold letters, and it should be washable.

Characteristics of Books for Pre-Primary Schoolers

Variety in the books selected for the pre-primary school library is important. Each pre-school group will enjoy a some what different selection of books, depending on their particular environments and the experiences they have had. In selecting books we must remember that the function of books for the young child is not to present new information, but to re-create for him the world he knows and by re-creation to strengthen his understanding of it.

Books to Security in Relationship

The pre-primary school child needs to feel secure in his relationships to each member of his family, his mother, father, and siblings in his home, his grandparents, who are frequently a part of his life. Many of the best loved books for pre-primary school children further a child's security in these fundamental relationships. Books about their own family members are favourite of pre-primary school children. Desirable relationships among thc children within a family are also interpreted to pre-primary school children through books. Books which help pre-primary school children to understand their relationships to other members of their family are a basis for understanding later the organisation of a family.

Books for Self-Confidence

The pre-primary school child can enjoy at each age level several books that help him appreciate his own worth. The child who is imaginative and follows Harold and the Purple Crayon on adventures can identify with household as an important person. He can enjoy Tommy and Dee Dee; a book about two little boys each in a different social order. The two boys are much alike in many important ways, such as having parents who love and appreciate them. Several books are use the setting of the animal world to bring out the importance of young to their parents.

Books to Meet the Need for Achievement

The theme of the hero who is able to overcome difficulty and gain recognition is found in books for three-year-old children. Harold and the Purple Crayon pottrays a hero overcoming difficulty and controlling his environment. Harold gets into difficult situations with his purple crayon, but since he has control of the crayon he can stop, back up, or proceed as is necessary to solve his problem. This demonstration of the ability to create and control a world gives the child a vicarious experience in a role of achievement.

Books for Meeting the Need to Belong to a Group

A basic need of pre-primary school children is to have a feeling of belonging to the pre-primary school group as well as to the family. How their need for security within the family is met interpreted for them through many picture books.

Books to Meet the Need for Safety

A child must not only be safe, he must also feel safe. The pre-primary school child, going into first experiences outside the safety and security of his own home, needs to have those early experiences free of fears, anxieties, and feelings of guilt. Several delightful picture books bring the pre-primary school child an opportunity to think of situations which bring him the pleasure of safety and security.

Books for Experience

Books which bring new ideas to pre-primary school children are numerous. The Ding Dong book brings many new ideas a few at a time to pre-primary school children. Such books introduce new labels for the child to use in talking about his experiences.

The teacher must plan carefully for using books with children. In planning, there are certain points and procedures to be considered.

A Well-Balanced Collection

Books of poetry, information, nature, holiday fun, folk stories, everyday experiences, inspiration and those that stimulate creative expression are essential. The teacher may use the following questions to help in evaluating a book. Does it have qualities that will appeal to the child's aesthetic sense and show possibilities for developing the child's artistic value and his love for beauty and harmony?

Does it deal with child like experiences and will it provide for the child's satisfaction and pleasure?

Does it have qualities that will challenge children's imagination and stimulate creative expression?

Does it contain information that will help in widening the child's horizons and deeping his understandings?

Does it deal with materials that will contribute to the child's understanding of human relations?

Using Books Collections

The well-selected collections of books is not enough. To be effective in the lives of children, it must be well used. Display books attractively on a table or on a low shelf. Flowers, a plant or cut-outs of character in the story may be used to advantage.

Arrange for children to borrow a favourite book to take home and share with their families. If the child wants a book, he brings it to the teacher and together they write his name on the book list and when the book is returned the child checks his namc off the list. Such procedure hclps children to develop responsibility in using and caring for books. A visit to a library can help to develop an interest in books and an understanding of how books are cared for. The teacher must not only select a good collection of books but nurture them effectively with children.

Classification of Literature

Following are the classifications of literature for children. It is classified as poetry, realistic stories, stories of folk love of fantasy and concept stories are suitable for the young children.

Poetry

Experiences with poetry can be happy and spontaneous ones for children. They enjoy the sounds around them, create sounds, laugh at unusual combinations of words, sense the rhythm of running, skipping and speaking. The spontaneous language of children is often poetic in nature. Poetry, if well selected and correctly used, can help the child to listen carefully; to learn new words and ways of expressing one's feelings; to develop increased auditory awareness or acuity; to improve the quality of one's own voice; and to feel secure in the groups as one participates in saying poetry with the group poetry can bring laughter and happiness to the child.

Selection of Poetry

Children enjoy a wide variety of poems including those about the situation familiar to the children-playmates, clothing and pets; poems about nature—the seasons, the wind, the falling leaves or signs of spring; poems that are fanciful and imaginative; holiday poems; humorous verses, and those filled with the repetition of unusual sounds with a singing quality. The content of the poem should be sufficiently related to the child's experiences that he can understand something of the meaning expressed by the words.

Realistic Stories

Realistic story is an imaginative writing which accurately reflects life as it was lived in the past or could be lived today. Realistic stories are about the excitement, the humour, the winning and losing and good and bad in everyday life. Children's classics are old fashioned. The speeches, the clothes, the customs are all different from those of today and they contain some essential identity which children recognize as being for them.

Some of the modern books, which are overflowing in the markets of today for children may deal with animals, everyday experiences of adventure and fantasy. They also come in a variety of forms to break the monotony. The visual art form of picture story books provides children with their first hand experiences with art and literature. The beauty and colour of expression make them appealing to children as well as simplify the way that the message is bold. Realistic fiction takes children into the outer world of people, times and places. Stories involving conflict and problem solving help children to interpret their experience through characters with whom they can identify. Another novel and modern trend in children book market is the evaluation of music books that give some sweet melodies when the book is handled by children and they are of special interest and appeal to young children.

Fantasy, Folk Love and Legend

The roots of the different types of folk literature myths, and legends, fables and heroic tales, folk-family tales, deeply embedded the past, can still charm and interest the children. Three things are necessary to produce and present fantasy and folk love: Story tellers, creative minds and imagination.

Cumulative Tales

Young children are more fascinated by the repetitions in stories. Anything like, "I'll huff and I'll puff and I'll blow your house" in "The three little pigs" is enjoyed by children. All folklore have this repetition of details which build up to a quick claimax.

Beast Tales

Children enjoy stories in which the animals speak and act like human beings. Talking animals appear in stories of all culture and take on many of the roles of children as well as adults.

Wonder Tales

Any wonder tale, that is about magic and the super-natural is called a 'fairy tale' by children. Some wonder tales resemble poetry such as Mother Goose in their strong rhythm and movement. There are stories such as, 'Jack and the Bean Stalk', 'Snow White the Seven Dwarfs' and 'Cindrella'. These tales are meant to be read or told for they originated in the spoken word of the story teller. Through many of the wonder tales, children have build up feelings of suspense and adventure that they would like to express through various forms of interpretation.

Concept Books

Concept need to grow from first hand experience as young children observe, explore, listen, compare, examine and discover. Children need to know the names of letters as they begin to associate the spoken word with the printed word. ABC books are frequently used as a way of presenting objects or animals for the young child to talk about.

Many concept books present a cumulative procession of objects with some typed story to hold them together. Books which help children discriminate colour are sometimes very informational. There are innumerable modern books that give varied concept to children, like house and family, flowers, animals, fruits, vegetables and numbers etc. Books on nature, time, weather, seasons and sounds are also within the experience of young children. Picture books and picture-story books give them wide experiences. Children's books that are now available are, 'Science for you', Children's Knowledge Bank, Children's encyclopaedia, the world famous series with 18 titles of discoveries, religions civilizations, great lives etc., 101 Science games, Play and learn, Maths for you, etc.

Reading Media of Childhood

Newspapers and Magazines

The newspaper is one of the best media to which the child is introduced. When children first begin to read newspapers, the main interest is the comic strips. Gradually as a result of their studies and their discussions of current events in schools, they begin to read the news of the day. At all ages they prefer magazines which are brightly coloured with many interesting advertisements.

Comic

The child's early interest in comics arises as early as 2 or 3 years. Long before the child cares about reading the news of world, he has become a daily reader of the comic, strips and this interest persists even then. Boys and girls have different tastes in comics and boys at every age, read more comics than girls. Then appeal of various kinds of comics follows a predictable pattern, among pre-primary schoolers. The favourites are those in which animals such as Micky Mouse, The Bear, etc. dress and talk like human beings.

If we could develop interest in reading at the young age itself, the child will not find it difficult to do literary work in future.

24

Readiness Programme

Readiness is the adequacy of the child's existing capacity in relation to some instructional objective. Readiness is an essential ingredient in all kinds of learning; whether it be formal or informal, simple or complex, involving motor or mental skills, or whether it be in the home or community. It has often been referred to as 'ripeness' for a new learning experience. In other words, it is the most propitious time to introduce any new learning experience.

Readiness period is the time at which the child is just beginning cycle at growth. The main aim of readiness to learn is to ensure a smooth transition from home or pre-primary school to school through enabling children to successfully meet the demands of the school. The pattern of development is the natural foundation for all learning. A child cannot be expected to learn a given task until he is ready for it. So readiness is an essential factor for any learning.

Importance of Readiness

Readiness is like a catalyst that needs to be present for an affective reaction of learning to precipitate. Readiness for school is important. Because entrance to first grade is a very novel and a unique experience for the children. They are on the threshold of all formal learnings and therefore, thcy should be ready and well equipped to confront all that first grade offers to them. The foundation of all future learnings are laid down in the first grade. Readiness can help to build a sound, strong foundation for the later educational structure to be built upon it. The later learnings in succeeding grades are likely to be shaky and weak on a poor foundation in the first grade.

Readiness and Maturation

Development is a product of inheritance and environment. On educational terminology, development is often described as readiness and maturation. Readiness is frequently confused with a related but different concept-maturation (Ausubel, 1959). Maturation refers to biological growth which occurs largely under the influence of heredity. In maturation, certain structural changes must occur before a certain behaviour can appear. So, maturation is regarded as the process of growth and development which takes place within the individual without any special training, practice or any other type of stimulation. As the result of maturation, the children normally start crawling, sitting, writing, standing, walking, speaking etc. at a particular age.

Readiness is a product of both training and maturation. Several studies show that training is largely wasted if the child has not reached the pre-requisite level of maturation. Lack of readiness is a product of lack of training: the teacher must increase readiness. Maturation alone will not manifest in the child, the readiness to speak grammatically, read skillfully, and compose limericks with consummate poetical skill.

Importance of Reading Readiness

Reading, Writing and Arithmetic are the three basic subjects taught in all first grades universally. A child cannot write meaningfully until he can read what is written, nor can he decipher numbers correctly unless he can read them. Since reading precedes all formal learning, readiness for reading is of paramount importance. Reading is not only a skill needed for learning first grade subjects, but it is that skill on which all the formal learnings, in all the subjects, and in all the grades depend. Reading skill is an essential requirement in today's literate world. It is a functional activity pursued for various reasons like communication, gaining information, solving problems, or for recreation and pleasure.

Reading is the ability to transform printed words into oral responses. Reading is the meaningful interpretation of symbols—a process through which we understand and it is a process of communication between readers and writers (Chall, 1967).

Thorndike (1917) defined reading readiness as reasoning. It is the meaningful interpretation of symbols—a process through which we understand. It is the process of communication between readers and writers and a means to an end.

Reading readiness is what teachers look for in children during their first year at school. It is stage during which a child is ready and is able to start reading properly and it is a time when reading may take off in a rush, given adequate practice and help. (Andrew and Penny Stanway, 1983).

Reading is very highly a perceptual process, involving discrimination among visual forms (letters) and co-ordination of information from two senses hearing and sight (Helen Bee, 1985).

Reading readiness means gaining meaning from the printed words, and learning the relationship between written symbols and spoken sounds (White and White, 1980).

Readiness for Writing

Writing readiness is developed by means of a large number of activities involving paper and pencil spontaneous drawing, copying, tracing, fitting and completing.

Children often begin writing in Kindergarten by learning to write their names. The beginnings of letter-writing actually start even earlier. Children in pre-primary schools have experiences in using crayons and paint brushes.

Children can be provided with pencils in the pre-primary school for both drawing and beginning writing. They can be helped in informal situations to make the strokes which include the circle and the horizontal, vertical and slant strokes.

For writing readiness, we need the eye-hand co-ordination and sustained muscle effort. The process of writing implies finer muscular readiness. It implies the development of small muscle control eye span and the eye-hand co-ordination, so that children are able to use their physical skills in written expression.

The physical growth of children should be taken into consideration in planning the programme of handwriting instruction. The growth patterns of children as they relate to handwriting may be briefly summarized as follows:

1. Handedness has usually been established between ages five and seven. Most children in this age group, have not fully developed co-ordination of the smaller muscles of the hands and fingers. Some irregularities in handwriting may be expected, and standards should not be unreasonably high.

Frequent use of large areas, such as the chalkboard permits use of the better co-ordinated large muscles.

2. Co-ordination of smaller muscles has improved by the time the child reaches the ages of eight to ten. Writing is reduced in size and it becomes more uniform in quality.
3. By the end of the elementary school years, the average child can produce handwriting of good quality at an acceptable rate of speed.

Children who get a good start in reading usually show a keen interest in writing. By the time, the child reaches four or six years of age, activities for the development of readiness for writing should be introduced. The process of writing implies finer muscular co-ordination, eye-hand co-ordination through activities to drawing of straight lines, curves, joining dotted lines.

Arithmetic Readiness

Learning number concept is a difficult task for the child. The child is not ready to learn numbers until he is 6 years old. But he can be prepared for learning number by such activities as number games. Number concepts are introduced to children through concrete objects, like models, pictures, objects etc.

Words relating to numbers are used soon after the child starts to speak. This early use of number words, is merely a form of "Parrot Speech" without giving real meaning to the numbers they repeat.

Young children's concepts of number above ten are generally vague and confused example they often think of 100 and 1000 as similar.

Important aspect in arithmetic readiness is matching identical shapes to know that it is necessary to recognise how things are alike and how they are different. This helps the child to learn to match identical objects.

Activities for development of Reading, Writing and Arithmetic

Activities that we provide in pre-primary school could promote the readiness for reading, writing and arithmetic:

Reading Readiness

Providing opportunities to children for free conversation, for listening, the recorded programmes of songs, stories, dramas etc. Participation in story telling both listening and repeating, dramatization etc; and recitating rhymes will promote readiness for reading. Giving opportunities to handle the books promotes eye-hand co-ordination and thus promotes readiness for reading.

Writing Readiness

Introduction of activities pertaining to drawing of straight lines and curves joining the dots and filling the gaps facilitate the skill of writing at a later stage.

As the children have to learn to hold the pencil, crayons and brushes, art activities like easel painting, finger painting, crayoning, writing in the sand, clay modelling, tracing, cutting and pasting of various shapes should be introduced, to promote readiness for writing in the pre-schools.

Larger area or papers should be provided for drawing, tracing and painting, so that they can move their hand freely.

Arithmetic Readiness

Telling children the concept of a circle, square etc; asking children to name some of the objects having different shapes, cutting paper in different sizes and shapes, giving coloured balls to the children and asking children to match the colour, serial counting, counting beads, matching and naming shapes and sizes and singing number songs will promote the readiness for arithmetic.

The teacher should identify a number of activities and create programmes of her own to help the children to be ready for formal instruction when they enter the primary school system.

The teacher could also introduce numbers while taking attendance in the class. Children could be encouraged to have concrete meaning every child present and the child who is absent. Similarly, number games could also be introduced to make them identify and count.

Pre-primary school programme thus could play a vital role in promoting the readiness for learning 3 Rs—Reading, Writing and Arithmetic through concrete activities.

25

Nature Walk

Nature walk helps children to get direct experiences. Nature walks should be given as much importance as the other programmes in the pre-primary school. Children enjoy going around rather setting in one place or inside the school. Hence the Nature walks help children to know about the flora and fauna; and makes them acceptable to new situation. Nature walks give chances to children to involve in several activities which help them to know the social surroundings and to make them good citizens. Nature walks give chance to see, hear, feel, touch and taste several things. Nature walk is a planned activity which gives a chance, relief and happiness to the children. Children start having a love for nature.

Places Suitable for Nature Walk

Nature walks depend on financial position, transport facilities, total number of children and their age. Children in rural areas can go to gardens dairy farms, poultry farms, spinning and weaving mills. If a rural school has enough finance and transport facilities, the children can go to near by bus stand, railway station, post office, police station, zoo, parks and markets.

Children of urban areas can make a trip to rural areas to see the rural beauty. Urban children can visit the very important industries, radio station, T.V. station, shops, hospital and zoo.

Stages of Nature Walk or Field Trips

There are four stages in nature walk, (*a*) Planning, (*b*) Preparation, (*c*) Execution, and (*d*) Evaluation.

Planning

The teacher and her pre-primary school children have to know the aim of the nature walk of trip clearly. Trips should be made only after the teacher has clearly in her mind the reasons for taking the trip and feels that the trip offers the most effective method of helping the children to develop certain understandings and appreciations and to acquire certain knowledge and facts. A time table should be prepared for their programme. While planning the teacher has to consider the following: (*a*) Starting time, (*b*) Mode of transport, (*c*) Safety of children, (*d*) Children's need, (*e*) Food, (*f*) Enough money, (*g*) Boarding place, (*h*) Places of visit and its time. Planning is a primary stage of field trip.

Preparation

After planning the teacher has to get the prior permission from the parents and the owner of the visiting places. The teacher has to inform the owner about the children's age, experience and expectations. So that the owner of the visiting place could make needed preparations. Prior visit by the teacher is important to make sure of gaining a lot for children and to attain the needed objectives.

If a trip is too long, the teacher has to arrange transport facilities. If it too short they can go by walk with the help of the staff and with their parents.

Execution

It is the third stage after planning and preparation. The teacher has to induce the children to raise the questions about what they see. The teacher and the guide have to answer suitably and clearly and satisfy their curiosity.

(*a*) *Obtain administrative permission*. Investigate school policies covering field trips and observe these in planning for the trip.

(*b*) *Obtain written permission of the parents*: It is important, to notice parents of each trip away from school. Such notice helps parents to understand the value of the trip and to know the details involved which may influence the clothing which the child wears that day, and the schedule for bringing and picking the child.

(c) *Visit site before taking children*: This is essential in order to determine whether or not the site is appropriate and can fulfil the purposes of the trip. Safety hazards should be noted. Talk with adults who will serve as guide and talk with the children.

(d) *Arrange transportation*: When private cars are used, be sure that the parents have adequate liability insurance. Two adults should be in the car, one in back seat another in front seat. The number of children per car should be limited so that there is room for each child to sit. If the group is walking, the number of adults will vary with the age of the children. With three-year-olds there should be at least one adult for every two children. For four-three should be at least two adults for every five or six children.

(e) *Invite parents to assist*: Select parents whose presence in the school situation does not overstimulate their own child. In order to help the adult "keep up with" the children assigned to her, each child might have a name tag, the colour of the children's tag matching the colour of the tag worn by the adult. Discuss with the parents the purposes of the trip.

(f) *Plan with the children*: Talk about what we hope to see, to observe, to learn. Be sure that they know why they are taken out. Count the children before leaving school and frequently during the trip.

(g) *Evaluate the experience*: Variety is needed here. Too often the group only discusses the trip of paints, pictures about it. Although pre-primary school children do not read or write about the trip, the comment reflects the child's reaction to the exclusive use of one type of evaluation.

Nature walk or field trip has immense value in the life of the child. Child's curiosity to know the world around could be satisfied by taking it out. Child enjoys free and fresh air freedom to roam about and have first hand experiences. Trips need not be costly or time consuming. A resourceful teacher will make use of the farm around, the markets, bus stand, railway station, dairy and poultry farm etc. to give first hand information to her children.

26

Festivals in the Pre-Primary School

The pre-primary school is a home away from home for young children. It should stimulate all round development of a child. The activities in the pre-school should help the children to understand the outside world through its activities and it also helps them to know how to adjust with the society. Celebrations of festivals in a pre-school is one of the major activities which enables them to develop an awareness of the world around them, and the customs and traditions of the people in the world.

Objectives of Celebrating Festivals

Celebrating festivals in the pre-primary school builds up better home school relationship, as certain festivals form recognition and extension of home environment. All festivals are not celebrated at home, whereas in a pre-primary school, all festivals are celebrated. They give an opportunity to participate at home. Festivals are celebrated in pre-schools to understand and keep up our cultural heritage and values, at the same time to develop a desire to understand the culture of others and respect them.

Celebration of different religious festivals, builds a sense of tolerance and acceptance of various forms of worship. Through this, children come to generalise that basically people are the same besides the religious differences. Celebration of national festivals impart national spirit in children and builds a sense of patriotism. It provides an opportunity to explain the meaning and significance of the festival.

Celebration provides fun, enjoyment, pleasure and relaxation. It reduces the monotony of life as celebration of the festival makes the day different and breaks the routine. Children learn to work in groups to complete a task at hand, while celebrating a festival. This promotes a feeling of co-operation and a desire to complete a task.

Kinds of Festivals

Different types of festivals are being celebrated throughout the year in our country. They are festivals at the time of prosperity and even at the time of famine. Our country celebrates festivals to thank the nature and God. There are festivals to develop the feeling of patriotism and to keep up our cultural heritage and values. Thus the festivals could be classified into three types such as Seasonal festivals, Religious festivals and National festivals.

Seasonal Festivals

Festivals are being celebrated according to the changes in nature. There are festivals like, Pongal, Onam and Holy, celebrated after the harvest is over to thank God and nature. Chaitra Full Moon Day is being celebrated at the time of changes in the season. Before the farmers start farming, they celebrate Adi festival to invoke the Nature to help them in farming.

Religious Festival

The birth of Lord Krishna and Lord Muruga, are being celebrated as Krishna Jeyanthi and Karthigai. The birth of Jesus Christ, Mohammed and other religious leaders are celebrated in the pre-primary school to help them understand their preaching and significance. Celebration of Diwali, Navarathri etc. also makes the children feel happy and enjoy the occasion.

National Festivals

Independence day, Republic day, birth and death days of national leaders are being celebrated in pre-primary schools. In addition to that, the days of soldiers who sacrificed their lives in the freedom struggle is also celebrated to salute the departed souls as a mark of respect. This promotes patriotism among children. The days of important writers and poets who were responsible for registering the feeling of oneness in the minds of people through their writing, is also celebrated in the pre-primary school.

Methods of celebrating Festivals

Celebration of festivals in a pre-primary school is not only a fun. When the festivals are celebrated in the pre-primary schools, we must bear in mind why do we celebrate a particular festivals and how to ensure objectives of celebration. The children should also have the pleasure of planning and working out the mode of celebration themselves. It should not be done by the teacher alone. A joint planning helps the children to take up the responsibilities which promotes leadership qualities in them. All religious festivals should be celebrated in pre-primary schools. Because religious festivals are celebrated by the people who follow that religion, others do not celebrate at home. So pre-primary school is the place where they can see and participate along with children from various religious and share their joy and happiness. It gives opportunity to the children to understand the significance of celebrating religious functions.

Children should participate in the function in every action from planning for celebration and to the end of the function. The children should be encouraged to take active part in the celebration so that they understand their responsibilities also. The teacher should be well informed, creative and co-operate with the children and show enthusiasm in celebrating the festival.

In short celebrations of festival in pre-primary schools make the children familiar with some of the best tradition of the past. They help the children to be secure, imaginative, creative and enable them to take the first step towards a reverent and appreciation of the glories of the past. They stimulate wholesome feeling, and give children an opportunity to express their emotions beautifully in marching, dancing and singing.

As the children grow elder, a study of the history of these festivals and the different ways of celebrating them, leads not only to a study of the lives and customs of other people, but also gives them the glimpses of the spiritual life. Celebration of these festivals, lights, teaches the continuality of history, the oneness of the race of the brotherhood of mankinds. It is therefore suggested that celebration of festivals should become an integral part of the pre-primary school curriculum.

27

Activities

1. Identify the curriculum followed in different system of pre-primary schools.
2. Choose specific themes and write programme for a week and lesson for a day.
3. Write outdoor activities suitable for 3-4 years old children.
4. Observe the common play habits and the speech pattern of the children of 4-5 year old and prepare a language curriculum for them.
5. Collect stories suitable for children of various age groups.
6. Prepare aids for story telling.
7. Learn to tell stories to children.
8. Collect rhymes suitable for young children and maintain a book of rhymes.
9. Learn to sing and teach action songs.
10. Write rhymes for pre-primary schoolers.
11. Make low-cost musical instruments to be used by pre-primary schoolers.
12. Prepare a list of creative activities suitable for various age groups in the pre-primary school.
13. Write the values of each activity and materials needed.
14. Collect samples of creative activities done by children in the pre-primary school and prepare an album.
15. Choose a story and make your pre-primary school children enact it.
16. Identify the type of roles the children play in the pre-primary school Dolls' corner.
17. Prepare list of equipment and other materials required for creative drama.

18. Prepare a list of Science experiences for various age groups in pre-primary school.
19. Maintain a record of Science experiences, materials required, methods and values.
20. Introduce Science experiences which you have identified and find out their relevance and suitability to the pre-schoolers.
21. Prepare a list of places where pre-primary schoolers can be taken for field trip, around your place.
22. Arrange for a trip to a railway station, during your teaching practice period.
23. Choose a topic under social study experiences and make the pre-primary school children learn the different concept in it.
24. Prepare a list of topics for pre-primary schoolers.
25. Find out the local festivals that are celebrated and the mode of celebration.
26. Find out the significance of celebrating each festival.
27. Make children prepare greeting cards and gifts for exchange among themselves and others.
28. Make a collection of books under the classification of children's literature and provide facilities for your pre-primary school children to read them.
29. Choose few books for children and review them.
30. Prepare a readiness kit.
31. Test the activities and the materials prepared by a group of pre-primary schoolers.

28

Learning through Play

Play is an integral part of the life of any child. Play is a non-serious and self-contained activity engaged for the sheer satisfaction it brings to children. For an adult, play may be just a time filler or a recreation, to a child play is a serious business. By engaging in this serious business, he develops his mind and body, integrating social and emotional functions and the intellectual functions of thinking, reasoning, problem solving, talking and imagining.

Play differs from work which is an actively towards on and in which the individual carry out the activity not because he wants the end result. Piaget describes play as a form of adaptation through assimilation. Indeed the principle business of childhood, it is the vehicle of improvisation and combination, the first carrier of rule systems through which a world of cultural restraints replaces the operation of childish impulses (Burner, 1975). In play there is a realization of effort; a child exercises, solidifies and extends reaction patterns that have emerged during the course of his development. In play situation, the child decides his own action and becomes aware that every object and action has a meaning.

Play satisfies the individual's urge for a freedom of action. It is an expression of the creative activities of the child. It is marked by freedom and joy. Play cultivates human values in children. It is very necessary for the growth and maturation of the physical and mental powers of the child. Just as a poet cannot restraint himself from writing a poem, or a musician from singing, so too the child cannot restrain himself from play.

Play for a child under three is a serious game. Serious play for a very young child means that he plays without reporting the imaginary situation from the real one. From the child's points of view the best definition of play is 'The way a child learns what no one else can teach him' (Matterson, 1977).

In play situations he imitates, repeats, explores, experiments and as his memory capacity develops he is able to make judgements and categorizes what he knows. Through play, opportunities are provided to related the words to something concrete, see, hear, smell, taste on experience right at this minute. For children and young people play is an expression of their desire to make their own discoveries in their own time and at their own pace (Lady Allen, 1971).

Theories of Play

There are many theories of play, as to the origin, purpose and function of play. They are grouped into psychogenic and sociogenic theories. The psychogenic theory stresses the fact that in play, the child uses former experiences and networks them or assimilates them. The sociogenic theory focuses on the role of novel responses as preparation for future adaptation. Play performs both functions.

Role of Play in development of the Child

Play is especially important for physical, motor, emotional, cognitive, social and personality development during the pre-school years. Through the use of toys and games, youngsters learn about each other and how to have interpersonal relationships. Children who do not have opportunities to play with age mates miss a vital social learning experience; as a result they may be slower than other children to become confident and surc of themselves in relation to people outside their family. Being away from home for brief periods to meet and play with new companions is a good preparation for the school years to come (David and Weiner, 78). Those who have rarely been away from their parents' side may find the transition to pre-primary school and the first grade a source of considerable anxiety.

Play increases, bodily functions; play is a form of exploration of oneself and of one's world. He manipulates objects and finds out the reality through play. Play is essential to physical growth in terms of a child's increasing awareness of his bodily functions. Through play the child reaches out into the widening world of intellect, and emotions. Play is the source of development and creates the zone of proximal development and physical space. Active play also acts as an outlet for the surplus energy, which is pent up, makes the child tense, nervous and irritable. Play is also a muscle builder; helps in developing better motor co-ordination.

Play Socialises

Play is a socialising force in the lives of young children. It promotes better social adjustment, co-operation and adaptation. They play in group and help the child to develop feelings of sympathy and understanding. Play is the best way to help the child adjust to the society in which he lives, his group, family and himself. By playing with other children, the child learns to establish social relationships and how to meet and solve the problems such relationships raise. Children learn to play the game fairly, how to lose with grace, how to win without arrogance, how to take criticism, how to submerge personal wishes in the interest of others, how to be loyal to one another and how to be part of a team. Imaginative play is important in the development of social competence. It permits the children to practise their own future roles as well as to play fully the roles and feelings of others.

Play promotes Concepts

Play has got educational value. While playing with toys and play equipment child learns the shape, size, colour numbers and the qualities of objects as well as their significance and also the textures of objects. As the age increases he is able to explore the physical and the natural world understands their significance. It increases the child's ability to deal with different situations and solve problems more efficiently and effectively.

Play is stimulating and pleasurable, because it is a way of satisfying an exploratory drive. Exploratory drive involves a need for new experiences and information and a curiosity about objects and events. As the children grow order and are able to process information more effectively they enjoy increasingly complex, novel and incongrous objects and situations for play. If an object is too simple or too familiar it does not give the child a sense of discovery and he becomes bored. If it is too difficult, he becomes frustrated, stressed and learning is not facilitated (Maris and Parke, 1979). Early opportunity to play has got a long-term effect on the child's cognitive and personality development. Pre-school children who are active explorers later curious, adventurers, independent and creative in the elementary school years.

A very young child tends to gratify his desires immediately through the medium of play activities. Experiments show that the development of play is arrested both in intellectually underdeveloped children and in those with an immature affective sphere (Vygotshy, L.S.). In play the child creates an imaginary situation. From the point of view of development, the fact of creating an imaginary situation is an intellectual activity. Wherever there are imaginary situations we observe rules and regulations. At the end of development the child starts applying the rules and regulations to real situations. Thus, the child learns the proper rules and regulations in the society at the same time his role in the society.

Play to learn Language

Play situations, play materials and objects help to promote the language development of children which is essential for cognitive development. In young children there is an intimate fusion between word and object. In the pre-primary school age, we first find a divergence between the fields of meaning and vision. In play, a child deals with things as having meaning, word meanings, replace object, and thus an emancipation of word from objects occur.

It is incorrect to conceive of play as activity without purpose; it is a purposeful activity for a child. In atheletic games you can win or lose, in a race you can come first or last. Thus, the purpose decides the game-purpose as the ultimate goal which determines the child's affective attitude to play. While running a race, a child can be highly agitated, distressed and little may remain of pleasure because he finds it physically painful to run, while he is overtaken he will experience little functional pleasure.

Play to release Emotional Tension

Play has the repentic value. Play could be used in number of ways and situations as a therapeutic measure which would help the children release their emotional tensions. In every day life, the child faces problems and tensions as a result of the rules and regulations imposed on him. In these situations, play becomes a vent to release his tensions and thus be relieved of. Play also permits the child to solve some of his emotional problems to learn to cope with anxiety and inner conflicts in a non-threatening situation. Play also provides a basis for meeting child's needs and desires which otherwise cannot be met. Children's peer interactions have been found to play an important role in the development of self-control and in working through or modifying problem behaviour in children.

Children who are undergoing psychological stress due to separation of their parents show a marked rigidity in imaginative play. They have fewer characters in play and are more bound to objects in play. They are less able to free themselves from reality. They rarely fantasize completely imaginary objects or people. They also show less diversity in both themes and affect. In disturbed children we could also observe that they are always pre-occupied with aggression and inability to assume the role of providing or caring for others in imaginative play. Children who show spontaneous imagination in play are likely to show a broader range of emotions and more positive emotions than less imaginative children. They smile more, be curious and interested in new experiences and express joy in peer relations (Singer, 1977).

Development of Play at different Age Levels

In the sensory motor stage the play is very simple. He is interested in his own body. There are random movements and stimulations of sensory organs. He is helpless, cannot do anything of his own. He has to relay on what others do for him. If his mother sings and talks to him, gradually gives him suitable play materials, provides opportunities to see, handle the objects and given encouragement he is off to an excellent start. At this stage he is not able to start learning about speed, distance, space, size etc., as he not yet able to use his body to find out for himself.

All babies need play materials and toys which are safe for them to handle. They such, chew, bring the toys near eyes, let the play things fall; they fall on to them in their play process. Hence, dangerous objects should be avoided. A good amount of well selected equipments encourage the child to be resourceful and social. Due to differences in intelligence, interest and many other factors, a child needs the type of play and play equipment, that will fit his needs. Play activities are also equally significant for the rapidly growing healthy youngsters. Suitable play things are those which give experience of colours, materials, textures, shapes, sounds and which encourage the development of motor and manipulative skills.

The next state is from mobility to walking. In this stage, the child starts moving about and exploring the space around him by crawling.

Bright colour balls, moving toys, pull and push toys, hammer, pegs etc., are much useful to this age group of children. He begins to learn more about how near and far objects are that he can crawl into a large box or under dining table but not into a small one or under a low table. He also starts learning cause and effect a little.

Toddlers (15-24 months) to 3 Years

The non-walker starts in this stage. He thinks once he can stand he can see more, reach more, use both hands more freely and once he can walk again gives him more scope for reaching, seeing, doing and thereby learning. During this period hand and eye co-ordination improves and manipulative skill is promoted. Big crayons and brushes, building block, large pieces puzzles, push and pull toys, dolls old clothes to dress up, hammering board, large sized picture books etc., are the best play and learning materials at this stage. The child could also be encouraged to play outside with sand, water, etc. They are interested in anything and everything but only for a short spell at a tune. They are easily distracted and quickly bored, because at this stage learning is wide rather than deep gathering information rather than understanding it.

Three to Four Years

Children of this age could be easily cope up with than the previous age groups. He can concentrate for little longer, has more skill, knowledge and can wait a little while for the help he needs, can play along side with other children without getting into many difficulties. He wishes to please others, as he enjoys praise and approval. This is a good training period because he is suggestable and co-operative. Boys and girls watch both father and mother equally and imitate them without sex difference. At this stage they can manage themselves without the mother.

At this stage as the children start walking and running with a curiosity to explore they need more space, more and larger play equipment. From the stage of playing along side other children a child will progress to combining activities almost accidentally with another child who is playing with the same materials, moving on to positively enjoying a joint game. Thus, there a more from parallel play to associative play begins at this stage and moves on to playing in small groups.

The child at this stage develops a wide vocabulary, learns to use it, learns more about colours, sizes, weights and textures, enjoys and remembers stories and learns to use all the raw materials more efficiently; skillfully on a tricycle. This is a very happy, busy, productive year. Although the whole pre-school period is important as laying the foundation for later development, this is the first stage in which outside agencies can make up for deficiencies in the home situation as they are more independent now.

Four to Five Years

The child at this stage still watches, listens and imitates but also can think of an idea and carry over interest in a game, start a game from where he left off instead of going back to the beginning. He can play with a group of children and benefit from their ideas and learns to lead a group and to be led, to play different roles, and accept a different status at different times. He has self-confidence and very competent within the limitations what he is allowed to do. His language develops very rapidly provided there is some concrete experience of situation associated with them. The adults are necessary to provide and structure internal, to add to an extra dimension to an activity and to encourage and stimulate conversation and communication. If a child does not go to a pre-school he had to entirely depend on the home, the parents and the experimental content provided by them.

Five to Seven Years

This group is content to play with all the materials they used before they went to school in more advanced and complicated manner. School children come home tired and seem to need to regress to the play behaviour of 2 or 3 years of age. They are influenced a good deal by what other children have and do. That means what the child is doing have been decided by child himself, rather than parent doing the thinking, deciding and providing. If there is parent involvement in school, the task becomes easier at the same time demanding. They can supplement and complement if they know the experiences provided in the school.

TYPES OF PLAY

There are sensory motor play, social play, constructive or creative play, imaginative play, adventure play and play which leads pre-skills. As it has been discussed already these plays occur at different ages. When children are one to two year old engage themselves in solitary play, sit with some toy and play alone; the 2 to 3 years old play side by side, but do not mix with each other—called the parallel play; the 3 to 4 start playing with another child—the associative play; 4 to 5 years old children play in small group following the rules and regulations of the game. As the age increases their involvement in co-operative, group play also increases.

Infants involve themselves in sensory motor play much. Pre-school age children participate in explorative and social play. They are also interested in constructive and imaginative makes believe plays, which lead to cognitive development and become pre-learning experience.

Factors Influencing Play

All the children do not play alike. There are individual differences which could be observed in the play patterns of children. When we analyse the causes for these differences it could be due to the health of the child, his motor development, intelligence, sex, tradition, season, environment, amount of leisure time available, play equipments and objects, encouragement provided by the adults and opportunities to play.

Healthy children play more than the sickly children. Healthy child releases its surplus energy through play. Motor development of a child determines the type of play in which he will engage himself. Poor motor co-ordination makes it difficult for a child to engage in running, jumping, throwing, catching, threading, etc. Bright and intelligent children are more active and participate in more imaginative and constructive play as compared to a dull child. Girls mostly engage themselves in make lecture play whereas boys in constructive and adventurous play. Culture and the tradition make the children play the games which are specific to those. Seasons of the year decide the type of play. For example, kite flying when there is wind. Children in town and urban areas engage in sophisticated games whereas the children in rural areas engage themselves in simple traditional games. Amount and type of equipment and toys available also decides the type of play of children. If they get plenty and variety of equipment the type of play will be according to that. For example, availability of blocks, clay etc., encourages constructive plays. A Doll's corner encourages dramatic, imaginative and fantasy play.

Conclusion

From the above discussion it could firmly be said that children could learn a lot through play experience provided at home and in pre-primary schools, especially during the early years of a child's life. It is important to note that not all of these play patterns are equally popular at all times during the early childhood years. Toys for example, become increasingly unimportant as early childhood draws to a close. And interest in games increases as early childhood comes to an end and becomes one of the dominant play interest of late childhood. Hence, providing a conducive atmosphere where a child will find the possibility of exploring, constructing, manipulating and imagining is a prime task of the adults.

Part III

Administration and Organization of Pre-primary School

29

Administration and Organization of Pre-Primary School

One of the primary objectives of administration in any organization is that co-ordinating the efforts of people towards the achievement of goals. In pre-primary school administration the primary aim has to do with the improvement of physical conditions, teaching and learning atmosphere and all the activities of the school administrator must be directed towards this end.

According to Luther H. Grulick and L. Urwick, "Administration has to do with getting things done with the accomplishment of the defined objectives. The science of administration is thus the system of knowledge whereby man may understand relationships, predict results and influence outcomes in any situation where men are organized at work together for a common purpose.

Effective administration depends on proper organization. An effective organization must have clearly defined goals and purposes. An organization should maintain an effective machinery for planning and decision-making. There should be short and long range plans aimed at accomplishing the specific objectives and general aims of the establishment. If an organization is to make satisfactory progress, it should develop an objective means of periodically evaluating its own programmes and policies in order to ascertain to what extent it is achieving its aims.

The operational areas of a pre-primary school administration may be loosely classified as follows:

(*a*) Curriculum development and programme of instruction.
(*b*) Children enrolment.

(*c*) Staff personnel.
(*d*) School Community relationships.
(*e*) Equipment and physical facilities.
(*f*) Records and reports.
(*g*) Finance.

If the administrator is to carry out the above tasks satisfactorily, there must be some sort of formal organization of areas of responsibility. In a typical pre-primary school the head will delegate tasks and responsibilities in lessening the degrees of importance to his deputy, the academic departmental heads, prefects, members of house, class and games organizations, clubs and societies. All of these organizations will facilitate the accomplishment of the objectives and goals of the institution. Since a school is a complex organization authority and responsibility will have to be delegated; the school head cannot possibly do everything alone. Yet it will often be necessary for officers to whom responsibilities are delegated to report directly to the administrative head.

Administration of pre-primary school can be diagramatically represented.

Management of Pre-Primary School

Objectives	Programmes	Resources
Philosophy	Curriculum	Equipment
	Activities	Physical set up
	Relationship with Parents and Community	Records

In next chapter, the learners is exposed to the above said different components of administration, organization of a pre-primary school centre. Physical aspect—the Pre-primary School Building, Playground, Play equipment, Furniture purchase, use and their stage; Records and reports to be maintained in a pre-primary school, their purpose; Teaching personnels—the teacher, her qualities, her role in running a pre-primary school; Teacher education programme for pre-primary schools; pre-school education and community—the parents working with them; Agencies in India which work for the welfare of the children; Nutrition and the nutritional requirements of pre-school, Deficiency diseases find among the pre-schoolers, common ailments in pre-school children and prevention etc., are being dealt in this paper.

30

Building and Equipment for Pre-Primary School

A pre-primary school is an institution which plays a vital role in physical and mental development of children. The physical set up of a pre-primary school—the building and equipment influences the human relationships in the school. It provides proper facilities which the children are deprived of at home and thus produces a good citizen. The pre-primary school must be a human relations laboratory. The successful functioning of a pre-primary school depends on its building and equipment to provide various opportunities and a good environment for learning.

The Pre-Primary School Building

The pre-primary school building is an important factor in determining the learning possibilities within a school. A well planned building makes supervision easy. A good deal of thought should be given to its planning. There are references available which describe functionally designed schools. A free flow of play between indoors and outdoors enables children to have more contacts with each other and to satisfy a greater variety of play interests. There are other less obvious ways in which the building which affect the behaviour of the people in it. Attractive, pleasing colour and the adequate space areas, sound proof if possible earning satisfaction to the users.

Selection of Site

Set up of a pre-primary school is very important. A pre-primary school should not be located in a congested or lonely area. If it is situated in a crowded area, the attention of the children would be diverted from doing activities or listening to the teacher. There would be a lot of disturbances including loud noise. If a pre-primary school is situated in a lonely area, the children are deprived of safety and proper homely environment. If it is a busy traffic area, they lose their safety. Hence it is necessary to be careful while selecting the site for a pre-primary school.

A pre-primary school building should be situated at the centre of the town so as to provide easy accessibility to all. The school should be away from traffic area to avoid accidents. It must be seen that the surrounding area should be clean. In an unhygienic area, children's health may be affected. If it is a town area, pre-primary school building should not be constructed near a factory or railway way and bus stand. As far as possible it should be away from industrial area. The foul from the factories may affect the children's health and mind. In a rural area, the building should be away from well and stream.

Structure of Building

A pre-primary school building must look pleasing and appealing to the children with proper facilities. Toilet facilities should be attached to the building. The building should also contain rooms for washing, sleeping and playing. Proper bathroom facilities could help to develop sense of hygiene in children. All these rooms should be easily accessible to children. The appearance of the building should be such to create self-confidence in children. Children will feel if the area is a larger one. Provision of space for each child should be minimum of 35 sq. feet.

Storage space must be properly planned. In the classroom, shelves for children should not be very high but should be easily accessable to the children, to take their things. The lock and key should be handled by the children themselves. This will promote self-help. A pre-primary school building should be planned on the basis of the teacher-pupil ratio. It is best to have 1:20.

The building should be attractive in colour and thus inviting the children. The building should inspire happiness, peace of mind and mental satisfaction to children. There must be a special sick room for children who fall ill at school. This arrangement will protect other children from contagious diseases. The doors of the toilet should be made such that the children should find it easier to open and close the doors.

The building should be constructed in such a way that there is enough space for the sunlight to enter in. The sunlight makes the children active and provides energy to their eyes. It should be well ventilated for proper circulation of air.

DIFFERENT AREAS IN A PRE-PRIMARY SCHOOL BUILDING

As there are different activities in which the pre-primary schoolers are involved there should be different area or corner for each one of these activities, so that children could go and play in these areas according to their interest and ability without disturbing other children and without being disturbed by others.

Small group activity area

This is the activity of explaining and demonstrating some points. Here attention of the children is very important for this activity. So the place should be peaceful and should not distract the attention of children.

Large group activity area

This activity is to be spacious enough for playing, dancing, exercizing and drilling.

Book area (Library)

Library should be located near the small group activity area, because library should be very calm. It should be provided with small chairs, small shelves and small tables which make the children to help themselves in book area.

Building Block Area

In this arca, blocks of various types and various sizes are provided. This activity develops creativity among children and concentration.

Manipulative toys and equipment area

This area is to be divided into sub-areas. Separate place should be allotted for keeping toys apart from other playing materials. Movable toys and immovable toys have to be kept in separate shelves.

Imaginative play area

In this area, several type of dresses, medical equipments' shop's equipments, dresses of drivers, and police equipments are provided. This creates imaginative tendency among children.

Arts and creative area

Paints, brushes, drawing equipments, papers, scissors, clay and gum are kept in this area to the imaginative power and this activity enriches their mental calibre.

Science area

Science area is purposively arranged to quench scientific thirst of children. Here pet animals, birds, scientific equipments, models, specimens, plants and flowers are kept. Here the teacher show them some simple experiments to the children.

Display area

Here things which are created or prepared by the children are displayed. Parents of the children will come and see the creative work of their children and appreciate them. This motivate the children to do some creative activities.

Special activity area

Here, testing material, tape recorders, record players, and radios are kept. It is a laboratory area where the teacher conducts the psychoanalysis test for the children to know their mental calibre.

Other activity area

It is the place where the children can take their food and rest.

EQUIPMENT FOR PRE-PRIMARY SCHOOL

In a pre-primary school, the teacher should be very particular about furniture. The furniture should be lightly painted in bright colours and suitable to the size of the children. It should be light enough for the children to carry individually from one place to another.

Factors to be considered while selecting the play equipment for Pre-primary School Children

The following factors are to be kept in mind while selecting the equipment for pre-primary school age children:

1. Age level of children.
2. Should be light and sturdy.
3. Attractive.
4. Long lasting.
5. Easy to maintain.
6. Less costly.
7. Made of indigeneous materials.
8. Should promote resourcefulness and imagination of children.
9. Total number of children in each class.
10. Location of the school (Rural or Urban).
11. Type of pre-primary school programme and its philosophy.
12. Expectations of parents.
13. Should be easily available.
14. Safety with regard to the materials used—the colour and the paints used; should not be sharp so that children may not get hurt while playing.
15. Should have multiple usc.
16. Should be of varied in shapes, colours and size and be challenging to children of different age groups.
17. Should have some educational value.

TYPES OF EQUIPMENT

The play equipment can be classified as indoor equipments and outdoor equipments. Further classification could be made as equipment for motor development, equipment for creativity, equipment for intelligence and equipment for promoting imagination.

Outdoor Play

The usefulness of outdoor play is not only restricted to play with large equipment but also helps to learn about nature and satisfy his curiosity about the moving world of living creatures and provides an opportunity to collect various kinds of things for his creative play. The outdoor play aids the child with growth and physical control as the child can climb, balance, swing, run, jump. The activity aids large muscle build up and stimulate the mental activity. The physical development helps the child to gain ability and confidence.

Factors to be kept in mind for Outdoor activity

Space is very important for the children to play outside of the classroom. Following factors are to be kept in mind while allotting space to conduct outdoor activity.

(*a*) A 120 sq. feet for children is needed per pre-primary school to conduct outdoor activity.
(*b*) A balance of space in the sun and shade.
(*c*) Ward surface area where when toys can be used and balls bounced.
(*d*) A grassy plot for playing, running and rolling.
(*e*) A corner for pets, garden and digging.
(*f*) A sandpit for sand play and manipulative activity.
(*g*) A space for water play.

Stationary equipment

(*a*) Swing
(*b*) Slide
(*c*) Jungle gym
(*d*) Merry go round
(*e*) Sand pit
(*f*) Sea saw

Movable equipmment

(*a*) Balancing Board
(*b*) Ladder

(*c*) Wheel toys
(*d*) Rocking toys
(*e*) Balls and bats
(*f*) Skipping rope
(*g*) Teniquiot
(*h*) Tricycle

Indoor Play

Indoor play provides the child with emotional and social satisfaction. Infants see and feel the world through plays. While selecting the equipments the teacher has to consider age, sex and capacity of the children. Indoor play stimulates the power of imagination for creative expression. Indoor and outdoor play could be either individual or organised. Through individual play, the child learns to assume responsibility for his own actions to respect others, to use materials, wisely and to develop moral and spiritual values. Individual activity provides the child with opportunities to become independent and to realise his potentialities and capabilities.

1. Materials that encourage sensory and artistic development

(*a*) Rattle
(*b*) Tinker toys falt
(*c*) Train of wooden block looked together
(*d*) Stuffed animals (Soft toys)
(*e*) Nest of boxes and blocks
(*f*) Push and pull toys
(*g*) Black board
(*h*) Colour chalk
(*i*) Washable dolls
(*j*) Wooden beads
(*k*) Building box and blocks
(*l*) Picture puzzles
(*m*) Colour cone
(*n*) Picture lotto game
(*o*) Toys of plastic, rubber, cotton and wooden
(*p*) Sand tray
(*q*) Mechano

(*r*) Picture books
(*s*) Form board

2. Doll's Corner

Articles for imaginative role play

Animals, Traffic signal, Household articles, bed, cradle, dolls clothed etc.

Science Corner

Collection of leaves, shells, flowers, seeds, nuts, sticks, stones, magnet, magnifying glass, litmus paper, candles, dissolving materials, mirror etc.

Equipments for Music, Dancing and Dramatics

(*a*) Sticks
(*b*) Gramophone
(*c*) Records
(*d*) Mettallophones
(*e*) Nails
(*f*) Triangles
(*g*) Rattles
(*h*) Drums
(*i*) Whistles
(*j*) Tambourines
(*k*) Drum with bells
(*l*) Bells
(*m*) Flutes
(*n*) Pipes
(*o*) Puppet and puppet theatre
(*p*) Constumes for children for dramatisation.

Arrangement of equipment

Group play often depends on the way in which equipment is placed. Space in the doll corner encourages its use by more children and reduces the number of their conflicts. Two things of a kind such as two dolls or two telephones mean more social play. Storage space where the children themselves can reach the equipments offers opportunity for them to be independent and self-sufficient. Even the use of the wheel toys depend on the type of hard surface and the space available. These are the ways in which arrangement of equipments influence the children's behaviour.

Care of equipment

Pre-primary school children should be taught the simple rules to make them understand how to handle and take care of the equipments. First of all, the children should know how to turn the equipment on and turn it off when they use it. For example if the children turn the water tap on they should know how to turn it off after using it. If they turn the light on, they should know how to turn it off.

Learning such rules in a pre-primary school group is one of the best kinds of training. These would help the children to make use of the home appliances more effectively and less dangerously.

31

Cost Effective Play Equipment

Introduction

The play equipment described here can be prepared from locally available cheap materials. Only a very little carpentry work is involved in the preparation. Any teacher who has got a little taste for painting and appreciation of fine arts with imagination and resourcefulness would be able to prepare these equipments. They are very cheap as most of them are made up of waste materials.

	Materials Used	*Method of Using the Materials/Equipment*	*Educational Values*
1.	Household articles: 1. Wood, 2. Store, 3. Paints, 4. Clay, 5. Iron	The child learns cooking by using these household articles. The child imitates the orders in this activity.	The child's imaginative and creative powers are developed through these activities. The child is prepared for the future by involving in these activities. Certain Indian manners and cultures are learnt even at this very early years.
2.	Bucket: Tin and iron rod	The child easily carries the water and other things in the bucket.	Finer muscle co-ordination takes place. They are trained to carry the water. It is a preparation for future life and work. He explores and orients himself to the actual world of things.
3.	Basket: Coir Wire	The child carries the basket by holding the wire handle.	The child comes to know the usage of a basket. Balance is promoted. Finer muscle co-ordination takes place as he carries the basket. The mathematical concept of volume is realised by the child.
4.	Tanjore Doll: Clay	Slights pat or a knock at the Tanjore doll makes it move in a balanced way.	Child's curiosity as to why the doll does not fall flat is aroused. The child uses his brain to find out the

(Contd.)

(Contd.)

	Materials Used	Method of Using the Materials/Equipment	Educational Values
			mechanism that is involved in doll. It will be a play materials for the child. His aesthetic and intellectual capacity is enriched by these play materials.
5.	Wheel roller with a long handle: 1. Wood 2. Paints 3. Rattle	The child makes the roller run by pushing the long wooden handle forward and the rattle inside it produces a rhythmic sound.	As the child's body involves in this activity, it develops the motor skills and muscular co-ordination. The concept of 'space' is introduced by this roller. The child can know how much distance he has covered by using this roller.
6.	Roller: (1) Wire, (2) Wooden roller		
7.	Vilva or wood apple wheel cart: (1) Vilva fruit (2) Sticks	The child has to make the wheel roll on the floor by pushing with the long stick.	Physical and motor development are developed while the child is running with the cart. He learns the mechanism of a cart through his own experience. His intellectual and reasoning powers are developed through such activities.

(Contd.)

(*Contd.*)

	Materials Used	*Method of Using the Materials/Equipment*	*Educational Values*
8.	Top: (1) Wood, (2) Nail, (3) Thread	The thread is wound round on the top from the tip of the nail till the three-fourth of the top. The top is left on the floor by releasing the thread from the top. The top speedily rotates on the floor.	Finer muscle co-ordination takes place as the child reels the thread on the nail of the top. This play promotes physical growth and motor development. The child uses his intelligence when winding the thread on the top. Mastering this skill gives him great sense of achievement and happiness.
9.	Kavattai: (1) Wood, (2) Rubber strip, 3. Stone	The wood is shaped in a 'V' shape and the rubber strip is tied at the top of the 'V' shape Kavattai. A stone should be placed at the centre of the rubber strip and it should be forcely directed to the objects we want to shoot.	There is opportunity for large and fine muscle co-ordination aiming and shooting is a skill and the child develops this skill through this miniature gun.
10.	Kitty Pillai: (1) Long wooden stick (2) Little stick	Make a small pit on the floor and place the 'pillai', (the little wooden stick) on it. Give a stroke on the 'pillai' with the help of 'kitty' (the long wooden stick). The 'pillai' will rise from the earth and fall down on the earth at a distant. The distance	The abstract concept such as space and number are improved. While they measure the distance covered by the 'pillai' they count it in numbers. These concepts are the foundation for their subsequent study of mathematics and

(*Contd.*)

(*Contd.*)

Materials Used	*Method of Using the Materials/Equipment*	*Educational Values*
	between the original place of the 'pillai' and the later place after the stroke, should be measured by the 'kitty' (the long stick).	geography. The play also helps in physical development as it forms a sort of exercise of the child.
11. Musical instruments: (1) (a) Hollow bamboo stick	The child blows air through the axial, role of the bamboo flute and plays his fingers on the top holes.	The child develops listening skill and auditory discrimination. The child comes to know the range and flexibility of his voice. It promotes appreciation and enjoyment.
(2) Bamboo Whistle: (*a*) Bamboo stick, (*b*) Whistle made of tin	The child passes air through central hole of the bamboo stick.	The sound produced, has a high pitch than the harmonious sound of the flute. The child is able to differentiate between the low and high pitch sounds. He develops the concept of 'pitch' while practising these instruments. It encourages discrimination in the choice of music.
(3) Bamboo Musical Pipe : (a) Bamboo stick	The child passes air through the central hole of the musical pipe.	The sound produced is in a low pitch and the child is able to distinguish between the music produced by the musical pipe and that of the former two.

(*Contd.*)

(*Contd.*)

Materials Used	*Method of Using the Materials/Equipment*	*Educational Values*
(4) Bamboo Musical Instrument: Bamboo stick	They are five bamboo rods. Each one is attached in a regular order by thread. The child has to produce sound by striking each bamboo rod continuously with the help of a bamboo stick.	The child can distinguish between sounds. Each bamboo rod produces a particular sound and so there is a harmonious musical sound. His taste for music can be enriched by these play materials.
(5) Rattles (*a*) Dry Palmae leaf, (*b*) Sticks, (*c*) Bebbles, (*d*) Paints, (*e*) The fruit of 'villva' tree	The child shakes the rattle.	The pebbles inside the rattles made of different materials produced different sounds. The child is able to discriminate the sound produced and this creates interest in the child to have taste for music. He becomes aware of different sounds produced by the rattles and his auditory discrimination and listening skills are developed.
(6) Drum: (*a*) Tin, (*b*) Thread, (*c*) A stick to beat the drum	The child beats the drum with the help of the stick.	It provides tactile experience and opportunities for manipulation and coordination. The child understands the concept of beat. He could know the regular beat as well as could differentiate between the slow and fast and light and heavy beats. As he beats the drum finer muscle co-ordination takes place.

(*Contd.*)

(*Contd.*)

Materials Used	*Method of Using the Materials/Equipment*	*Educational Values*
(7) Coconut shell drum: (*a*) Coconut shell, (*b*) Paper, (*c*) A stick	The child can beat the drum with the help of the stick.	It develops an awareness and sensitivity to sounds as well as auditory accessity.
(8) Cylophone and metalphone: (*a*) Wood (*b*) Nails (*c*) Bamboo (*d*) Tin plates	In metalphone the tin plates are attached to wooden hands. With the help of a wooden stick the child has to touch all the tin plates from the top to bottom. In cylophone bamboo sticks are attached instead of tin plates.	The harmonious sound produced by the cylophone and metalphone attracts the attention of the children. The child learns to discriminate the sounds. Children who are deficient in auditory acquity are responsible for faulty pronunciation. Cylophone forms the foundation for phonetic instruction which may be introduced in later years.
(9) Bottle caps musical instrument: (*a*) Bottle caps, (*b*) Thin iron rods, (*c*) Wood	Just hold the iron rod or the wood and shirk it.	This enlarges the musical experience of the children. The children learn more about music and other aspect of sound. While singing songs this musical instrument can be accompanied. The child can associate soft and melodious music with that of the music produced by this musical instrument.

(*Contd.*)

(*Contd.*)

Materials Used	*Method of Using the Materials/Equipment*	*Educational Values*
12. Concept formation: (1) Concept of shape (*a*) Chart Paper, (*b*) Varnish papers, (*c*) Tin, (*d*) Paint	Different shapes such as triangle, square, trapezium, right angle triangle, circle, semi-circle, rectangle are formed. Each shape has different colours. The child has to match these mathematical designs and should form other forms of shapes.	The child has the first hand experience with these shapes. The child may make his own design with these cutout shapes, and this explore shape in relation to design. Each shape has its educational value. For example, the shape of a circle, can develop the concept of the world as a round entity and thus lay a foundation for latter study for geography. He develop a correct attitude to mathematical shapes and designs.
(2) Bamboo construction set: Bamboo big and small sticks	The hollow bamboo big sticks have number of holes in them. There are thin sticks which should be fitted into these holes of the big sticks. By this the child can construct number of designs.	It provides finer muscle activity. This type of construction with bamboo sticks provides children with endless opportunities for the creation of shapes and forms. They are practical too in that they can be used for the basic structure of many activities.
13. Cigarette box trains and cars: Cigarette boxes	The cigarette boxes are shaped as trains and cars. The child uses these locomotives in their play.	These miniature cigarette cars and trains helps the child to visualise in his mind the real cars and trains. The purpose of cars and trains are realised

(*Contd.*)

(*Contd.*)

Materials Used	*Method of Using the Materials/Equipment*	*Educational Values*
		by the children. The social implication of science in relation to community activities help children to understand why transportation is important.
14. Puppets: Rod Puppets and paper mesch puppets—(*a*) Paper (*b*) Sticks, (*c*) Paints	Different kinds of puppets are shaped with the help of the mesched paper. The teacher has to conduct a sort of puppet show while telling the stories.	The dolls and puppets play provide good opportunities for the children to express themselves fully in a group atmosphere. These puppets can be used as an aid in story telling. Instead of merely narrating the stories puppets help the teacher for realistic expression. merely narrating the stories puppets help the teacher for realistic expression.
15. Mask: (1) Chart paper, (2) Colour paints	The chart paper is cut-out in different shapes so as to make them a sort of masks. The child can wear these masks and play the roll of the animal that are represented in the mask.	Provides opportunities for creative expression and the development of a sense of design and form. These masks can be used in role-playing. We can make the children participating in dramatics by making use of these masks. (*promotes social development).

(*Contd.*)

(Contd.)

Materials Used	Method of Using the Materials/Equipment	Educational Values
16. Structure construction with pitch and maze stem: (*a*) Thermocol, (*b*) Maze stem, (*c*) Colour paints	Different shapes like table, cart and cot are made and these can be used by the child as play materials.	The child's imaginative power and constructive ability develops through these activities. As he used his fingers in these activities finer muscle co-ordination takes place and he has the correct perspective of things around his worlds.
17. Collage work (butterfly); (*a*) Chart, (*b*) Seeds, (*c*) Nuts, (*d*) Flower, (*e*) Waste materials	The shape of the butterfly is formed by using these seeds nuts, flowers and leaves.	'A thing of beauty is joy for ever.' The child develops his aesthetic domain by seeking these artful play materials and promotes the eye hand co-ordination while doing the college work promotes the concept of colour tool.
18. Wooden toys, wire toys and cardboard toys: (*a*) Wood (*b*) Wire and wastage thread (*c*) Cardboard (*d*) Paper (*e*) Paints (*f*) Nails	These toys can be used in story telling or in class teaching by showing the toys to the children.	These toys can be used in story telling. These toy characters will remain in the child's mind for ever just as the flesh and blood characters. The child themselves can make such toys and these will be play materials for them.
19. Puzzles: (*a*) Wood, (*b*) Paint, (*c*) Cardboard	1. Different kinds of birds and animals are cut-out from the wood and cardboard. The child has to	The child has to use his intelligence to fit the birds in their respective places. The child has the knowledge of the

(Contd.)

(*Contd.*)

Materials Used	*Method of Using the Materials/Equipment*	*Educational Values*
	replace these figures in their respective places.	different shapes of the birds. His intellectual capacity is enriched by this kind of puzzles.
	2. There are many cut-out pieces of the same figure. The child has to join these pieces and should form its full shape.	The concept of shape and space is developed.
20. Paper following: Varnish paper	Step by step children fold the papers of different shapes and figures.	Creative effort and strain is needed to make these paper figures. Thus the child uses his brain and it improves his cognitive domain. As his figures are involved in these activities there is greater scope for finer muscle co-ordination.
21. Pannanguli: Wood	The child plays pannanguli with tamarind seeds. There are 12 round pits in it. Two persons have to play this game. The seeds are put in all the small pits of the pannanguli in equal numbers. The child should take off the needs from a particular pit and should put one seed each into the other pits.	The concept of number is promoted.

(*Contd.*)

(*Contd.*)

Materials Used	Method of Using the Materials/Equipment	Educational Values
22. Kolattam: (*a*) Wooden stick, (*b*) Paint	There are two sticks. The child has to hold one stick in each hand and should produce a rhythmic sound by striking each other.	The child can dance with the help of these sticks. This activity promotes the large muscle co-ordination. Sense of rhythm is developed.
23. Clarionet: (*a*) Plastic, (*b*) Paint	Just below the air, through the hole of the clarionet.	The child can distinguish between the sounds produced by each musical instrument.
24. Walking cart (pushing): (*a*) Wood, (*b*) Paint	The child has to push forward the cart.	This is used by the child when he starts walking. It helps the child to walk with support. Large and finer muscle co-ordination takes place.
25. Building Blocks: Thermocol	The child has to build structure by using these blocks.	The child's cognitive domain is enlarged by this type of activity. His constructive ability and intellectual capacity is developed.
26. Plaugh: (*a*) Wood, (*b*) Paint	There are different pieces which the child is to assemble.	Large and finer muscle co-ordination takes place through these activities. Constructive ability of the child is provided.
27. Swinging Parrot: (*a*) Paper, (*b*) type strip, (*c*) Silver paper, (*d*) Hush and piece of cloth	Just make the parrot swing by shirking the type strip.	The child can enjoy while the parrot gone up and down. He is able to appreciate and admire beautiful things in future years.

(*Contd.*)

(Contd.)

Materials Used	Method of Using the Materials/Equipment	Educational Values
28. Number game: (*a*) Chart paper, (*b*) Sketch pencil	There are several numbers in a chart paper. There is also one number in one small piece and cardboard. The child has to find out the respective number and thus should match it.	This is a play way activity to learn the numbers easily. The child can easily learn and can remember the numbers by this play way technique. His intellectual capacity is improved.
29. Concept of colour: (*a*) Card-board, (*b*) Paper, (*c*) Paints	Several circles are drawn in a card-board. Each circle has different colours. There are also cut-out circles. The child has to match these circles in relation to their colours.	The child learns the concept of colour as well as the circle. The child can discuss the sizes of various circular objects and the colours of various objects.
30. Colour Wheel: (*a*) Wood (*b*) Cardboard (*c*) Colours (*d*) Nails	Just rotate the handle of the wheel. The wheel turns.	The wheel is painted with different colours. This play material is used to develop the concept of colour.
31. Chettiar Doll: (*a*) Paper (*b*) Paints	Gently strike the head of the doll. The doll moves its head to and fro.	This kind of dolls can be used in story-telling. The moving doll attracts the children.

32

Games without Equipment

Ordinary Tag

One of the players is selected as "It" who at a signal tries to chase and tag any one in the group. He who is tagged becomes the new "It" and he continues the game. All must keep within the boundary.

Nondi Tag (Hopping Tag)

Similar to ordinary tag except that "It" should tag others by hopping on one foot. The new "It" continues the game.

Squat Tag

Similar to ordinary tag. Players squat when "It" comes to touch them. It should be constantly moving. Squatting is allowed only three times for each and after this, the player must run and escape being tagged. Squatting is allowed only for a few seconds each time.

Slap Jack

Join hands and form a circle facing inside. "It" runs round outside and touches one in the circle, who runs in the opposite direction. They both complete, running on opposite direction to reach the gap on the circle. The one who reaches late continues the game.

The Hunter and the Bird

"It" is the hunter and the rest are birds. They gather behind the hunter and they follow him. After leading them to some distance, the hunter shouts (Bang) and suddenly turns and chases them to the starting line. All tagged, could become the hunters and continue or else the one tagged first could be the next hunter.

Flowers and Winds

Divide the players into two equal groups; one group as "Flowers" forming a line and the other as "Winds" forming another line 40 yards away. Select the name of a flower say "Jasmine" amongst them without the knowledge of the "Wind". "Flowers move to the wind line and from a distance of about 3 yards demand the "Winds" side guess the name one by one as Lily, Rose, Sun Flower, etc., and if they guess the name one correctly as "Jasmine", the "Flowers" must run back to their line. Then they are chased and caught by the "Wind". This continues till all the "Flowers" are caught. The name of the flower is changed each time.

Frog in the Pond

"It" is the frog round whom others form a circle. They come near the "Frog" and tease him like "Frog" in the sea, could you catch me, could you catch me, "When the frog, suddenly leaps at them and touches them till they reach the circle. He who is tagged becomes the "Frog".

Spider and Flies

Ground marking. Two parallel lines (goal lines) 50 yards apart and a small circle 10 yards in diameter marked in between the lines at the centre.

"It" is the spider seated in the centre of the circle and the others are two "flies" walking around, clapping, waving hands, as though flying and making a buzzing noise. Suddenly the spider jumps up and gives them a chase till they reach the goal lines. All those tagged become spider and they work under the command of the original spider. The last fly caught becomes the first spider for the new game.

Come with Me

Except "It" all are assigned places marked in dots round a circle 20 yards in diameter. "It" goes round inside the circle with the magic wand ("1" stick) and pointing it on some one commands him. "Follow me" and thus three or four are gathered, and they walk around. Suddenly "It" shouts "Go Home" when those who followed him must dash back to the places vacant on the circle. "It" also tries for a vacant place. He who is left out, takes the magic stick and continues the game.

Shadow Tag

A game suitable on a sunny day. "It" attempts to step on the shadow of the runners. The player whose shadow has been stepped becomes the next "It" to continue the game. Move, bend, or twist the body so as to shift the shadow from "It".

Good Morning

Form a circle, leaving "It" out who runs outside the circle tapping at the back of someone and continues the run. One who is tapped leaves the circle and runs in the opposite direction. They meet on the other side of the circle, stop, shake hands saying "Good Morning" three times, and dash to the gap in the circle. He who could not reach the gap earlier becomes "It" and continues the game. All must get chances to be "It".

Potato Race

Divide the players into three teams of ten each and form a file of each team behind the starting line. In front of each team, mark 5 small circles about 2 yards away from one another in a straight line and place one potato in each of the first four circles thus leaving the last one empty. On signal the first one from each team runs and transfers one potato at a time, and all the potatoes to the last empty circle and returns to touch the second in his team at the starting line. The second person distributes the potatoes to each of the circles one by one as originally placed and touches the third. The last player will finish at the starting line.

Clasp Tag

Players are spread out within the play area. "It" runs in and tags the players. Those tagged hold the waist of one another thus forming a CHAIN and under the direction of "It" touch the rest.

All Change

Assign a place for every player on the circumference of a circle 30 in diameter. Mark each place on the circumference with a small circle. "It" takes his place in the centre and shouts "CHANGE" when all must change their places and "It" also would seek a place for himself. The one left out without a place is the next "It" to continue the game.

Four Corners

Four teams of equal number occupy the four corners of a 15 yards square. One is selected as the "It" who occupies the centre of the square. On signal the teams cross over diagonally to the opposite corner, when they are tagged by "It". All those who are tagged are eliminated or can join "It". The team which has retained the largest number after four changes is the winner.

Human Obstacle Relay

Station four players as obstacles in front of each relay team in between the starting and the finishing lines 10 yards apart from each other. The first and fourth stand erect, the second stands with feet wide apart and the third bends forward, holding the ankle. On the signal first man of each team, runs round the first obstacle dives through the second, vaults over the third and rounds the fourth and returns directly to the starting line to touch the second player.

Centipede Race

Relay teams are arranged in pairs standing one behind the other with the back player holding the waist of the front player. On signal each pair runs round the turning point which is about 25 feet from the starting line and touches off the next pair.

Backward Running Relay

Teams are arranged in file behind the starting line. A turning point is marked 40 feet away in front of each team. The player runs backward round the turning point and returns to touch off the next player. The finish is at the starting line.

Chain Tag

Players spread out, within the area marked. "It" runs and tags others. Those tagged join hands with "It" and the end players alone touch the rest without breaking the chain. The game ends when all have joined the chain. All must keep within the area.

Couple Tag

Players are paired and each pair clasp their hands right through the game. One pair is selected as "It" who chases the rest and touches any other pair. The pair that is touched becomes the next "It".

Whip Tag

"It" has a whip in hand with which "It" chases the other players within the marked area and hits. If some one is hit "It" drops the whip and the other takes the whip and continuous the game as the next "It".

Flying Dutchmen

All the players join hands and form a circle except two. These two are the "Flying Dutchmen" who join their hands and run around the circle outside, and one of them strikes the joined hands of two players on the circle. The two who are struck, at once break away from the circle and run on opposite direction and thus compete with "Flying Dutchmen" for the gap in the circle. The pair that could not occupy the gap, continues the game as the next "Flying Dutchmen".

Luggage Van

Trains are formed by the five players holding the waist of one another in a file. Three such trains are formed. One is selected as the luggage van. He is away at a distance of 20 feet from the trains. On signal the luggage van tries to attach itself with the tail end of one of the trains by hooking him arms around the waist of the last player in the train. The front player in the train with outstretched arms jumps about, turning the train to and front to avoid the luggage van. The luggage van tries all the three trains and if he succeeds the player at the head of the train becomes the next luggage van.

Brownies and Fairies

Two teams play this game. One team is called Brownies, and the other is called Fairies. Each team has the same number of players. One player on each team is chosen as a Lookout. He does not turn his back, but watches the other team.

Each team stands behind a goal line at opposite ends of the gymnasium. First the Fairies turn their backs to the Brownies and cover their eyes with their hands. The Brownies go toward the Fairies on tip-toe. When they are almost there, the Fairy Lookout calls, "Look out for the Brownies" and then the Fairies chase the brownie back to their goal line. If any Brownies are caught, they have to go with the Fairies and play on their team.

Cat and Rat

We love to play cat and rat. In this game everyone joins hands and makes a circle. Two children are chosen. One is the Cat; the other is the Rat. The Cat is outside the circle. The Rat is inside looking out.

The Cat says, "I am the Cat" The Rat says, "I am the Rat" The Cat says, "I will catch you" the Rat says, "Oh no, you won't". Then the fun begins.

The Cat tries to catch the Rat. He holds up our hands to help the Rat through, but we stoop down when the Cat tries to go under our hands. If the Rat is too quick, we choose two Cats to chase him.

When the Rat is caught, he and the Cat choose two new ones. Then we play again. We never get tired of playing this game.

Fire Engine

We play this game in teams, with four on a team. Each player has a number: One, Two, Three, or Four. We all stand on a home line, and there is a Fire Line on the opposite side of the playground.

In front of all the players stands a Fire Chief. Watch him, because he may give you signal to run to the Fire Line. First he claps his hands; once, twice, three times, or four times. If he claps his hands twice, and your number is Two; get ready, because when he calls "Fire", you and all the other Twos will run to the Fire Line and back home. The one who gets back first is the next Fire Chief. Sometimes the Fire Chief calls, "General Alarm-Fire!" Then everyone runs to the Fire Line and home, and the fastest runner in the whole class is the next Chief.

33

Essentials of Records and Reports in Pre-Primary School

It is essential to maintain records and reports in a pre-primary school, since the pre-primary school serves as a guide to the child's growth and development. Records and reports are to be properly maintained because it will be of great help to plan the programme and guide the children. A best, effective programme should be based on the children's needs, wishes and their abilities. The experience the children have in a pre-primary school should be useful, enthusiastic and promote development in various realms. Records and reports would make the teacher realise the school readiness of the children. Records and reports of a particular child, when taken to the primary school along with the child and handed over to the teacher it would help the teacher to know the child's physical, emotional, social and intellectual development and his deficiencies as well.

Systematic recording of the children helps a lot in detecting the cases early enough for referral services and give proper therapeutic treatment on time. Thus it can be community's first like of defence in the battle of mental health. In this regard proper maintenance of the records of children are of great value to the researches. Hence, it is necessary to have records and reports in pre-primary schools. The following records and registers are to be maintained in a pre-primary schools:

1. Attendance Register.
2. Admission Register.
3. School lunch record.
4. Record of income and expenditure.
5. Stock Register.
6. Visitor's Record.

7. Parent education programme Record.
8. Daily Diary.
9. Monthly report.
10. Record of programme planning.
11. Health report.
12. Cumulative Record.
13. Record of Early planning. These records can be classified into two:
    (*a*) Records of children, and
    (*b*) Maintenance and Administrative Record of pre-primary school.

Records of Children

A child, while coming to a pre-primary school comes from different circumstances. The future life of the child depends on the changes that a child undergoes in this stage. Pre-primary school plays a vital role by bringing changes in physical, language, mental, motor and social development. The following records of children are very important such as health records and cumulative record.

Health Record

The main aim of this record is to make the parents and the teacher realise the gradual development of each child. A pre-primary school teacher should note down every month the serial number, name of the children, age, month, weight and height in a health record. The activities in a pre-school will be done skillfully by the children while they enjoy good health and development. "Health is wealth". This record points out the interest of the children in various activities and the ability and development of the children shown in those activities. When this record is handed over to the next class it is easy to guide the child in the right direction.

Cumulative Record

Normally the collected data about a child are kept in the form of a Cumulative Record. The pre-natal history, birth history, developmental history from birth, disease and vaccination are some of the points that are most important to the pre-primary school teacher. The teacher should record the interest of the child in various fields and their involvement in a work. This will serve as a guide to the child in job oriented education and education suitable for his future life. Generally, a cumulative record contains details of personal data, home background, habits and interest of the child, health and general remarks of the teacher.

Records of Administration

Attendance Register

The names of the children who attend the school should be written in attendance register serially. The attendance of the children should be marked both in the morning and evening daily. Two different colours may be used to differentiate the names of boys and girls.

Admission Register

This Register should contain the names of the children, names of the parents, or guardian, their occupation, income, caste, religion, address, child's date of birth, native place and date of admission. The names of newly admitted children should be written continually after the name of discontinued children, without committing them.

Record of Income and Expenditure

The record of income and expenditure should have the particulars of the sources of income and the expenditure of the school. This will help them to make both ends meet, successfully.

School Lunch Record

There should be a school lunch record to write down the menu every day and the expenditure for it. This would help to check up whether the children enjoy a balanced diet or not, to find out the expenditure for each of meal and to enable changes in the lunch scheme, if necessary.

Stock Register

This register should contain the date, the name and number of articles and the value of them, whether the article is a donation or bought by the school, particulars about condemned goods, stock, signature of the Secretary and other particulars. Stock Register to be maintained for each type of item such as furniture, equipment, books etc.

Visitors Record

Whenever there is a visit to the school by officers or guest, they should be made to record their opinion about the school and the performance of the children. They can also give their suggestions.

Parent Education Programme Record

There may be gathering of the parents, weekly or monthly under the chairmanship of the pre-primary school teacher to discuss the problems or some issues. For example, subjects like nutritious food for children, child care, problems found among pre-primary school children and solution may be discussed. Particulars regarding such meetings should find a place in parent education programme record.

Daily Diary

The pre-primary teachers should record their daily routine—the programme they have during the whole day in the pre-primary school. Particulars like date, starting of school, attendance, prayer, free conversation, planned activity, outdoor play, song, indoor play, and visit of guest should be marked in the diary.

Monthly Report

It is essential to have particulars regarding the number on roll both of boys and girls at the beginning and at the end of the month, working dates, particulars about the classes taken, health check up and other activities of the whole month.

Yearly Planning Report

This record would contain programme for the whole year. Extra curricular activities and other activities for the whole year should find a place here. Total number of working days, holidays, and activities for each month would be written separately in this record.

Inspection Report or Supervisor's Remarks

The supervisors and inspectors who are visiting the pre-primary school should have the aim of guiding the teachers for the betterment of the school. At the same time, the advices and suggestions for improvement of the school given by the inspectors would help the teachers to do their duty properly and successfully.

A pre-primary school teacher, who works with small children should keep a keen eye on the children to observe the various development of the child and record it. This would help to form an idea of the total development of the child, its ability and to promote the child to the next class according to their growth and development. Proper education can also be provided to the children based on their ability and interest. All the pre-primary school teachers should know the importance of records and reports in a pre-primary school and develop the skill in maintaining them.

34

Parents Education and Working with the Community

A child's growth and development depends-both on his heredity—what he is born with and his environment—what the parents and community provide for him during the formative years. These two influences are very closely interdependent. A child's parents are his genetic background. They are also his earliest guides, educators and companions. They set the atmosphere for his moral and ethical standards, his physical well-being, his aesthetic appreciations, his concept of family life and his philosophy in general. Generally, a child's experiences in the family remain a permanent part of his life and childhood is an extremely impressionable age. The kind of person a child will depend so much on the kind of livings he and his family live in. Hence, it is essential that the parents rearing the child should know the nature, ability and interest of the child so that he could have a proper development. Due to the various changes in science, a lot of changes have occurred in child rearing practices. A pre-primary school may be of great help to the parents and the community to know more about the rearing practices. Hence, parent education programme and working closely with the community should be stressed in a pre-primary school.

Objectives of Parents Education

The parents whose children are mostly dependent on them may find it difficult to accept his liking for pre-primary school. If the mother also has found that the child cannot do without her supervision then she will also become reluctant to put him in pre-primary school. It is important to change this type of ideas from both of them. The programmes for parents are the important aspects of the pre-primary school programmes. The pre-primary schools however efficient they are, cannot stimulate the optimum development of the children unless they work in close collaboration with parents. The major responsibilities of children's growth remain with the parents. Now-a-days parents are also becoming aware of the new trends in educating children and they would like to know more about parental duties so as to bring up healthy and well adjusted children. So today the task of the pre-primary school teacher is not merely to guide the children but also to educate the parents.

The home-school relationship should be very close at all stages of education but specially so at the pre-primary school stage. The pre-primary school should be an extension of the home and should supplement the home to make the child not to be last in the first time and facing the world outside. To do this the teacher must have sufficient information about the home of the child and should be able to work in close co-operation with the parents, thereby the parents also get to understand the objectives of the school and may be able to help the school to achieve its aims. In addition, it helps in avoiding conflicts that arise in children's mind. The difference between school and home could be minimised through the best parents education programme.

Specially in rural balwadies the programmes for parent education should start even before the child starts coming to the pre-school to create consciousness in parents about the primary needs of children and the objectives of pre-primary school education. Hence, Gandhiji said that the first stage of education is parent education *i.e.* immediate after the conception.

Parents Education Programme

For conducting any parent education programme, the main thing is to get the parents and the community in the programme. Involvement does not mean just getting their names registered or signed up for it but really getting them involved with the programme is essential. All of us can not be parent educators and be the social workers. It needs certain amount of skill and techniques. The following are some techniques which would bring success in this programme:

Techniques

1. Be friendly and really interested in parents, their children and family.

2. Make home visits once in a week and have informal talk with the parents about the ability of their children.
3. Listen to the parents in order to pin-point individual and community needs.
4. Encourage parents to arrange for regular meetings, prepare the schedules, agenda for meetings, decide the chairperson, days and hours of meetings. There should never be hindrance to their work.
5. Help parents to work on an issue of their choice.
6. Find out ways to collect some funds for parent programmes and let the parents manage the funds.
7. Encourage everybody to speak in the group. Let no one be left out without participating in meetings.
8. Have a suggestion book that parents can use without even having their names.
9. Start some schemes such as small savings, chit funds, poultry unit, tailoring etc. Just to encourage them to come regularly.
10. Invite some prominent members of the locality to attend the scheduled meetings without involving much on politics; specialists in child development and other allied subjects are of good choice.

Methods of Parents Education Programme

Group Discussion

Topics are selected and given preference on the basis of priority. Either the teacher or any group member can be the leader, but the selection of the leader should be by the group. It can either be formal or informal. The success of the group discussion depends to a great extent on the efficiency of the leader.

It often happens that two or three people dominate the whole discussion and other do not find any chance to speak at all which would create lot of dissatisfaction among the members. The leader should sense the feelings of the group, and see that the whole discussion revolves around the main topics and not carried away in the different channels. The leader should keep recording the main issues and points and bring them together to a conclusion. Towards the end the leader should read out the finding and conclusions of the whole group.

Lecture Method

Specialists can be invited at times to give talks on any particular subject or topics on which most of the parents are interested and their felt needs. Sometimes even the teacher can give talks on various subjects.

Audio-Visual Aids

This is one of the effective methods of parent education. Now-a-days documentary films are available almost in all the subjects which are very useful to parents. Audio-visual aids are much suitable as mass media of communication.

Demonstrations

On the spot demonstrations are highly effective than sheer lecturing. Selections of topics can be done mainly from day to day living. This method is a very effective one.

For example new recipies, method of cooking, selection of fabrics for daily occasional use, their care, stain removal storage etc. Preservation of foodstuffs, proper method of storage are more of interest to the parents.

Sending Pamphlets to Parents

This method can effectively be used among educated parents. Ideas of specialists of particular topics may be printed or written and sent to the parents. The parents should be asked to voice and send their opinions regarding these. This method would be useful for the parents who could not visit the school often and who are interested in the welfare and progress of their children.

Sending Progress Report

All parents are interested to know the development and progress of their children. Hence, it is necessary to observe the growth of pre-primary school children. The teacher should keenly observe the growth changes that occur in the children and inform the parents. The parents should be made to realise their duty too. Progress reports provide information about the growth and progress of the children. This helps in eradicating defects immediately and enables the teacher and parents to serve as guides to their children.

Parent Conference

Parent conference represent one of the most profitable ways in which teachers and parents can share their experiences. This contact can be established even before the child starts coming to school. So that the teacher can learn about the attitude of the parent towards the school, and how far they are interested in sending their children to school, their experiences etc. Teacher can also function as a counsellor to the parents as well as to the children.

Home Visits

The teachers should make frequent home visits. Such visits will give the teacher a clear concept of the child's home environment, financial status neighbourhood relationship with his parents, siblings; relations etc. The teacher could explain the parents the general policies of the school, its regulations, what she expects from them as parents. This method is especially more useful to those who find it difficult to come to the pre-school.

Parents should never visit the school during working hours to discuss the problems. It would lay a hindrance to the teacher as well as to children. Children will be disturbed and may not be willing to stay in the school.

As pre-school teacher must be a fool to widen the cognitive domain of the parents. The teacher who educates the parents through parent education programme should have a clear knowledge on all these matters.

Suggested Topics of Parents Education Programme

1. Parent child relationship.
2. Importance of pre-primary school education.
3. Child's health and nutrition.
4. Pre-natal and post-natal care.
5. Safety of the children.
6. Behaviour problems of children and ways of handling them.
7. Family planning.

8. Small savings.
9. Kitchen garden.
10. Poultry and dairy.
11. Selection of clothing, laundry techniques, stain removal tailoring.
12. Sanitation.
13. First aid.
14. Problems of over weight and under weight.
15. Modern child reading practices.
16. Home decoration.
17. Methods of cooking.
18. Community improvement activities.

Parents Day Celebration

This is important that every pre-primary school teacher knows the importance and methods of celebrating parents day. Parents day may be celebrated in order to create enthusiasm and an awareness. Local leaders like panchayat president, women and members of panchayat, Mahila mandal convenors, school teachers, headmasters, primary health personnels may be invited for the function.

A brief report of the progress of the pre-primary school may be read by the concerned teacher at the beginning of the discussion. Then there can be particular topic or plan for the next year programme. The following is a model programme for the celebration.

8.00 a.m. to 1.00 p.m. :	Preparation and arrangements of exhibition of the creative activities, crafts, educational equipments and other hobby, collections of the children.
4.00 p.m, to 4.30 p.m. :	Exhibition
4.30 p.m. to 6.30 p.m. :	Reading of report, Discussion on the improvements of present, parents contribution and free services. Responsibility of the village towards balwadi. Resolution regarding and issues.
6.30 p.m. to 7.30 p.m. :	Cultural programme by the pre-primary school children and balsabha of children. After vote of thanks, the function may come to an end with National Anthem.

35

Child to Child Programme

The older children looking after the younger ones is a quite common phenomena in most of the developing countries. In the child to child programme which is a new concept emerged from the Institutes of Education and Child Health at the University of London, by Dr. David Morley emphasised that the older children look after the younger ones not only at home but also in the schools.

This programme has been launched by the Institute of Child Health's Tropical Health Unit in 1977. Since then hundreds of countries have started following this programme as the result of which an International Committee has been set up. During the month of November 1979, experts from the field of Child Health and Education, representing different parts of India met in Madras, Calcutta, Chandigarh, Barailey, Hyderabad and Vellore to study the possibility of implementing the Child to Child Programme in India. A National Committee on Child to Child Programme has been formulated in the International Workshop on Child to Child Programme held in Hyderabad from 5th to 8th November 1979. This Committee consists of representatives from Medicine and Education.

This Child to Child concept is not a new concept as far as India is concerned. It could be seen that the elder children especially girls in most of the villages carrying and looking after the young ones at home when the parents are away either in factories or in the farms. This has become an inevitable activity especially after the breaking down of joint family system in India.

The children to children concept even in the schools used to be followed during the ancient Gurukula system of education where the Guru used to teach a few who are called the Monitors, in turn they used to teach the rest of the children.

The Objectives of Child to Child Programme

The Child to Child Programme aims at popularising the concept of elder children looking after and passing on the information to the younger ones on simple health aspects which includes preventive and curative. It also aims at stimulating the pre-primary school children to develop good health habit and food habits. It encourages the older and the younger children to actively participate in the health programme of the home and the community. When the children are educated properly and are conscious of health and hygiene and good food habits, it will become easier to bring about changes in the homes and the communities.

Procedures to Implement the Child to Child Programme

If it is to become a scientific and popular activity both at home and school, it is essential that we make the child to child programme an integral part of the school curriculum. In every class the older children should be made responsible for looking after the younger ones. They should be encouraged to bring the children to the school regularly. They should be made responsible for looking after the cleanliness of the younger ones. They should also see that the younger ones eat right type of food and free from illness. All the children in the school should be taught the simple medical care and simple treatment. For example, the concept that it is essential to give plenty of water when a child is suffering, from diarrhoea as there is dehydration to be taught. Simple activities could be given to illustrate the dehydration and in the same way looking after the sick child, feeding it and entertaining it should also be introduced.

The child to child programme should also be included in the teacher training curriculum so that they in turn will encourage the children when they become the teachers. The existing curriculum of health and hygiene at the teacher's training institute should become a practical oriented curriculum. The teachers should encourage the practice of health and hygiene and also encourage the elder ones to help the younger ones in simple health and hygiene activities such as cutting the nails, combing the hair, putting on the dresses, cleaning after the outdoor play, cleaning the hands before eating etc.

The subjects which the children learn in the school should have a practical implication. The application of knowledge gained should be encouraged. Science should never be taught as a subject for gathering information, facts and principles.

Children should be encouraged to involve themselves regularly in the field work. Thus they could be made to understand the problems relating to health, food, nutrition and education. This awareness should be made use of an active participation in solving the problems relating to health and hygiene, food etc.

When the children understand an importance of the immunisation, innoculation and other preventive aspects of health, they will encourage even the elders to follow these. They would take steps to see that all the children and adults at home get immunisation and innoculation at the time of epidemic.

In the present system of secondary education that they should have the socially useful productive work experiences. The Kothari Education Commission of 1964-66 has recommended that at every level at the school we must introduce work experience. The fruit of such type of work experience should be enjoyed by the very young ones at the primary and pre-primary levels. For example the products from the school garden such as green vegetables etc. could be given to the mid-day meal programme and thus help the younger ones to improve the nutritional status. When the older children work in the carpentary unit they could be encouraged to prepare toys for the younger ones, and thus entertain them.

The children in the primary schools could be encouraged to look after the children in the pre-primary school and in creche. The children should take it up even as a leisure time activity or as a part of the regular extra curricular activity.

In every pre-primary school and in the primary school regular periodical meetings of the mothers should be held, as Gandhiji says, education starts not after the birth of child, but at the time of conception. That means the mothers are to be educated first to bear and rear the child properly. The mothers are to be provided with health and nutrition education. They should be encouraged to accept their children when they come with new concepts on nutrition, health and hygiene. This type of acceptance will encourage the children to learn more and more and put them in practice.

Every school should have as a regular periodical health check up for the children. This type of school health programme could be taken up with the co-operation of primary health centres nearby and the pedeatric departments of the hospitals. The health check up should have practical implication. Children should be advised and motivated to take nutritive and clean food, and follow good health habits. Periodically exhibitions, film shows and talks on different aspects of nutrition, health and hygiene could be arranged in the school as well as in the community.

Implication of Child to Child Programme

I. It is observed that the children drop-out from the schools especially in rural areas. Some children drop-out in the first standard itself, some before they reach Fifth Standard and a few before they reach 10th Standard. The reasons which are given for this drop-out in rural areas suggest that they keep the older children to help them either in farming or in grazing the cattles. The older children are stopped from school to look after the younger ones at homes in the absence of the adults. If child to child programme is implemented, the older ones could take up the responsibility of bringing the younger ones either to creche or to pre-primary school centres and they could be looked after there in a better atmosphere and thus reduce the problem of drop-outs.

II. A sense of responsibility is created in children. The older ones take up the responsibility of looking after the younger ones and bringing them to creche or pre-primary schools where they get a stimulating environment.

III. Child to child programme can create an awareness of the different aspects of life in the whole community and the school and hence promotes good relationship between school and community. Both parents and the school teachers work together in order to promote the sense of responsibility in the young minds.

IV. Psychological security to the whole family is created when older ones take care of the younger ones. This leads to better understanding and adjustment among the members of the whole family. And thus good social adjustment could be brought about.

V. Child to child programme will improved and promote good health habits in young children. The problem of under nutritional malnutrition could be reduced a little as they develop right type of good habits.

We could see from the above discussion that child to child programme if properly implemented, can promote the all round development of the child and the community at large. To conclude, it could be said that child to child programme, a new innovation in the field of child welfare, health and education could easily be adapted and practiced at every level of education without much special preparation or financial commitments; specially at the pre-primary school level if we could implement this child to child programme when the children are in the formative period we could conceive of a healthy child and a healthy nation.

36

National and International Organizations in Child Welfare

"Some of the significant parameters of the quality of life of any nation are the infant mortality rate, incidence of malnutrition, the morbidity picture and the literacy rates" (National Policy on Education, 1986).

Providing good nutrition, health facilities and cognitive stimulation become the essential aspect of any development and welfare programme. These services are inevitable especially to the children who are coming from deprived families and areas for a better human development. From birth to pre-primary school it is a crucial period in the life of a child. Our concern should be to the whole child whose needs should be adequately reflected in all our plans and actions, which is turn results in a better human resource development in future.

Social progress and economic prosperity depend on the full use of human as well as natural resources. Realising this Jawaharlal Nehru has said "ultimately, of course it is the human being that counts and if human being counts well, he counts much more as a child than as a grown up."

Attempts have been made to take stock of its human resources and to involve systems that will ensure more efficient national productivity and even a more dynamic contribution to national development by improving the human resources. Governmental as well as voluntary agencies try to provide alternative strategies for delivery of child development services and to identify manpower training and resources for these services, throughout the globes. Meeting the development needs of children is not only an investment for future but also a matter of their rights as individuals.

An Overview to the Human Development Services

In early days the services to needy children as such was started only with orphanages especially by religious missionaries throughout the world. These were attached to monasteries or mosques or temples. No other services, other than these were provided to children (orphanages were created to satisfy the conscience of a man who had fathered an illegitimate child, as such as a child was not accepted by the society, man's guilt was probably the reasons for starting such type of services in those days. But most of the services, if we analyse, came as the result of recognition of a problem principally disturbing adults or the society.

A new concept of child care was thought of in Europe about 300 years ago. In France a centre for the medical care of mother and child was started in 17th century. Besides medical service, this also provided, day care centres for working mothers, family allowances for poor families and free public education. French Revolution established that assistance to poor was a national obligation. Religious institutions started orphanages and workshops for poor boys. Between 1904 and Second World War various enactments were made to protect women and children in France.

Montessori system was another hallmark in the education of pre-school children. Though a medical woman made use of her knowledge which she gained while treating the young children, especially those who were mentally retarded, to give proper education.

In United States 'Head Start' programme comes to help the poor Negro children. The prime objective was to give Negro children a head start through pre-primary education, so that the disparities between white and the black could be reduced.

In Britain during 17th century an Act of Parliament decreed that children should be placed in foster homes. It also took care of orphans, the illegitimate, the aged, the handicapped or insane. It prohibited child labour and social consciousness was slowly beginning to develop. This also paved the way for humanitarian consideration and proper human development.

Human development and their problem in developed and developing countries seem to be different and the solutions were also different in these countries. The types of problems, magnitude of problems, of human development in these countries and the methods adopted to solve these problems were to be different because of the differences in socio-economic conditions as well as the cultural ethics of those countries.

A developing country like India never had the problem of delinquency, drug addiction and broken homes. India had to and even today has to face poverty, poor health, child mortality, mal-nutrition, over-population and improper education.

In socialist countries, like Soviet Union, China, Yugoslavia and Cuba, child welfare programme assured a new perspective in 20th century. Marxists thought that capital formation in economic terms also meant preparation of human capital. Hence, priority was given to the development and care of children from infancy to adolescence.

This overview gives an idea of the different stages of development in child welfare programme around the world. Now let us see the role of national and international organizations which are involved in human development services. Today national and international responsibilities are becoming our local responsibilities. These organizations have to concentrate on health, nutrition and the education of children.

Types of Organizations

On the basis of the type of services provided to the human development, the organizations could be classified, as the agencies which provide health services, nutrition services and the educational services. They are also classified as national and international organizations.

Organizations

International Organizations

1. UNICEF
2. UNESCO
3. OMEP
4. WHO
5. FAO
6. CARE
7. SOS
8. IUCW

National Organizations

1. NCERT
2. IAPE
3. CSWB
4. ICCW
5. NIPCCD
6. ICMR
7. IARI
8. ICSM
9. NCF
10. KGNMF
11. CASA
12. NCB

International Organizations

UNICEF (United Nation International Children's Emergency Fund)

United Nations International Children's Emergency Fund came into existence in 1946, as one of the organs of United Nations General Assembly. The immediate purpose was to provide urgent relief to children in Europe who managed to survive the Second World War. Nearly 60 nations joined to provide food, medicines, clothing, footwear. The basic, daily needs of around 6 million children were met and thus an entire generation was saved from malnutrition and deprivation.

The mandate of UNICEF today is "to save succeeding generations from the courage of war and to promote social progress and better standards of life in larger freedom.

When the declaration of General Assembly emerged from the thinking of many agencies who had battled with the terrible problems of death and disease, in the aftermath of war, it also helped to synthesise a new universal approach to the problems of children for the first time in human history, "Mankind owes the child the best it has to give", states the declaration of the Rights of the child adopted unanimously by the General Assembly in 1959. The Nobel Peace Prize won by UNICEF in 1965 was an affirmation of the simple truth that the well being of today's children determines the peace of tomorrow's world.

Resources: UNICEF is financed by voluntary contributions from governments (133 of them in 1982) in both industrialised and developing regions as well as from organizations and individuals. Income is derived also from other sources like getting card sales, fund-raising campaigns and allocations for specific purposes from the United Nations system.

India has the largest UNICEF programme for any country. UNICEF came to India in 1949 and started in a small way with relief supplies to children in need: Skim milk powder; drugs, vaccines.

With the worldwide observance in 1979 of the IYC, the focus fell sharper on the unmet needs of the children. As a result, new programmes were developed by UNICEF around the world to meet the neglected problems like, the decline of breast-feeding, improper weaning practices, infant diarrhoea leading to avoidable deaths, child mal-nutrition; non-protection of children against common childhood diseases even where vaccines were freely available. The UNICEF look at it as a prime task to make adults aware of all these problems, and thus these concerns have become priorities and being built into every programme supported by UNICEF. It takes greater interest now in associating itself not so much with the material symbols as with children growing up better feed, healthy and educated with a purpose to their active place in building tomorrow's India.

UNESCO (United Nations Educational, Scientific and Cultural Organizations)

UNESCO was created at a conference held in London in November 1946. There are 155 countries which have enrolled as members of UNESCO, and they meet twice a year to discuss the programmes.

The main activities of UNESCO is to help its member states to implement programmes that will promote the status of education, scientific research and help in strengthening the culture of a nation. It also assists to implement universal and compulsory education, curriculum construction, writing textbooks for children, non-formal education, adult education and training the pre-primary school teachers. Number of projects have been undertaken in different countries to train the teachers and to produce books for children. During the International Year of the Child, UNESCO helped to review the programmes for children in each country tend to plan new programmes in the light of other local experiences.

Besides the resources made available for the educational projects by the UNDP, World Bank, and UNICEF various other funds have been created around specific problem areas, population issues, the environment, prevention of drug abuse, promotion of science and technology which open opportunities for educational action.

OMEP

OMEP was born after the concerns of many for the well being of the young children in the aftermath of World War II. In 1946 Lady Allen of Hurtwood from Great Britain travelled the Scandinavia lecturing. She met many people interested in early education and discussed with them how to create an international organization that would promote greater understanding of young children and bring closer together those working in the field.

As a result of her discussions with a group of people from different countries met together to form a preparatory committee. This group subsequently held a meeting at UNESCO headquarters in Paris to which were invited outstanding early childhood educators, representatives and individuals from many countries. Their plans to form a World Organization for Early Childhood Education were then taken to the UNESCO Assembly where they were warmly supported.

A world conference on Early Childhood Education was held in Prague in August 1948 and a constitution for OMEP was adopted. Thus, the OMEP was born. Following that conference other countries decided to form National OMEP Committees and took up the early childhood education programme. The major objective of the organization is to use every possible means to promote for eaoh child the optimum conditions for his well-being development and happiness in his family, institutions and the society. It also creates and promotes a worldwide consensus regarding the crutial nature of early years and the need to provide early childhood education to all children.

CARE (Co-operative for American Relief Everywhere)

CARE is a non-governmental organization created in 1946 for the immediate purpose of sending food from American donors to people in war-devastated Europe. As the post-war emergency programmes neared completion its programmes were extended to other countries and to other kinds of aid besides food.

CARE began its operation in India in 1950 since 1961, CARE has been helping India in the mid-day meal scheme for primary school children. This is the largest school feeding programme in the world outside of the U.S.A. Besides the feeding programme CARE was given help in the fields of medicine, literacy, vocational training, agriculture and is a small way of helping schools to grow more food by provision of garden tools and improved seeds. In the field of medicine vans, X-ray machines, diagnostic test, eye glass and frames, medical books, medicines and vitamins are distributed.

WHO (World Health Organization)

WHO is a specialised non-political health organization of the United Nations with its headquarters in Geneva. The constitution which was drafted in 1946 came into force on 7th April 1948 which is being celebrated every year as World Health Day.

Objectives of WHO are given below;

1. To provide highest attainable standard of health which is the fundamental right of every human being.
2. To control the diseases especially the communicable diseases among the human beings.
3. To promote the health of the child which is the basic requirement to live harmoniously in a changing total environment.
4. To extend to all people the benefits of medical and related knowledge which is essential for the attainment of good health.

WHO diverts and co-ordinates the international health work through its network programme on a voluntary basis. It tries to prevent and control specific diseases and also genetic disorders, mental disorders, drug addiction and dental diseases.

In India, WHO extends its activities to the primary health care, environmental health and health statistics. It also takes up bio-gradical research throughout the world especially in developing countries.

WHO acts as a clearing house for information of a health problem and makes available literature on different issues and problems in the field of medicine and health. Thus, the contribution of WHO to the human development through its varied types of programme is great.

FAO (Food and Agriculture Organization)

FAO was formed in the year 1945 with headquarters in Rome. It was the first UNO's specialised agency created to look after several areas of world co-operation with the following objectives:

1. To help nation's raise in standard of living.
2. To improve nutrition of the people in the globe.
3. To increase the efficiency of forming forestry and fisheries.
4. To raise the conditions of especially the rural people through all these means by widening the opportunity of all people to involve in productive work.
5. To increase food production to keep pace with the ever growing world population which means better quality of life and human resource development.

National Organisations

IAPE (Indian Association for Pre-school Education)

In 1964 when a small group of pupils who were interested in pre-school education had a gathering. They formed the Indian Association for Pre-primary School Education. This association started gaining momentum by making all those who were interested in pre-primary school education in different parts of the country to take membership. The first annual conference of IAPE was held in Delhi in December 1965. Today it has grown a number of branches all over India.

Objectives of IAPE

1. The prime task of IAPE is to bring together all the workers who are involved in promoting pre-primary school education.
2. To discriminate the new concepts and innovations in child development and pre-primary school education.
3. To undertake projects related to pre-primary education and child development.
4. To be a forum for discussing and debating the different issues in pre-primary school education.
5. To organize seminars, workshops and conferences on different themes for the teachers, the experts, the teacher educators and the public.

These activities are being carried out by IAPE as well as its branches in different parts of the country. This association IAPE is mainly focussing on the education of young children so as to promote the human development.

NCB (National Children's Board)

The constitution of National Children's Board was formed on September 15th 1975 under the Chairmanship of the Prime Minister of India with ministerial and departmental representation from the states. Its major objectives are:

Continuous planning, review and co-ordination of all essential services. The Prime Minister in her opening remarks in 1975 said, "We have so many Boards that I am a little way of yet another one, and I can only hope that this will not remain a more forum for talking but will be able to get down to the grassroots of some of the problems we face".

As a continuation of this, the Government started another programme.

National Children's Fund (NCF)

NCF was created by the Government of India, Ministry of Social and Women's Welfare in the International Year of the Child (IYC) 1979 with the view to augment resources from the community for assistance to voluntary organisations actively engaged in the child welfare department for undertaking to meet the needs of the children of poor families in backward areas, particularly the scheduled castes and scheduled tribes.

NCF concentrates on providing funds for the voluntary agencies which are involved in promoting child welfare services in India, organizing pre-primary centres and recreation programme for destitute children and organizing vocational training for the destitute children.

NIPCCD (National Institute of Public Co-operation and Child Development)

The NIPCCD was sponsored and registered by the Planning Commission on February 28th, 1966 as an autonomous organization. Its functions under the Ministry of Social Welfare. The main functions of the Institution are given below:

1. Research and evaluation studies in public co-operation and child development.
2. Training of Government Voluntary section personnel engaged in social development, child development and allied activities.
3. Dissemination of information pertaining to child development and public co-operation through documentation and publication.
4. Technical advice to central and state government to promote and implement the policies and programmes for child development.
5. Liason with international and regional agencies, research

institutions, universities and other bodies engaged in similar activities.

NIPCCD is actively engaged in organizing seminars and workshops training and evaluation related to human development and organization of pre-primary school programme. Its contribution to the functioning of ICDS programme throughout India is remarkable. Wherever there is an ICDS programme the expertise knowledge comes from the NIPCCD.

ICCW (Indian Council for Child Welfare)

ICCW is one of the major national organizations for human development. Today with branches in every state it came into existence in 1942. When there was famine in Bengal, ICCW with its branches throughout the country mobilized voluntary activities. This was a pioneering organization for planning society for children not only linked to women's welfare but also to the care of the handicapped.

The main function of the council is working for the promotion and implementation of child welfare activities in the country. It has been training a new cadre of child welfare worker's called Balsevika for the established Balwadies in villages, slums, tribal areas and cities. The BST programme initiated in the early sixties laid the foundation for the 5th and 6th plan and ICDS programme of the Government. ICCW also awards the National Awards to children for acts of outstanding courage every year on 26th of January.

CSWB (Central Social Welfare Board)

CSWB was established in recognition of the work of the voluntary organization for social and child welfare in India. This is being financed by Government with a paid Chairman and a small administrative cell in the centre.

Child care programme, welfare extension projects, training programmes and specialised projects, such as organization of creches, balwadies in rural areas, holiday homes for children, orphanages and homes for the widows.

CASA (Church's Auxillary for Social Action)

The real origin of CASA starts from the communal trouble that started after the partition in 1947. From a very small humble but dedicated beginning CASA has grown in such proportion and dimensions that it is now being recognised as one of the major international voluntary organizations in India. From the role of being a mere food distribution agency to the children and needy institution CASA has emerged as a relief and rehabilitation organization with Christian inspiration. This is possible because of the generous contribution made by the international church bodies like World Council of Churches, Church World Services, Luthern World Relief, Central Evangelical Agency of West Germany. CORSO (Council for Relief Services Overseas), Newzealand and similar inter-church and agencies in Britain, Australia, Holand and Denmark, donates supplies of foods, medicines, clothing, hospital equipments, agricultural implements and other goods are made available to the poor and needy irrespective of caste creed or religion.

Relief in Emergencies

CASA is undertaking to provide help during emergent and natural disaster over the years. CASA has offered relief and rehabilitation to the victims of natural catastrophies, flood, fire, famine, cyclone, earthquakes and situation resulting from political and military clashes. CASA continued its services during the liberation war of Bangladesh and the rehabilitation period.

Activities of CASA

Food for the work was the main activity of CASA in the beginning. Construction of wells, lakes, dams, ponds, laying of rural roads, building up community centres and houses for low income families are of a few developmental activities achieved by the programme.

Mobilisation of voluntary services was another activity of CASA. It attempted to provide opportunities for young students to stay and take up projects such as construction of cheap houses, land reclamation, digging of compost pit for sanitary wells, constructing wells etc.

Third type of activity undertaken by CASA was providing financial assistance to institution was supporting the handicapped such as the blind and polio affected children. Drugs, clothing and other gifts are distributed to hospitals and health centres which take care of the handicapped children.

Feeding programme was also undertaken by CASA. High protein mixtures like wheat, soyabeans, soya fortified oats and soya fortified bulgar are cooked and distributed through MCH centres to the pre-school children expected mothers and lactating mother who belong to vulnerable segments of the population. It also conducted orientation courses and seminars on themes on nutrition.

Voluntary Organizations

Besides well established organisations there are also voluntary organizations like the Children's Garden Society, Kasturba Gandhi Memorial Fund, SOS villages, Lion's clubs, Rotatory Clubs, Children's Aid Society, Nutan Bal Shikshan Sangh in Gujarat and Maharashtra, Guide of Services and many more are involved in promoting human development through varied types of activities for children. All these agencies believe in full development of the potentialities of the child and their programmes strive towards achieving the goal.

Conclusion

IYC helped in enhancing the awareness of the special needs of children on the part of decision-makers and the public. It has also made every one in this country who is interested in the welfare of the human being, recognize the fact that programmes for children should be an integral part of economic and social development plans.

In carrying out the programmes to achieve the goal of wholesome development along with Government organizations, the voluntary organization takes active part. All these programmes represent an abundant set of good intentions and also a ray of hope that something positive may well emerge in due course to benefit the child in India.

37

Pre-Primary School Teachers and Their Training

Qualities of Pre-Primary School Teachers

A pre-primary school teacher who is to work with very young children should have love and affection for children and their needs. She should be a substitute mother for the children who leave the mothers for the first time. She should also have an aptitude to work with young children.

The pre-primary school teacher should be able to deal with different types of problems found among young children. As she is being entrusted with the young children she must see that comfortable safe and healthy working conditions are provided to them in the pre-primary school.

She should be a healthy and active woman with pleasant personality, bright and cheerful temperament and capacity for broad human understanding, should be friendly with children, ready to work hard and willing to help children. She should work closely with patents and establish a link with the pre-primary school, the home, the community and other agencies in the village and town.

Integrated approach to pre-primary school teacher education is the logical outcome of the thinking in recent years regarding the attempt towards providing integrated services for the pre-school child. Combining health, nutrition, education and welfare services in a meaningful manner and offering a package deal to the pre-primary school child would entail developing a cadre of trained workers at the professional and para-professional levels. For the successful implementation of the combined health, nutrition, education and welfare programmes, resources will be required by way of trained personnel as well as physical facilities. Ultimately, the success of these programmes will be determined by the quality of the teacher who will deal with the pre-schoolers, their parents and the community workers, in day-to-day interactions.

The training atmospheres must be flexible, warm and permissive. Young adults can develop into successful teachers only if their own personalities are permitted to expand and flourish in relationships with children and others in the school and community. Threats to the student teacher's perception of herself will make her defensive and anxious and will interfere with her successful preparation for teaching.

The student teacher should be encouraged to develop her own approaches to young children. She should be helped to develop a sense of self adequacy and develop new skills through exploration and experimentation. Ultimately the student teacher must develop the concepts, methods and attitudes that are more meaningful to her.

Pre-primary School Teachers and Their Training

The presence of number of programmes of child care and education services necessitates proper provision for training the personnel. Varied types of training facilities are made available to suit the need both regular as well as ad hoc. There are variations in curriculum and methods. Some follow Montessori approach, few Kindergarten, progressive play-way methods and few others a combination of all these. The duration of the training also differs. There are two year training programmes; and also short-term training programmes. The minimum qualification for training ranges from X std. to a first degree. Some are highly theoretical and academic whereas a few are of practical oriented. There is no uniformity in the training procedures followed.

Two Year Teachers' Training Programme

Two year teachers' training programme is being carried out by two agencies in Tamil Nadu, Children's Garden School at Madras and Pre-Primary Training at Kasturbagram at Erode; each having its own procedures, curriculum, methodology, examinations and administrations.

Children's Garden School was founded in 1937 by Mrs. Ellen Sharm of Germany and Dr. V.N. Sharma. A beginning was made by this private institution to introduce training programmes in Brindavan

Trainining Centre. Later their efforts bore fruit and the programmes came to be recognised by the Government of Tamil Nadu in 1947.

The training section for Kindergarten Teachers comprises of three different groups: (1) A two-year courses for the Kindergarten Teachers' Examination (Recognised by the Government of Tamil Nadu). (2) A three month refresher course for experienced teachers in Kindergarten methods. (3) A one-year Creche-Helper Training Course recognised by Social Welfare Board.

The Kindergarten Teachers' Training course is offered in Tamil Medium. The candidates are selected with a basic qualification of pass in XII standard. The selection is done annually and each batch has a maximum of 40 candidates in the age group 18+ to 25. A free education is provided and after the completion of the courses, the Government conducts the examination and a Government recognised certificate is issued to the successful candidates.

Specialised methods like playway method and project method, as introduced by the founder, are encouraged for widespread use in classroom through the training programme. Apart from these methods of teaching, three other subjects as prescribed by the government like Psychology, Hygiene and school administration are included. In practicals, the trainees are taught drawing, music, handicrafts and needle work suitable for children. They visit various pre-primary schools and training institutions in and out of the city.

Another institute which offers two year Pre-Primary Teachers' Training is Kasturbagram in Periyar District. This training institute was started in 1954 under the Kasturba Gandhi Memorial Trust to prepare pre-school teachers to go and work in the pre-schools mainly in villages. Minimum qualification for admission is XII standard passed and they have to appear for an examination conducted by the State Government, like the Kindergarten.

This is an aided training institution and the staff are paid as per the government rules. The Headmistress is a graduate with teachers' training qualifications. She is being assisted by a Craft teacher and two officc assistants.

Once in two years 40 candidates are admitted in a batch. They pay a sum of Rs. 500/- per year for buying note books and for preparing teaching materials.

On completion of the course these teachers are permitted to teach upto fifth standard. The available job opportunity for these teachers are not bright even in government schools. Hence, the management has decided to close the training institute by next academic year. Probably, this may be due to lack of co-ordination with the governmental agencies and other agencies which are involved in pre-primary school education at the state level.

Creche Nurse Training

A Creche Nurses training programme of two years duration is offered at CSI Creche Nurses Training and Model Day Care Centre at Kotagiri in Nilgiris District. The training course has been operating from 1969 and so far 216 creche nurses have been trained. Students are admitted once in two years with 16 in one batch. The candidates qualification for admission is S.S.L.C. pass and the medium of instruction is Tamil.

It is completely a residential institute. The present batch has four institutions sponsored candidates and the other 11 are CSICC German sponsored.

The institute has three staff members on its roll. Two teaching staff and one office assistant: Ms. Cushing, the founder of the institute, teaches Craft, English and book-keeping. The Principal takes care of the other subjects like Child Care and Development, Care of sick children, Nutrition and Cooking, Hygiene, First Aid. In a weekly rotation 8 girls are in theory class and the other 8 in practicals.

In practical training period students spend time in creches, learning how to care for pre-school children and how to plan the daily routine and play activities. They spend few weeks in a hospital learning to care for new born babies and sick children. In the course of the practicals they are exposed atleast to one normal delivery in the hospital and they also learn ante-natal and post-natal care.

Visits are arranged to such places as welfare clinic, residential nursery, Home for handicapped children, dairy etc.

One Year Teachers' Training Programme

(a) Indian Council for Child Welfare is conducting one year training programme in two different centres, at Madras and at Munanjipatti in southern most part of Tamil Nadu. Another voluntary agency Vidya Vikasini Society at Coimbatore has one year training programme funded by Social Welfare Board under a scheme called vocational training.

The ICCW Balsevika Training Institute at Madras and Munanjipatti Tirunelveli District design their programme to meet the all-round needs of pre-school children. They offer eleven months course. The course has been functioning from 1962 at Madras and from 1980 at Munanjipatti. Fifty candidates form one batch and the course commences in April and ends in the following February. The students are given a stipend of Rs. 75 per month by Central Social Welfare and Rs. 100 for buying materials. Hostel facilities are available.

Minimum qualification for selection for the course in S.S.L.C. and the age limit 18+. The course covers various areas such as:

1. Child Welfare/Development
2. Pre-school Education
3. Nutrition
4. Health/Hygiene and Environmental Sanitation
5. Social Welfare
6. Training in First Aid.

The trainees are also exposed to practical experience of working with and among children, undertaking house visits, preparing educational aids, visits to educational institutions. Preparation of a kit (consisting of different types of teaching aids) is included in the practical part of the syllabus. Block placement forms an important feature of this training programme.

The institution is staffed with one principal and two instructors. They are postgraduates in Child Development or Nutrition. The Principal is on the pay scale of Rs. 1700 and the instructors Rs. 1100 each.

(b) A voluntary organisation Vidya Vikasini Society at Coimbatore funded by the Tamil Nadu Social Welfare Board under the vocational training programme, offers a one year pre-school teachers' training programme. The programme has been in operation from 1979 and has 30 students in one batch. Minimum qualification for admission is S.S.L.C. Free education provided for sponsored candidates with stipend and non-sponsored candidates pay Rs. 1000 per year as fees. There are seven staff members out of which five are teaching staff. Among these five, two are honorary members. Approximate expenditure for each batch is Rs. 40,000.

The course offers both theoretical as well as practical subjects of study. The subjects taught are Psychology, Child Development, Nutrition and Hygiene and Pre-school organisation and administration. Under practicals they learn preparation of materials and have intensive teaching practice in pre-schools.

Short-Term Courses

Creche Workers' Training

The ICCW also conducts creche workers' training for untrained creche teachers. This course comes directly under the auspices of Social Welfare Board. It is a five-week full time course. So far 12 batches have completed training. All the candidates are sponsored candidates with a stipend of Rs. 350 per month.

The course covers both theory and practical subjects. It includes the following areas of study such as Organisation of a Creche, Child-Development and Pre-school education, Health and Nutrition.

Brindavan Training Centre, Children's Garden School offers a course in pre-school and Creche Helper training. The chosen candidates have a minimum qualification of appearing Xth examination and in age group of 18+ to 30. The Children's Garden School Society issues a certificate after a successful completion of the course. The candidates are selected annually and are sponsored by Social Welfare Board. Training is free and the medium of education is Tamil. Number of candidates per batch is 20 to 25. These trained candidates have employment opportunity in Balwadi/Creche/Noon-meal schemes and creche teacher project.

The same institute also conducts 5 week orientation training for workers in balwadi/creche/mid-day meal scheme etc. It is a sponsored programme by the Social Welfare Board and a certificate is issued by the Human Resource Development Ministry to successful candidates.

Child Welfare Organisers (Noon Meal Programme)

When Noon Meal Scheme was initiated, the noon meal instructors were given training, mainly on nutrition for one month in Sri Avinashalingam Home Science College, Coimbatore. They in turn gave training to the Child Welfare Organisers (CWDS) for a period of 3 months.

Subsequently the CWDS went to different institutes for one month course. But the department (Social Welfare Directorate) found that it was not very successful. As a result the Social Welfare Directorate has an arrangement with the Education Department for the training.

Training of the Key Resource Persons (KRPS)

Higher Secondary School teachers were requested to be deputed for one month training programme. These teachers were chosen from different blocks. They were given training for a period of one month in Lady Wellington College of Education, Madras; Lakshmi College of Education, Gandhigram; Institute of Rural Health and Family Welfare Trust, Gandhigram; Balsevika Training Centre, Munanjipatti; Tirunelveli District and Kasturba Pre-Primary Teacher's Training School, Kasturbagram at Erode.

ICDS (Integrated Child Development Scheme)

Till 1982 the Anganwadi Workers (ANWS) were trained in different institutions, as done in other states. But there came a shift from institution based training to project based training from January 1983. For every project an instructor was appointed. She was responsible for training ANWS in that particular block for a period of 75 working days. As a follow-up activity these instructors visited the Anganwadies concerned and participated in the day-to-day activities. This scheme of training continued till 1985. With a gap of one year, there came another innovative training scheme in July 1987.

The Mobile Team

In July 1987, seven Mobile Teams consisting of three instructors, in each team were appointed and were made responsible for training the teachers.

Duration of the Training

The untrained ANWS in each block are trained for a period of 72 working days at a stretch, except on Sundays and other public holidays. As the training is block based the ANWS make arrangement for lunch and take attendance before 9.30 a.m. in their concerned centres. Later they go to the training centres to under go the training. In the absence of the ANWS (undergoing training) the Anganwadi Centres are managed by Anganwadi Helpers (ANWHS). The training course continues from 10 a.m. to 5 p.m. for 72 days. Each batch of trainees consist of 50 ANWS.

Qualification of the Anganwadi Workers

Earlier, prior to 1982, even the XI standard failed candidates were selected, given training and appointed. After 1983 S.S.L.C. passed untrained candidates are recruited through Employment Exchanges and appointed. They are given training when they are on the job by the Mobile Team.

Helper's Training

The local women (even illiterates) are appointed as helpers. Then they are given on the job training for a period of 6 days on health and hygiene, nutrition, story telling, music and the proper ways of handling children.

Distribution of a Kit

After the completion of the training the ANWS are given a kit consisting of play materials to be used in their centres. In the course of the training they are taught the proper use of the kit while teaching.

Middle Level Training Centres (MLTC)

The Middle Level Workers to be the supervisors in ICDS programme, are given training for a period of 3 months in Madras by ICCW. The training is being imparted at two levels:

1. Job training for ICDS supervisors for 3 months, and
2. In service, refresher courses, after 2 years of the completion of job training. These are being funded by NIPCCD Human Resource Development Ministry, New Delhi. Each batch consists of 33 to 50 candidates.

An evaluation of the various strategies followed in training the ANWS for ICDS schemes in Tamil Nadu, shows that an attempt has been made to be innovative. ICDS being the second largest scheme in providing childcare services in Tamil Nadu, has made an attempt to reduce the cost effect of training its functionaries by shifting courses from institutions to the centres concerned. Moreover, when the training is localised it becomes more meaningful, catering to the needs of the local situations.

Other Agencies

Apart from these regular training programmes some of the agencies like UPAST, Vivekananda Kendra and Christian Missionaries conduct their own short-term ad hoc training for their workers wherever they are in need of. The duration of the course varies from 10 days to 2 months and the content from nutrition, health and to that of a comprehensive child care programme.

University based Programme

Different Universities in India offer Pre-school education either as an elective or as an optional objects at the graduate and post-graduate levels. In Tamil Nadu Madurai Kamaraj University offers Pre-school Education as an optional subject in the Colleges of Education. The teacher trainees (B.Ed.) study both theory and practicals for one academic year, as part of the regular B.Ed. curriculum. Pre-school education and Child Development form part of two theory papers and preparation of low cost toys and other teaching materials, observation of children and maintenance of case studies and teaching practice for a period of 10 days as part of the B.Ed. practicals. They are examined in all these subjects.

Annamalai, Alagappa, Avinashalingam Institute of Higher Education and University of Madras offer Pre-primary education as an elective at thc B.Ed. course. Both pre-primary school education and child development are theory papers and a written examination is taken in both, at the end of the year.

In B.Sc. and M.Sc., Home Science students learn pre-school education as part of Child Development with practicals and teaching practice.

Madurai Kamaraj University offers certificate course in Family and Child Welfare through its distance education programme to the XII standard passed candidates. Therc arc two thcory papcrs, onc among of them is pre-school education and Child Care. This course does not offer any practical experience which is the weak point of the programme.

In few Higher Secondary Schools Child Care is offered as one of the Vocational Courses for a period of two years. Along with principles of Nutrition they learn pre-school education which includes both theory and practicals.

38

Creative Activities

1. Observe a pre-primary school centre and list down the type of administrative activities going on there.
2. Visit a pre-primary school and assess the suitability of the location of the building and its structure.
3. List the equipments and furniture available and assess their suitability.
4. Identify the locally available play equipment and find out their values.
5. Design suitable play equipment for indoor and outdoor play.
6. Identify the artisans in your area who could make play equipment and furniture for young children.
7. Observe different types of non-equipment games played by children of various age group.
8. Visit different types of pre-primary school centres and note down the type of records they maintain.
9. Learn to maintain the records and reports which are essential for a pre-primary school.
10. Prepare pamphlets on important themes to be sent to the parents.
11. Organize a parent education programme in a pre-primary school centre.
12. Identify the interest patterns of parents for parent education programme.
13. Prepare a set of activities through which you could implement child to child programme in an urban pre-primary school and in a rural pre-primary school.
14. Observe the activities where the older children help the younger ones and maintain a record.

15. Identify the national and international organizations in your area which are involved in child welfare programmes.
16. Observe the activities of voluntary organizations which undertake child welfare activities.
17. Visit a pre-primary school teacher training institute and study its curriculum.
18. Identify the strong and weak points in different training programmes.

Bibliography

Balchandra Mayadevi, *Pre-school Education-Rural, National Policy for children*, Proceedings of the National Seminar, New Delhi, the Indian Council for Child Welfare, 1964.

Bernard, Spodek (Ed.), *Early Childhood Education,* (Part II), New Jersey, Prentice Hall, Inc, 1973.

Block, N., Foreign Language in the Kindergarten, *The Educational Review*, March, 1970.

Cole, Luella, *A History of Education. Socrates to Montessori*, New York, Holt, Rinehart and Winston, 1962.

David and Mary Mindess, *Guide to an Effective Kindergarten Programme*, New York, Parkar Publishing Co., Inc, 1974.

David, Elkind, Pre-school Education, Enrichment of Instruction in Bernard Spodek (Ed.), *Early Childhood Education*, New Jersey, Prentice Hall, Inc, 1973.

DeBoer, John J., *The Teaching of Reading*, Calcutta: Oxford and IBS Publishing Co., 1967.

Desai, K.G., Effectiveness of Kindergarten Education, New Delhi, Report of an Investigation, National Council of Educational Research and Training, July 1972.

Fred, M. Hechinger (Ed.), *Pre-school Education Today*, New York, Double Day and Company, Inc, Garden City, 1966.

Fuller, Mechem Elizabeth, Early Childhood Education, Inchester W. Harris (ed), *Encyclopedia of Educational Research* (3rd ed), New York, The Macmillan Co., 1960.

Gardener, D.E.M., *Education under Eight*, London: British Council, Longmans, Green and Co., 1949.

Gardner, D. Bruce, *Developmemt in Early Childhood*, The Pre-school Years, London, Harper and Row Puplishers, 1964.

Harry Passow, H., *et al.*, *Education of the Disadvantaged: A Book of Readings*, New York, Holt, Rinehart and Winston, Inc, 1967.

Hirlekar, Yamunabai, *Kindergerten in Germany*, Bombay: The Popular Book Depot, 1970.

Holland, Bernice, C., *How to Individualize Kindergarten Teaching: New Approaches using the Key Sensory Modes*, New York, Parker Publishing Co., Inc, 1974.

Hymes James, L., Emerging Patterns in Early Childhood Education in Michael S. Auleta (ed), *Foundations of Early Childhood Education Readings*, New York, Random House, 1969.

IAPE, 1969.—— (Ed.), *Systems of Pre-school Education in India*, New Delhi, IAPE publications, 1968, ——, Home stimulation and Child Development, *Indian Educational Review*, Vol. 5, No. 2, July 1970, ——, Play Preferences of Nursery School Children, *Indian Educational Review*, Vol. 7. No. 2, July 1972.

IAPE, Cognitive Development and Pre-school Education, Report of the 4th Annual Conference of IAPE, New Delhi, NIE Campus, N.C.E.R.T., 1968.

IAPE, Source Book for Pre-school education, Baroda, Indian Associate for Pre-school Education.

Khaladina, Margret, The Pre-school in Rural India, *NIE Journal,* NCERT, Vol. V, No. 2, 1970.

Kohn, Ruth, Cognitive Development in Pre-school Programme—Concept Formation can be Guided, R. Muralidharan (ed), *Cognitive Development and Pre-school Education*, New Delhi, IAPE, 1968.

Krown Sylria, *Threes and Fours Go To School,* New Jersey, Prentice Hall, Inc, 1974.

Lee, Betty, *Canda's Kindergarden in Columbia Reader's Digest*, London, the Macmillan Co., 1971.

Malani, Indra, Recent Trends in Pre-school Education, R. Muralidharan (ed)., *The Systems of Pre-school Education In India*, New Delhi, IAPE, 1968.

Michael S. Auleta (ed)., *Foundations of Early Childhood Education Readings,* New York, Random House, 1969.

Miller, Mabel Eyelym, *A Practical Guide for Kindergarden Teachers*, New York, Parker Publishing Co., Inc, 1974.

Ministry of Education and Social Welfare, Report of the Study Group on the Development of the Pre-school Child, Delhi-6, 1972.

Moghe, Shalini, Pre-school Education in Urban Area, A National Policy For Children, Proceedings of the National Seminar New Delhi, The Indian Council for Child Welfare, 1964.

Muralidharan, R., (Ed), *The Systems of Pre-school Education in India*, New Delhi, IAPE 1968, Learning Through Play Experience in Freny

Tarapore, (ed) Child's Rights to play, SNDT Collage of Home science, Pune, Pre-school Education, the Indian Publications Ambala Cantt, 1994, *Pre-School Education* (Tamil) 4th education, Lakshmi Sevasangam, Gandhigram 2002.

Muralidharan, Rajalakshmi, Cognitive Development and Pre-school Education, Report of Annual Conference of IAPE, New Delhi, 1968, *Pre-school Education as an Instrument of Change in a Developing Society*, New Delhi.

Nanle, S.N., Pre-school Education (A Short working paper on the Subject), A National Policy for Children, Proceedings of the National Seminar, New Delhi, The Indian Council for Child Welfare, 1964.

Panandikar, S., The Place of Pre-school Education in The Educational System, *NIE Journal,* N.C.E.R.T., Vol. V, No. 2, 1907.

Pankajam, G., Class Room Practices in Pre-Basic School, *NIE Journal,* N.C.E.R.T., Vol. V, No. 2, November 1970.# ——, The System of Pre-Basic Education,

Paul, C. Burns and Leo M. Schell (Ed.), *Elementary School Language Arts*: *Selected Readings*. Chicage, Rand Mcnally & Co., 1969.

Ramji Marsi, T. and B.R., Goyal, *Programme and Activities for Balwadies*, New Delhi, N.C.E.R.T. 1972.

Read Katherine, H., *The Nursery School: A Human Relationships Laboratory*, Calcutta: Oxford and IBH Publishing Co., 1960.

Schmidt, W.H.O. *Child Development*, *The Human Culture and Educational Context*, New York, Harper and Row Publishers, 1973.

Singh, Gurbax, Compulsory Primary Education and the 1961 Census, *Indian Journal of Educational Administration and Research*, Vol. II, No. 1, May-June 1961.

Swaminathan, Mina (Editor), Proceedings of the National Seminar On An intergraded Approach to the Pre-school Child, Indian Association for Pre-school Education, Bangalore, October 1972.

Verma, Amita, The Role of A Laboratory Nursery School, *NIE Journal,* N.C.E.R.T., Vol. V, No. 2, 1970.

Weber, Lillian, *The Engligh Infant School and Informal Education,* New Jersey, Prentice Hall, Inc, 1971.

Whitebread, Nanette, *The Evolution of the Nursery Infant School,* London, Routledge and Kegan Paul, 1975.

Wright, F. Robert, Observational child study in paul, H. Mussen (ed) *Handbook of Research Methods in Child Development*, New Delhi, Wiley Eastern private Ltd., 1970.

Index